# The Meaning of Helen

## IN SEARCH OF AN ANCIENT ICON

ROBERT EMMET MEAGHER

Bolchazy-Carducci Publishers, Inc.
Wauconda, Illinois USA

2002
Bolchazy-Carducci Publishers, Inc.
1000 Brown Street, Unit 101
Wauconda, IL 60084
www.bolchazy.com

Printed in the United States of America
by United Graphics

Library of Congress Cataloging-in-Publication Data
Meagher, Robert E.
  [Helen]
  The meaning of Helen : in search of an ancient icon / Robert Emmet Meagher.
      p. cm.
Originally published: Helen. New York : Continuum Pub. Co., 1995.
Includes bibliographical references.
  ISBN 0-86516-510-6 (pbk.)
1. Helen of Troy (Greek mythology) I. Title.
  BL820.H45 M43 2002
  305.42--dc21
                                                    2002071745

*for*

I am the first and the last.

I am the whore and the holy one.

I am the wife and the virgin.

I am the mother and the daughter.

I am the members of my mother.


Why have you hated me in your counsels?

I am the one who has been hated everywhere

and who has been loved everywhere.

I am the one whom they call Life,

and you have called me Death.

I am the one whom you have despised.

I am the one whom you have hidden from.*

* Freely excerpted from "Thunder: Perfect Mind," introduced and translated by George W. MacRae and edited by Douglas M. Parrott, in *The Nag Hammadi Library in English,* James M. Robinson, General Editor (New York: Harper & Row, 1988), pp. 297-303. In fact, this poem defies sure classification, and whether it should be called "Gnostic" at all is a matter of dispute.

# Contents

FOREWORD   vii

INTRODUCTION   1

1 • HELEN AND HISTORY   6

2 • THE MANY HELENS   23

3 • THE DUALITY OF HELEN   49

4 • THE FIRST HELEN   70

5 • THE TRUTH OF HELEN   92

CONCLUSION   112

APPENDIX: HISTORY AND IMAGINATION   115

NOTES   125

# Foreword

Endings and beginnings have always been mates. They make each other possible. Only at the end can we afford to look back and wonder about the beginning, which is what I intend here, with considerate brevity.

This project has gone on for years, at least ten. It began with a telephone call. I let it ring twice as is my compulsion. Then, with few words and little room for declining, Irene Papas commissioned from me a new translation of Euripides' *Helen*, which led to years of unforgettable conversations and schemes, so many brushfires lit by Irene's irrepressible imagination. She was quite simply in Helen's thrall, as I suspect Helen was in hers. Their companionship was tangible. For years I was privileged to overhear their conversations. Soon I too was haunted by Helen.

My own search for Helen took as it would a scholarly turn. Like the moles in my yard, I went underground, tunnelling through the stacks of various libraries, leaving a determined mound of writing behind me. The industry of moles is one of our planet's small mysteries.

Like any scholar, I found a world in my subject. Helen turned out to be a *Matrioshka*. Nested within her were other women, other stories, which on second thought were not "other" at all. Helen began to shed appreciable light not only on the past but on the present, and I learned all over again that the past is never really past.

The story of Helen is the story of woman, loved and hated beyond human recognition. No woman from the ancient past is more notorious to this day. No woman remains at the same time more silent. "The woman I needed to call my mother," writes Adrienne Rich, "was silenced before I was born." Breaking that silence is a long labor, to which this volume, I can only hope, makes some small contribution.

I ask the reader not to be distracted or annoyed by the sometimes over-whelming accumulation of notes provided to the text. Back for a moment to the mole. There is always the tunnel *and* the mound. The one produces the other, and they inevitably trace an identical path. Here, the noteless body of the text tells the whole story, without detour. The reader is there-fore invited to follow the mound and to stay to the "surface" of every chapter, unless driven "below" by instincts I happen to share.

I will limit my vast "accounts payable" to three women. My deepest thanks to Irene Papas for launching this project and for putting such relentless first winds in its sails. To Betsy, my spirited wife and incom-parable companion, I owe the sheer joy of the voyage. Finally, I am again indebted to the inimitable Dr. Laurie Haight Keenan, editor extraordi-naire, who has piloted this volume to press with her accustomed wit and skill.

In conclusion, searching for a few suitable words to all those who have already contributed to this book and to all those who will eventually read it, I come upon the words of Theoklymenos, with which Euripides con-cluded his Helen:

> In the name of Helen, the noblest of spirits,
>    and for that reason an exceptional woman,
> I bless you all.

Robert Emmet Meagher
*The Clearing*
East Hartland, Connecticut

# Introduction

It is a truism that Helen's face launched a thousand ships, to say nothing of countless books, dramas, poems, paintings, and operas. She is arguably the most notorious woman in Western culture. Yet she remains strangely faceless. Removed from the spotlight, she becomes unrecognizable, commonplace. Without her thousand ships, how would anyone pick her out in a crowd? Helen's beauty, like anyone else's, is relative and among the world's most ephemeral phenomena.

What, then, makes her so engaging, so consequential? Like an ancient wall layered with millennia of graffiti, Helen preserves the human record. She has become what others have said about her, done in her name, suffered in her stead, created in her honor. Her story and our story are not to be plied apart. More specifically, she is woman as we have idealized, worshiped, slandered, celebrated, constructed, and deconstructed her. Helen, for better or for worse, in all her metamorphoses, represents the complex, intact fossil record of woman in Western culture. The story of Helen is the story of woman.

In recent memory, say for the last five thousand years, that story has been one of contradiction, a contradiction summed up in what Gisèle Halimi has labeled "Doormat-Pedestal" tactics. Woman has been idolized and demonized, adored and degraded, relieved of the workplace and deprived of the courts, been the last to wage wars and the first to suffer from them. She has been a creature of extremes, rarely of her own making. One moment she brings bliss, the next she is said to be the source of all misery, the misery at hand and the as-yet-distant misery only feared. Readily granted divine or bestial standing, or both, woman has been consistently denied any sure footing in the middle. Humanity, gravity-ridden and yet upright, has been mostly reserved for men. The exceptions have serviced the rule. The "otherness" of woman is still operative.

The "official" story of woman is, in a word, the story of misogyny, the story of a consistent, however ambivalent or dissembling, hatred—not only the hatred of men for women but also the self-hatred of women instilled by the culture of misogyny, so seamless for so long. In Western culture, Helen has only two long-term rivals as the preeminent archetype or icon of misogyny: Eve and the Virgin Mary. Neither Eve nor Mary, however, tells the whole story. They divide between them the essential contradiction imposed by misogyny. Eve owns the doormat, and Mary is secure on her pedestal—the one a temptress-whore and the other a sublime virgin, the one driven from paradise and the other lifted bodily into heaven. Between them they encompass the dual expectations and fates of woman, but not as more ordinary women experience them, conflated and confused. Enter Helen, uncontested queen of beauty, every man's wildest dream, encased all the same in hate.

Who, if anyone, conceived such a creature? When and where and how did she begin? The canonical answer to these questions is enshrined in the myth of "Leda and the Swan," retold in this poem by Yeats:

> A sudden blow; the great wings beating still
> Above the staggering girl, her thighs caressed
> By the dark webs, her nape caught in his bill,
> He holds her helpless breast upon his breast.
> How can those terrified vague fingers push
> The feathered glory from her loosening thighs?
> And how can body, laid in that white rush,
> But feel the strange heart beating where it lies?
>
> A shudder in the loins engenders there
> The broken wall, the burning roof and tower
> And Agamemnon dead.
>                     Being so caught up,
> So mastered by the brute blood of the air,
> Did she put on his knowledge with his power
> Before the indifferent beak could let her drop?

Helen's origins are demonstrably violent. She is conceived in rape, no less brutal for its being so fantastic. Bred in violence, Helen will go on to breed violence. The great war with its legendary savagery and carnage is engendered with her in the same instant, in the same womb.

Mother and daughter, Leda and Helen, designated by the same violence, soon part ways. Leda, unable to live with her shame, hangs herself, while Helen, after causing no little chaos, is awarded immortality and lifted away to the Isles of the Blessed. Apparently, no rules need be observed by women nor in the treatment of them. Like gods and brute beasts, women—the unstable hybrid of both—are either above or below whatever measure or standards otherwise apply. Their exemption may be seen as a singular honor or as a singular slight. Either way, it is equally distorting. Either way it comes down to the same exclusion from humanity.

Faced with an imagined foreign breed or alien presence in their midst, the challenge for men has been to tame women, to neutralize their otherness, to win them over, with force or with favors, whatever the situation demands, whatever works. In short, the solution has been to marry them. The bride was and is to be the final solution to the problematic presence of women, a solution both defined and defied by Helen. Helen is at the same time the mold and the one who broke it in pieces.

The woman who unlearns her fear of man is, according to Nietzsche, a woman who has surrendered her most womanly instincts. Woman's great art, he claims, is the lie, while her defining concern is with her appearance. Cosmetic deception lies at her core. If man is not taken in, he may find distraction and enjoyment in what is essentially a game of cat and mouse, provided that the man remains the cat. Nietzsche's virulent misogyny is remarkable only for its blatancy. Otherwise it is utterly orthodox.

There is surely no need either to define or to document further the existence of misogyny. Like racism, it is a reality as undeniable and irrational as the weather. Unlike the weather, however, we have conjured it from within.

One of the most remarkable characteristics of misogyny is its doctrinal integrity. No blind belief, no creed has remained so incorrupt for so long. Nietzsche and Hesiod, Aeschylus and John Paul II, Gorgias and Clarence Thomas, for all of their differences, recite the same lines with respect to women. It is as if they went to the same school, studied the same text, entitled *Helen*.

If the long history of misogyny is one of rote learning and monotonous repetition, it is not for that reason inevitable. It had a beginning; and anything with a beginning can and will have an end. It is finally only a habit, and habits can be broken. Here too Helen and her story are revealing. Tracing the story of Helen to its origins takes us back beyond misogyny, and following that same story through its revision by Euripides brings us to the brink of misogyny's theoretical demise. In sum, we glimpse in the image and story of Helen the beginning and the end of misogyny. Regrettably, the memory of the one and the anticipation of the other have been long lost; and what has confronted women and men for several millennia is a reality seemingly without beginning and without end. Misogyny, for all we have known, always was and always will be. Recently—more recently for some of us, less recently for others—we have come to understand that misogyny, on the contrary, is only an episode, an aberration to be put behind us. To many this may seem a superhuman task. But "superhuman," as Camus once wrote, is merely the name we give to things we take a long time to accomplish.

There are those, I know, who will resent such words as these, as well as the book they introduce, all coming from a man. There are those who would argue or simply assert that men are unequipped or at least unauthorized to shed any light on the historical reality or experience of women. A male feminist is, to some otherwise thoughtful minds, an oxymoron. Let men write about ants or gods or the solar system or one another; but only women can write about women. There is poetic justice, to be sure, in the silencing of men; but poetic justice, however immediately satisfying, is rooted in revenge. It leads us deeper into the violations it addresses, not out of them.

Speaking for myself and on my own behalf, imaginative, emotional, or intellectual separatism is unthinkable. I am the son, the father, and the committed companion of a woman. More abstractly, but with no less conviction, I know that I share with every woman a common humanity, no slight bond. Furthermore, I exchange questions and ideas daily with my students, who irrespective of gender teach and learn from me things we mutually come to treasure. It was precisely this lived consortium of male and female that propelled me further and further into the study of Helen; for this study instructed me, as nothing had previously, regarding the extent and the limits of the misogyny I had witnessed, wondered about, and struggled with all my life.

What was so revealing in this study and at the same time so exhausting was the density and entanglement of what I uncovered. They say that the devil is in the details, but so is the truth. The sheer accumulation of circumstantial evidence is what forces whatever conclusions I draw here.

Anyone who would study birds or butterflies or insects must acquire an appetite for and a fascination with fine detail and innumerable differences. The same holds true when we study one another, across time, culture, and gender. To simplify any further the story told here, the story of Helen, would both ease and impoverish the journey.

Dylan Thomas, in *A Child's Christmas in Wales,* tells how he as a child received a book that told him everything about the spider except *why.* A similar hiatus is to be found in this book, which, while it has something substantial to say about the history of misogyny, has very little to say about the *why* of misogyny. Notwithstanding the speculations and suggestions which I offer in the course of *Helen,* the *why* of misogyny remains a mystery to me. War is always hell, always madness; but individual wars are usually relatively brief, fueled by a discernible ambition or illusion. Exhaustion, pain, and disillusionment eventually make way for sanity's return. The multi-millennial war of the sexes is another matter. It makes no sense, serves no one's interests, disfigures everyone involved, and seems interminable.

For this reason Helen remains an enigma. Why what is most desired and loved must be hated beyond recognition; why a species so singularly prone to loneliness, alienation, and eventual self-doubt would sever itself in two, deny itself the intimacy, recognition, and comfort of equals; why the embodiment of beauty and life would be fashioned into an icon of shame—all this is beyond any light cast by this book. The sight of a massive whale, self-beached, drying up, lapped by the waters it needs to live, perishing patiently and resolved, without, it seems, any second thoughts, such a sight presents perhaps a comparable enigma. One difference, of course, is that few whales engage in such behavior. Most know and do better.

In sum, I know of no more urgent or encompassing challenge than the understanding and overcoming of misogyny; for humanity would best be wholehearted and common-minded in confronting its precarious future. A species divided against itself cannot stand. Neither do I know any more fruitful place to initiate such an understanding and overcoming than in the rediscovery and exoneration of Helen.

# 1

# Helen and History

Is there a word suitably elusive and archaic to name the enterprise undertaken here, one that will provide at the least a point of departure and at best a goal? I would propose "encomium," a celebration, in this instance a celebration of Helen.

Helen is, of course, already a celebrity; and her encomium has already been written. In short, there is a precedent of sorts for what we do here, since an illustrious fifth-century orator and author, the Sicilian-born Sophist Gorgias, once composed a work he called his *Encomium of Helen*.[1] Gorgias seems to have meant by "encomium," however, something other and less than a celebration of his subject; for what he wrote took the form of a defense, more specifically a legal defense. As if assigned to plead, before an Athenian court of law, the notorious case of Helen, indicted for her infamous adultery and its chaotic consequences, Gorgias wove Helen's defense with the specious skill that had already become the byword of his profession.

After equating woman (*gynē*) with body (*sōma*) and claiming that the proper fulfillment of both lies in beauty, Gorgias admits that Helen's beauty was divine and that "in very many she created very strong amorous desires; with a single body she brought together many bodies of men"[2] to war, of course, and to death.

Conceding this much to the prosecution, which he admits is legion, Gorgias advances his argument for the defense, which it is pointless to take seriously when he did not. More revealing of his light purpose than anything else he says is the very last word of his encomium. This is the name he gives to the whole: *paignion*.[3] In the end, Gorgias calls what he made his "plaything" or "amusement." In contriving a defense of Helen, Gorgias by his own admission was amusing himself and others with a mere exercise in wit. If, indeed, the test of the Sophist was to defeat an intrinsically stronger case with an intrinsically weaker one, then Gorgias had set to himself the ultimate test; for there was no case weaker than Helen's. In defending her, he was defending the indefensible. Nothing could be more ludicrous—more playful, if you will—than to argue the innocence of Helen. The verdict on Helen was, after all, already in.

Had Helen's case ever come to trial and Gorgias presented his defense, we may assume that he and she would have lost. A jury of men, as it would have been in any ancient court, tainted by prior exposure to the particulars of the case and already partial toward the prosecution, would have handed down a sure conviction, provided they were never allowed to gaze upon Helen's epic beauty. Of this much the tradition assures us. Helen, convicted daily out of court, was simply the most notorious woman in Greek literature and art, a virtual icon of feminine ill repute. In a time and a place wherein it was "the greatest glory of a woman . . . to be least talked about by men,"[4] Helen was a household word.

What I propose here, at the very least, is to reopen the case of Helen, to reexamine the evidence and to add to it, considerably. My intent, unlike that of Gorgias, is no mere display of casuistry; for the matter of Helen is no ludicrous, no laughing, matter. The original decision against Helen set an infectious precedent for the perception and treatment of women in the ancient world and beyond. Her infamy was and remains generic. Her conviction never did apply only to her; it was a slander upon all women. Her offense, analogous to that of Eve's, represented, as it were, an "original sin" inbred into the race of women. In reopening her case, then, I am necessarily reopening the case of women in the ancient world, though most pointedly in the poetic tradition from the archaic to the classical periods, from Homer and Hesiod to Euripides.

To reopen a case and to appeal a previous conviction, ordinarily one must either offer new evidence or claim that earlier evidence was significantly misinterpreted. In this case, it is easy to do both. The archaeological finds of the last century alone, together with the most advanced techniques for reading those finds, suffice to challenge the traditional verdict against Helen. Additionally, there is the immeasurable contribution made by feminist awareness and criticism, which has served to open the eyes and expand the imaginations of already several generations of scholars, women and men alike. Too slowly for some and too rapidly for others, past oversights and misreadings have been called into question and left behind. What is more, a new integration of disciplines within an overly partitioned academy has contributed to an increasingly holistic under-standing of the ancient world. Clearly, with so radical a change of venue, it is possible now to plead Helen's case afresh.

Before beginning in earnest, I wish to point out in advance the direction of my argument, a direction suggested by Helen's own sister Klytemnes-tra, whose voice in the *Agamemnon* of Aeschylus is one of the few voices in classical poetry defensive of Helen. The dramatic moment I have in mind occurs after the slaughter of Agamemnon, when Klytemnestra emerges from the palace, red-handed, and confronts the hostile Chorus of Argive men, composed of those too old and frail to have been useful to the war effort. Stunned by the death of their warlord king and searching for the root of their pain, the Chorus turn first, as if by habit, to far-off Helen instead of to her murderous sister, who stands before them with their king's blood spattered across her face. "Helen, wild Helen," they sing:

> Loose beyond your wits,
> One woman for so many men,
> Exhaling their lives,
> Beneath Troy's shadow.
> Like a flower,
> Your truth
> Is in the blooming:
> Blood, too much blood
> To wash away,
> Or to forget.
> Eris[5] stalks this house,
> Breeds between its walls.
> She is man's curse and, eventually,
> His death.[6]

In response, Klytemnestra lashes out, reminding the Chorus that they have enough problems already without virtually asking for the same fate as their lord's. "Furthermore," she goes on:

> As for your rage against Helen,
> Your "Man-slaughtering Helen,"
> The "open wound in man's side,"
> As if every Greek corpse in Troy
> Were her private handiwork . . .
> Let it go.[7]

The senseless carnage that was Troy evokes rage, but that rage has no place at Helen's door. In short, the angry Chorus are barking up the wrong tree. Ironically, in Euripides' *Trojan Women,* from the opposite side of the war's pain, a similar opinion is voiced by Hecuba, the uncontested queen of suffering. Although her hate for Helen is venomous, Hecuba, perhaps unwittingly, offers testimony obliquely useful to Helen's defense when, after chronicling her own pain—sons and spouse slaughtered, daughters dragged off by their hair, and now her own imminent exile to the house of Odysseus—she laments that "all this—all that has been endured and all that is yet to be endured—on account of one woman and her bed!"[8] While lividly contemptuous of Helen, Hecuba reveals the gaping disparity between Helen's indiscretion and the chaos it engendered. Indeed, she seems on the verge of asking the obvious: How can one woman's love ignite ten years of savagery? Even without the help of Hume, causality has become a tenuous concept here. Helen made love and tens of thousands of men made war. Cause and effect? Even Hecuba appears to be wondering about that. Perhaps she too is barking up the wrong tree.

Klytemnestra's point is elementary. Helen slew no one at Troy and had still less to do with the slaying of Agamemnon. The Chorus of old men simply doesn't know what is going on. The question remains in the *Agamemnon* and in the *Oresteia* as a whole: Who *does* know what is going on?

For Agamemnon "it" all began with the theft of Helen and ends on this day with his return from Troy, while for Klytemnestra the relevant beginning was the murder of her daughter at Aulis and the end will be her murder of the murderer, also on this day, the day of his homecoming. Aegisthus has in mind another ending, another homecoming, his own from exile, an exile that began long before Helen's war. Agamemnon, Klytemnestra, Aegisthus, and nameless, countless others, not surprisingly, tell the only stories they know, the stories whose beginnings and endings are marked by their own private wounds and hopes. The Furies, unseen as yet (except by Kassandra) and silent for now, look deeper still into the past and the future for the beginning and ending of this day's slaughterous spectacle; but even they lose the scent of the past and fail to divine its outcome. There are pages missing, it seems, in everyone's book. So many pawns all, thinking out every move they make, when in truth they move nothing, not even themselves. Eliot's Thomas might as well have had them in mind when he said: "Only / The fool, fixed in his folly, may think / He can turn the wheel on which he turns."[9]

In the *Oresteia*, only Zeus, *Zeus Teleios*,[10] the one who brings to completion all that is coming to be, knows and controls the whole story, whose end marks the close of the old world and the dawning of the new. His is the plot; all else is subplot. The end, the consummation of his scheme, is the Athens of "Olympian" Perikles, imperial Athens, in which man is the measure of all things and the master of women. In this story, set into song and dance by Aeschylus, Helen is but a plaything, a pretext, an eventual irrelevancy, finally neither cause nor effect. Klytemnestra and Hecuba were right, it seems, in suggesting that Helen was truly beside the point.

There is, however, another story, outreaching that of Zeus and of Athens, a story to which Helen is altogether central. It represents the tragedy not of the house of Atreus but of what for now and for lack of a better name we might call the house of Helen. It is the story of woman, divine and human woman, a story both lost and lingering in the archaic and classical figure of Helen—goddess, wife, consort, whore—the epitome of woman to the Greek eye. In ancient Greek poetry and art, Helen was indeed always more than *a* woman who brought on *a* war. The Trojan War, whatever its actual insignificance may have been, stood as the paradigm for all war; and Helen, its reputed cause, was the avatar of the feminine, the provocatrice of all mischief and pain, the original *femme fatale*. This synecdoche by which Helen was seen as all women and by which all women were seen as "Helens" was a simple liberty taken by the ancient tradition and operative, in one guise or another, ever since.

The triumph of the Olympian regime, in cosmos and polis, celebrated in the *Oresteia*, may have seemed at one time to encompass the reach of history, to tell the whole story. But even the Olympian gods, much less their history, is finite. The gods, after all, reigned for an *aiōn*, not forever. An *aiōn*, compared to the fleeting lives of mortals, is easily mistaken for eternity; but "aeons" too come and go. Even *Zeus Teleios*, given a sufficiently long view, may reveal himself as a minor player, if not a plaything, in what is coming to pass. Doubtlessly, the story of Helen requires a long view, well beyond the regime of Zeus and the mystique of classical Athens, well beyond the misogyny and androcentrism at their core. None of these was nor is forever. Helen was before them. Her regime belongs to another aeon, another seeming eternity, prior to our own, which may now seem never to have been.

Already this would-be encomium has taken a decidedly historical turn; for, before we can celebrate Helen, we must find her. In fact, most of what follows falls within the scope of *historia* as the Greeks understood it, a word encompassing inquiry, observation, narrative, and myth. And at least one modern understanding of history strikes close to the core of our endeavor. Martin Heidegger's distinctions between *Geschichte* and *Historie*, between *die Vergangenheit* and *die Gewesenheit* undeniably clarify our purpose, nearer to poetry than to science;[11] for the object of our search is not something past and gone, over and done with, but rather something ancient and ever-present, an event waiting to re-happen. Even more importantly, immersed as this study will soon become in the past, it must affirm always the priority of the future.

One further distinction is clearly indicated here, at the beginning. While this study might well be called "a historical search for Helen," it surely is not "a search for the historical Helen." Whether or not there ever was a "historical Helen"—a singular, flesh-and-blood woman blessed and cursed with "Homeric" beauty, the sort that launches fleets of ships and drives men out of their wits and into war—is something we are likely never to know.[12]

No matter. Even if there were a discernible Helen at the core of "her own" tradition—the granular irritant somehow responsible for the pearl —she would not be the object of this study. By the time Homer—much less Aeschylus, Gorgias, or Euripides—wrote of Helen, she was no longer *a* woman. She was, instead, an image; and, as she was to them, so she is to us. The history of Helen is inevitably the history of an image.

Any woman, or man for that matter, who either never existed in the flesh or no longer does so, is an image. Up until the moment when each of us dies and is buried away from the living, we are always here and not there, or there and not here. Afterwards, however, we could be, and often are, literally anywhere, summoned by imagination, not ours but someone else's. C. S. Lewis came to this same commonplace yet startling realization when he lost his friend Charles Williams, a story worth retelling here.

Lewis tells how he, learning that Williams had been taken to Oxford's Radcliffe Infirmary and having no reason for thinking him to be in any danger, brought his friend a book. At the infirmary he received the news that Williams was dead. Lewis comments that he was no more prepared on that day, an otherwise ordinary Tuesday, for his friend's death than he was for his own. It belonged to Lewis now to bring the news of Williams's death to their common circle of friends, who as it happened met each Tuesday morning to share their work. "The world seemed to us at that moment," writes Lewis, "primarily a *strange* one."[13] He goes on:

That sense of strangeness continued with a force which sorrow itself has never quite swallowed up. This experience of loss (the greatest I have yet known) was wholly unlike what I should have expected. We now verified for ourselves what so many bereaved people have reported; the ubiquitous presence of a dead man, as if he had ceased to meet us in particular places in order to meet us everywhere. It is not in the least like a haunting. It is not in the least like the bitter-sweet experiences of memory. It is vital and bracing; it is even, however the word may be misunderstood and derided, exciting.[14]

The point here for us is not, of course, grief, but rather the living imagination that grief may evoke and sustain. Those who live in others' imaginations—whether they no longer exist or never did—live all the same. Their reality is unquestioned and, I would argue, unquestionable. Often, as in the case of Helen, their reality is found to be vital and bracing and exciting. Indeed, the Helen who is the object of this encomium, the Helen whom we seek to celebrate, is not a flesh-and-blood woman but an image or, more honestly, a complex of myriad images. Consequently, her reality cannot be known nor appreciated without imagination.[15] To enter her realm is to enter a world of images, which is the way Plato described the world in which we mostly live anyway, wittingly or unwittingly. Imagination is the very medium of Helen's historical existence.

The historical search for Helen is inevitably a search for and amidst images, images of Helen, who if she ever existed left no certain trace; and unlike Helen "herself," Helen's images provide discrete objects for historical inquiry. Each of Helen's images, whether iconic or textual, considered in this study dates from the distant past and is the proper object of historical understanding. The identification, dating, and contextual interpretation of any icon or text, while not the sole property of archaeology and history, are surely within their legitimate reach, and tracing the history or story of Helen raises problems, historical problems, which in turn call for certain broad practical guidelines regarding evidence: where we look for it, what constitutes it, and how to read it.

The central historical problem of our study has been pointed out already: the fact that its object is imaginary. Helen, for all we know, is a figment of the ancient imagination, nothing more and nothing less. She is encountered only in images, read in texts or seen in art. She is the real yet elusive presence within every mention or depiction of her. Not only does she seem to be other and more than the sum of her explicit mentions or appearances, but she seems to be present even in myths, stories, and images that contain no direct reference to her.

More concretely, the problem is this. We may speak of Homer's Helen or, more accurately, Homer's Helens, the Helen of the *Iliad* and the Helen of the *Odyssey*. To these we may add the myriad diverse Helens sung in lyric verse and portrayed in Attic drama, as well as those painted on vases. Together these raise the question of who or what they are about, if they are not about a once existent individual. Who or what does the history of those images reveal? What real presence lies behind them? But the problem is far more complex than this; for those who set out to search for Helen invariably find her, for reasons soon to be considered, where she is not supposed to be, where she literally is not. They see her in Aphrodite, in Ariadne, in Pandora, in Eos, to mention a few. She reflects them or they reflect her, or both. Their stories seem to retell each other. Then, because each of these "other Helens" has roots and resemblances of her own, Helen becomes associated with the likes of Sumerian Inanna, Canaanite Hurriya, Hebrew Eve, and Vedic Uṣas. If Helen reflects Aphrodite and the others, then she reflects, at one or more removes, whomever they reflect. Her story grows accordingly until the Helen we first knew by name becomes a mere episode in that story. She turns out to have been only a clue. But in saying this, we are far ahead of ourselves.

The immediately pressing question concerns the historical status of those resemblances cited above and others like them. When we notice a resemblance, a striking resemblance, between two people, we often put our perception to the test and ask them if they happen to be related; and it is rare that we dispute their response. After all, it is possible for two individuals to have no discoverable connection apart from the fact that they appear all but identical to each other. Similarly, the fact that striking resemblances occur in the myths and icons of peoples living in times and places utterly remote from each other suggests that cultures too can produce virtual, yet unrelated, twins.[16] All the same, faced with similarity, in people themselves or in their artifacts, we search first for actual connections, blood relations, or simply influence.

What, we are led to ask, are Helen's "connections"? More precisely, if we begin with the Helen we know by name in the Greek poetic and iconographic tradition from archaic to classical times, from Homer to Euripides, which of her myriad resemblances are attributable to actual historical influences? Clearly, within the Greek-speaking world, the answer is relatively simple. We may begin by assuming that anything later may have been influenced by anything earlier. The scope of this assumption has been widened considerably by the relatively recent decipherment of Linear B, the written language of the Mycenaeans, and the accompanying determination that the spoken language that Linear B represents is an early form of Greek.[17] For the purposes of this study, therefore, Helen's home culture, within which broad diachronic influence may be assumed plausible and likely, is the Greek-speaking world from at least the middle of the second millennium to the fifth century.[18] To say that influence is generally plausible and likely is quite a different matter, however, from saying that it actually occurred in any specific instance. It was barely yesterday, after all, that we acquired the ability to prove direct genetic descent from one generation to the next without reliance on perceived resemblance, personal testimony, and trust. By comparison, tracing Helen's lineage is sheer guesswork. In a mostly oral culture, which the Greek-speaking world was, well into the fifth and even fourth century,[19] the meanderings of myths and stories are anyone's guess; and images, until the reintroduction of writing by the late eighth century, are anonymous. Helen's name first enters positive history in the poems of Homer; and the only ancient images actually bearing her name follow, temporally and thematically, the emergence of the written poetic tradition. From that point on, few would doubt the enduring, pervasive influence of Homer, while the prehistoric Greek influences on Homer remain matters for surmise, supported by a general assumption of baseline continuity within Hellenic culture from the Bronze Age to the classical age, despite the various disruptions endured during that span of time. In short, we may assume that any myth, story, or image invented or received by the Mycenaeans could have made its way to Homer and from Homer to anyone else, with or without leaving any lasting trace of its journey.

Once we assume the possible survival and transmission, in archaic and classical Greece, of myths, stories, and images dating from the Mycenaean period, the scope of Helen's possible "connections" widens appropriately to include all those cultures with whom the Mycenaeans, or for that matter their heirs, are known or thought to have had contact; for any contact marks a possible influence. This is, of course, true whether the contact is direct or indirect. When a Mesopotamian seal is found in the Peloponnese and dated from the late Bronze Age, or a Mycenaean pot is uncovered in the Nile Delta, these finds, in isolation, may mean either direct or indirect contact between Mycenaean Greece and both Mesopotamia and Egypt. Pots and seals, after all, may be carried from their original to their final homes by a single set of hands or passed along the way through many hands. With enough pots and seals and an occasional bill of lading to examine, plausible patterns of traffic and trade may be established, which may or may not describe the path actually followed by an individual seal or pot. No matter. If a single pot found its way from one site to another, directly or indirectly, through however many hands, so might a story have followed the same route, leaving slight trace of either its journey or its arrival.[20] It has, after all, "long been established—and is indeed common sense," writes Paul Friedrich, that "myths tend to be shared along trade routes."[21]

The traces left by foreign stories once told and retold in another oral culture are to be found in narrative lines, patterns, images, names, and words embedded in the recipient culture's oral and eventually written tradition. When, for instance, a monkey appears in the writings of Archilochos,[22] providing the first glimpse of a monkey in European literature, or when Aristophanes[23] makes reference to the story of the "The Eagle and the Dung Beetle," we may suspect foreign influence, as we may whenever we find pre-Hellenistic Greeks writing of lions or tigers or peacocks. To complicate matters further, imported stories, unlike pots and seals, may not only break but also break down as they are conveyed to a new place and appropriated by a new people. Quite obviously, stories are translated, both linguistically and culturally, until they mean something to the new owners and serve their purposes. A striking example of this process of absorption may be found in the *History* of Herodotus,[24] wherein we find a near-perfect replica of an older story of likely Indian origin, except for the fact that the original was an animal fable, while Herodotus's characters are all human. Otherwise, the two versions are virtually identical.[25] Clearly, if characters change species, they may change their names and practically anything else about themselves.

Immaterial trade—stories, myths, and ideas—can and likely does go wherever material trade goes. In fact, we might conjecture that the former often finds its way where the latter does not. In cultures wherein literacy was rare, books even rarer, mass media nonexistent, and entertainments few, hunger for and delight in stories must have been common and intense. Furthermore, anyone—merchants, warriors, slaves, sailors, priests, physicians, explorers, and kings—could be a storyteller or a listener, and probably was. Stories add no weight to anyone's load. Pots and seals wind up along established trade routes, whereas stories may be carried so far that their bearer never returns. There is much we will never know about the exchange of goods, much less ideas, in the ancient world.

What *is* known, then, about the contacts of the Mycenaeans with their neighbors and with their neighbors' neighbors? What were their commercial and cultural "connections"? What channels of imaginative influence might have flowed through them to our Helen? Needless to say, this is a vast question, as vast as the world into which it inquires, not something to be encompassed here to anyone's satisfaction. Some response, however, is required, if we are to imagine Helen and to know what to make of her many faces and names and stories. If our search for Helen is to be at all historical, we must know or be able to make an informed guess regarding the possible extent of her relations. Consequently, we must return to and broach the vast question at hand.

That the East Mediterranean world—encompassing Greece, Crete, Asia Minor, Egypt, Cyprus, Palestine, Phoenicia (Lebanon), and Syria—constituted a broad commercial and cultural consortium at the height of the Mycenaean period is by now a commonplace among historians. The history of that consortium—its trade routes, its wars, its shifting alliances, its balances and imbalances of power—defies concise synopsis. If we claim, however, that a myth, a story, a figurine, or an idea might have made its way, whether directly or indirectly, from any part of the East Mediterranean world to another, we hardly risk refutation. In this matter, absence of proof does not amount to negative evidence. Besides, there exists ample indication of extensive commerce throughout the region in question.[26]

A few examples are in order. "There is plenty of evidence," writes Colin Renfrew, "that already in pre-farming times the early inhabitants of southern Greece were traveling by sea."[27] If this is so, then it is no surprise to find that the Mycenaeans, many thousands of years later in the second millennium, were accomplished seamen and traders. Furthermore, if Renfrew's account of Indo-European origins and dispersion is correct,[28] then the Mycenaeans' own roots lay in Anatolia, roots that they shared with "cousins" in Crete. By any account, Mycenaean contact with Anatolia and Crete was extensive. Indeed, from their home cities in mainland Greece, the Mycenaeans partially colonized the Aegean coast of Anatolia, including Rhodes, and eventually controlled Crete.

The travels of the Mycenaeans north and west into Europe, although extensive, are of less interest here, since the older and higher civilizations lay mostly to the east and south. It is well worthy of mention, however, that the Mycenaeans reached Sicily and the Lipari Islands as early as the sixteenth century, and Ischia soon afterwards. Their trade connections, whether direct or indirect, reached as far as Britain, Scandinavia, central, and Eastern Europe.

To the east, following the lead of Minoan Crete, their apparent mentor in such matters, the Mycenaeans took a lively interest in the Levant; and, once they and no longer the Minoans presided over the Aegean, the Mycenaeans established for themselves what may have been colonies or perhaps only trading posts in the Near East, most notably in Syria, Palestine, and Cyprus. In turn, from the seaboard cities of the East Mediterranean, the Mycenaeans gained unquestionable access to the preeminent cultures of Mesopotamia, partly through the Hurrian-Mitanni-Hittite links with northern and central Mesopotamia. The seaboard cities, too, gave the Mycenaeans still another link with Egypt.

Mycenaean finds have been uncovered in numerous sites from Lower to Upper Egypt, as far south as Nubia; and the influence of Minoan-Mycenaean art on the artistic revolution of the Amarnian era of Akhenaten is evident to some.[29] In fact, Mycenaeans, who are thought to have fought with the Egyptians in the early sixteenth century against the Hyksos,[30] appear to have returned among the "Sea Peoples" to invade Egypt and the Levant in the late thirteenth century, completing the collapse of what had been a prosperous and relatively stable period for the entire region. The general crisis that followed the decline of the Egyptian and Hittite empires and the extensive raids of the "Sea Peoples" plunged the East Mediterranean and the Near East into "a long period of absolute decline, whose ferocity is hard to explain."[31] The Trojan War seems to have been a mere moment in that ferocity.

It would be well to pause here to consider further, briefly, the implications of Mycenaean travel and trade. Their direct contacts with Crete, Anatolia, Egypt, and cities along the Syro-Palestinian coast gave to the Mycenaeans at least indirect access not only to the cities and peoples of Mesopotamia but also to all of the other cities and peoples who were or had been trading partners with Mesopotamia and the Near East. With this realization, our circle of possible influences on Helen widens well beyond the Aegean and the Mediterranean to the Arabian Sea and crosses the vast reaches of Iran to India. There we stop, more out of exhaustion than lack of evidence leading us further.

Iranian and Indian influences might have made their way to the Mycenaeans by any number of circuitous routes, but the most likely font of that influence would have been Mesopotamia, with which the Mycenaeans were in at least indirect contact through the coastal cities of northern Syria. There is convincing evidence of Mesopotamian trade with the Indus Valley already in the Sumerian period, as early as the middle of the third millennium.[32] The earliest trade may have been along overland routes, in which Susa and Baluchistan[33] were likely hubs; but sea trade soon followed. The Semitic conqueror of the Sumerians, Sargon of Akkad, the founder of the first great Mesopotamian empire, whose reign spanned the second half of the twenty-fourth century, vaunted his own capital city's sea trade with Telmun (Bahrein), Meluhha (India?) and Makkan (the Arabian mainland?).[34] Bahrein, indeed, appears to have been the major entrepôt in the sea trade between the great cities of the Tigris and Euphrates and those of the Indus Valley, until the latter's decline in the mid-second millennium.

It is important to point out that not only raw materials, such as tin, ivory, and lapis, were transmitted across Iran to Mesopotamia and from there to the Mediterranean. Image-bearing objects, such as seals, pottery, and figurines, were common objects of trade as well. To cite one significant example, nearly identical replicas of a mid-third millennium chlorite bowl (uncovered in Khafaje, Sumer, and bearing elaborate images of the Lady of Beasts and Mistress of Water and depicting bulls not native to Mesopotamia) have been found at Mari, in the north, at sites in the Arabian Gulf to the south, and as far east as Mohenjo-daro in the Indus Valley.[35] In fact, what appears to have been a center for the manufacture of these bowls has been excavated at Tepe Yahya, in Baluchistan, located on the main trade route from Sumer to northern India.[36]

The influences of Iranian and Indian myth, art, literature, and religion on the Near East and eventually on Greece are, it may be suspected, much earlier and far more substantial than they are generally acknowledged to be. Cultural parallels and resemblances between the Greeks and the Indo-Aryans, are most often attributed to their presumed common Indo-European origin rather than to direct or indirect influence, one upon the other, whereas both attributions may well convey a measure of the truth. The Indus Valley civilization, its origins, and its demise remain shrouded in uncertainty. If and when its story is told with any assurance, we may be led to rethink altogether the relationship between the cities and peoples of the Indus Valley and those of Mesopotamia, Egypt, Anatolia, and Crete. For now, we have compelling evidence of early and sustained connections,[37] until the period of collapse and confusion which struck all of these sites in the last centuries of the Bronze Age.

It is unlikely that all international trade, much less contact, ceased following the upheavals—whether invasions, wars, or what Renfrew calls "systems collapses"—of the late Bronze Age; but it is safe to say that commerce and exploration were temporarily and dramatically diminished. Briefly, Greece found itself more isolated than it had been for many centuries, which is not to say that it lost its hold on everything it had once received. Myth, ritual, stories, and a people's imagination are not easily erased, whatever hardships and dislocations come upon them. Regardless, already by the late ninth and early eighth century, a second great "orientalizing" period was under way, still in good time to exercise a profound influence on Homer and Hesiod, the founders of the Greek literary tradition.

In the meantime, before the reentry of Greece into world trade, Egyptian, Phoenician, and Jewish ships were sailing in the Persian Gulf and were thus fully capable of having reached India. The Phoenicians, for one, are known to have had commercial links with India and, for that matter, to have sailed as far west as Gibraltar. In the wake of the Phoenicians, Greeks were soon to retrace the steps of their ancestors westward to Sicily and beyond, but once again we will focus here on their more significant contacts with the East.[38]

John Boardman distinguishes "four main areas in the Near East which were either penetrated by the Greeks, or whose cultures had a profound influence on them"[39] during this period: north Syria, Phoenicia and Palestine, Cyprus, and Anatolia. This was the period of Assyrian ascendancy, whose grip under Sargon II reached from Israel to Tarsus in eastern Anatolia to Eridu in southern Mesopotamia, which ascendancy brought Mesopotamian influence to each of the Greeks' Near Eastern doorsteps, perhaps most notably the north Syrian port of Al Mina. Al Mina, where Greek finds date from at least 800 B.C.E., was probably the earliest and most important of the new Greek trading posts in the Levant. Athens, Euboea, Samos, and Rhodes figured centrally in the renewed trade with Near Eastern markets, which developed during the eighth century. Geometric vases were in considerable demand during the eighth century and have been found in such disparate sites as Catal Hüyük in Syria, Assyrian Nineveh, Megiddo in Palestine, and near Sidon in Phoenicia. Ionian Greeks conducted trade, as well, with Phrygia and made likely use of the overland route across the Anatolian plateau, which route led to Urartu and Iran.

To suggest the range of Eastern experience had by Greeks in the archaic period, several random points of contact may be mentioned. Ionian sailors were in the employ of the Assyrian king, Sennacherib, while Greeks mercenaries, such as the brother of the poet Alkaeus of Lesbos, served under the neo-Babylonian king Nebuchadnezzar II. In Egypt, Greek merchants and mercenaries became commonplace. There is evidence that generations of Greek sailors and warriors in Egypt's employ sailed the Mediterranean and Red seas in Egyptian ships and fought in various Egyptian campaigns from Syria to Nubia. Eventually, King Amasis, "a great lover of the Greeks"[40] despite the fact that Greeks had fought with King Apries against him, gave to the Greeks their own trading colony at Naucratis, a city in which they might build lasting homes for themselves and temples for their gods, and from which they might administer Greek commercial affairs in Egypt. Ionians, Dorians, and Aeolians are said to have combined to found the Greco-Egyptian city of Naucratis.

Once again, Greek trade with the East brought Oriental images and ideas to Greece. As in earlier periods, contact, direct or indirect, commercial or military, between Greeks and Oriental "barbarians" in the archaic period had cultural implications. Not only merchants and mercenaries, after all, but poets and artists too have a keen interest in foreign "goods." "Greeks, and artists," writes Boardman, "are inveterate travelers. The more so, then, are Greek artists; and no less in antiquity than today."[41] The resulting Egyptian, Phoenician, Cypriot, Assyrian, Urartian, and North Syrian influences on archaic Greek art and literature are unmistakable. For example, an eighth-century Athenian grave has yielded five nude female figurines of the type associated with Astarte. They are, in Boardman's assessment, local Greek imitations of Mesopotamian originals, revealing techniques and ideas learned from Near Eastern craftsmen working in Athens.[42] Hera's earrings, as described in the *Iliad*,[43] are of Assyrian design, examples of which, dating from the ninth century, have been found in Lefkandi. Their design was apparently copied by later Greek artisans. Grotesque masks, closely resembling masks of the monster Humbaba, slain by Gilgamesh and Enkidu, have been found on Samos, Thera, and in Sparta. Related to Humbaba is the figure of the Gorgon, whose movement and metamorphoses have been tentatively traced from India to Greece.[44] Finally, it is all but inconceivable that myths and stories too were not imported, in even greater numbers, throughout the archaic period.[45] Surely the Greek iconic fascination with Eastern deities, animal forms, and fantastic hybrids had its counterpart in a rich oral narrative tradition, whose influence on Hesiod and Aesop is particularly evident. Both of these poets, Hesiod in the late eighth century and Aesop roughly a century later, had close connections with Asia Minor, as did Homer.

Eventually, then, with the recovery of literacy in Greece, this second period of orientalizing influence marked the emergence and spread of early Greek poetry and science. The Greeks of the eighth century acquired from the Near East not only the skill to write down their ideas but also many of the ideas which they first wrote down. The "Greek miracle," if we may speak in such terms, lay not in any cultural *creatio ex nihilo*, but rather in the sheer height and brilliance of their achievements in the ensuing centuries of Greek preeminence, achievements whose root system, elusively intricate and ancient, we have endeavored to trace.[46] These too are the roots of Helen, who shines still among the lasting splendors of Greece.

Our aim, after all, is to tell Helen's story, the full story, and so to arrive at the meaning, even the truth, of Helen. If "we define the myth as consisting of all its versions," and if the meaning to be found in myth "cannot reside in the isolated elements which enter into the composition of a myth, but only in the way those elements are combined,"[47] then it is essential that we be able to recognize each version of the myth of Helen wherever we come across it, whether it bears her name or not, and that we be able to discern the unity of Helen amidst her myriad versions. If Greek Helen is not a radical creation but rather, like Greece itself, a "new synthesis," then we must know where and how to look for the elements of that synthesis. We must, in short, be able to locate and to recognize the "avatars" of Helen, her "lines of descent." Helen's "avatars" (from the Sanskrit *avatāra*, meaning "descents"), of course, are, like herself, not embodiments but images, not incarnations but reflections.

The history of Greece and the history of Helen are, as it happens, entwined inextricably. Thus, when Jaan Puhvel outlines "the three main ingredients of ancient Greek culture in general, and of myth in particular,"[48] his outline closely coincides with Paul Friedrich's tracing of the historical sources of Homeric Aphrodite and so of Helen, whom Friedrich regards as a "variant" or "allomorph" of Aphrodite, or an "Aphroditoid."[49] Whereas Puhvel describes the roots of Greek myth as *substratal* (Aegean, Pelasgian, Minoan); *superstratal* (Indo-European Greek); and *adstratal* (the steady seepage from Asia Minor and points further east),[50] Friedrich describes the fourfold roots of the myth of Aphrodite, and thus of Helen, as Old European, Oriental, Minoan-Mycenaean, Proto-Indo-

European, whose influences he specifies as: Sumerian, Semitic, Egyptian, Phoenician, Old European, Minoan, Mycenaean, Proto-Indo-European, and Early Greek.[51] Allowing for differences in nomenclature and adjusting for variant accounts of the movements of ancient peoples, Puhvel and Friedrich concur not only with each other but with the general depiction of Helen's "connections" presented here. Indeed, as general a map of Helen's world, imaginative and historical, as has been drawn here presents little pretext for controversy.

In conclusion, the two central concerns of this chapter—imagination and history—converge in Helen; for her history is essentially imaginative. The world of Helen is a world of images; her history the history of an image. We are concerned, however, not only to collect and to catalogue the many images of Helen but to discover the meaning, the truth, refracted in Helen's myriad avatars. The line of her descent, like the "Divided Line" of Plato in the *Republic,* must be ascended, traced to its source, if the truth, the truth of Helen, is to be found out. This ascent is from the many to the one, from the many Helens to the one Helen.

# 2

## *The Many Helens*

In the Greek poetic, cultic, and iconographic tradition from the archaic period onwards, Helen is the mere fossil of her former self. Her fossil record, however, is plentiful and vivid and thus informative. Most noticeably, it is diverse and contradictory. There appear to be many Helens, too many to make sense of. Depending on the source, she is divine, semidivine, or merely human. Her sister Klytemnestra's mortality, however, seems never to be a matter of question, while their brothers, the Dioskouroi, are, like Helen, one moment human and the next divine. Helen is goddess, queen, trickster, witch, seeress, scapegoat, prize, curse, devoted wife, whore, weaver of tapestries and of fates, phantom, seductress, victim, the promise of bliss, and the assurance of doom. Association with her may bring immortality, whether in song or on the Islands of the Blessed, or it may bring dark oblivion. Indeed, at first glance, Helen might appear to be a mythic catchall, which as we shall see is not far from the truth.

If a coherent myth or story of Helen is to emerge from the history of her myriad images, those images must be, borrowing a phrase from C. H. Whitman, distilled into meaning. Again it must be made clear that the history under consideration is that of an *eikōn* or an *eidos*, an image or a figure, and not of an individual. We are not about to launch a search for the historical Helen, who if she ever existed and could be found out would likely be irrelevant to her own story. Rather, our aim is to discern the unity of Helen, the form of the forms of Helen, as it were, the original endlessly reflected Helen. This will be accomplished neither by selecting arbitrarily a manageable array of narrative ingredients and constructing a fairy tale, nor by collecting uncritically every least trace of Helen and amassing her archives. The key to the unity of Helen lies in the syntax of mythology, wherein meaning is the product of mixture rather than of separation. In the physics of color, pigments subtract from each other and accumulate into black, while lights add their colors to each other and accumulate into white, the fullness of the visible spectrum. Like the latter, the myriad images of Helen, when brought together and layered one upon the other, yield brilliant clarity, not impenetrable confusion.

The first task, then, is to hunt down and to gather the many faces, the many images of Helen, without immediate concern for coherence. Even a cursory inquiry into the lineage of Helen yields the kind of complexity and contradiction we are looking for.

In the *Iliad* and the *Odyssey*, Helen is known simply as the child or daughter of Zeus—*kourē Dios* or *Dios thygatēr*[1]—though her precise familial connections with the rest of the Olympian pantheon are never brought to light. Apart from several lesser figures,[2] such as Muses and nymphs, these two epithets belong solely to Helen, together with the preeminent daughters of Zeus: Aphrodite, Artemis, and Athena;[3] and she, Helen, is curiously the only so-called mortal among them.

Elsewhere, in a Hesiodic fragment,[4] Helen is said to be the child of a daughter of Oceanos, which coincides with a later tradition that Helen is the child of Aphrodite.[5] In a fragment from the *Kypria* of Stasinos, Zeus remains Helen's father; but her mother is "fair-haired" Nemesis, whom Zeus, we are told, had taken by force.[6] As for Nemesis herself, she is by Hesiod's account in the *Theogony*[7] one of baleful Night's dark daughters, born to be a *pēma*, a disaster, for the race of mortal men; but this is a late and shadowed Nemesis. Before the reign and the rapine of Zeus, celebrated by Hesiod, and afterwards, Nemesis was honored as a nymph, a goddess of earth, of animals and vegetation, and of the sea.[8] This is suggested not only by her name[9] but also by the fact that, as Zeus pursued her, Nemesis changed forms numerous times, from one animal to another, under water and across land, until at last she leaped into the air and took flight as a goose and was taken by Zeus in the form of a swan.[10] Appropriately, her child, Helen, was born from an egg.[11]

Leda, the wife of Tyndareos, may have been a somewhat late entry as "mother apparent" to Helen. Ambiguity surrounds her—and, for that matter, her spouse's—parentage.[12] Both Leda and Nemesis, in one tradition or another, produce offspring from an egg,[13] so that their common ornithic connections are clear. Less clear are the source and the contents of the egg or eggs. Sappho, writing in accord with the *Kypria*, says:

> People do gossip
> And they say about
> Leda, that she
> once found an egg
> hidden under
> wild hyacinths.[14]

Another legend suggests that Helen's egg dropped from the moon, reflective of an earlier moon-fallen egg, ferried to the banks of the Euphrates by fish and hatched by doves until it cracked open to reveal Astarte, Aphrodite's Syrian counterpart.[15] Which of Helen's siblings too came from eggs and which eggs they came from and whether they too had a divine parent are all too complex and too speculative to pursue in detail here.

Before we leave, however, the elusive figure of Leda, we might speculate further regarding her "connections." It is possible that she may be, like Nemesis, closely linked or even identical to Leto (Doric: Lato and Lat), the mother of Artemis and Apollo. After all, Artemis shared with Nemesis the title *Adrasteia*, "the inescapable one,"[16] originally associated with the moon[17] and later extended to both Nemesis and Artemis, and eventually to Helen, the daughter of Leda.[18] Furthermore, all of these mothers and daughters—Leda, Leto, Nemesis, Artemis, and Helen—are associated with swans.[19]

Before delving further into Helen's myriad identities, it may be well to reflect briefly on the speculative multiplicity of her lineage as we have uncovered it thus far. In the literal world of legitimacy and inheritance, any confusion, much less mass confusion, concerning one's parents is unfortunate; and having multiple—that is, more than two—biological parents is considered to be more discrediting than enhancing. In the world of myth, however, a world of images, one can't have too many relations, even parents. Lines of descent are lines of power. As in a spectrum, the wider the energy that can be gathered and focused, the brighter the light that is cast. Thus, as we shall see, Helen is both older than, and the child of, Zeus. She is born from womb and sea and egg. She descends both from the solar light of day and from the moonlit darkness of night. She is child and goddess of earth and sea and sky, hatched from the cosmic egg, heaved up by the primal waters. And always she is woman.

In both the poetic and iconographic traditions, the bond between Aphrodite and Helen, whether as mother and daughter or not, is the one most explicitly and extensively developed. The eyes, the face, the beauty of both are at the same time irresistible and terrifying. Helen might appear to be simply a mortal, incarnate Aphrodite, except that Helen too is, on occasion, immortal and disembodied. Regardless, Helen is, it seems, all but indistinguishable from Aphrodite, as from an other self. Thus Paul Friedrich speaks variously of Helen as an "Aphroditoid" or "allomorph" of Aphrodite, as "the 'faded Aphrodite,'"[20] and as Aphrodite's "alter ego."[21] Indeed, it might be said that Helen is the very image of Aphrodite.

The reflections of Aphrodite in Helen are too many to count, much less to examine here. Several must suffice. First, there is the irresistible beauty they share in all but equal measure. From an epic fragment,[22] we first learn of the famous beauty contest, occasioned by Strife, between three great Olympian goddesses—Hera, Athena, and Aphrodite—and of how Paris was made to judge between them. The powers of Aphrodite prevailed and Paris awarded her the prize. What is more, in choosing Aphrodite, Paris received not Aphrodite but Helen, her surrogate, as his lover. Aphrodite herself, it seems, for all the smiling pride she took in mating mortal women to gods and mortal men to goddesses, was far from inclined to cross that line in person, even for Paris. When, to silence her frequent boasts and to teach to her her own lesson, "even in Aphrodite's soul Zeus placed sweet longing to mate with a mortal man"[23] (in this case Anchises, the father of Aeneas), Aphrodite's response, after the fact, was one of shame. Yes, she lamented to Anchises, "great shame shall be mine before the immortal gods to the end of all time because of you . . . struck by great madness in a wretched and grave way, and driven out of my mind, I mated with a mortal and put a child beneath my girdle."[24] In epic poetry, shame frequently afflicts those who succumb to sexual desire.[25] Such desire is, after all, a form of compulsion, breaking or taming those on whom it is imposed. It clouds the mind and weakens the knees, as if it were a form of death. All too often Fair Desire brings not only brief delight but lasting embarrassment.

In liaisons involving mortals, Aphrodite mostly prefers to play the procuress. Without succumbing to the desire that she herself inflicts, the nearest Aphrodite may come to the beds of mortals is to send Helen in her stead. That Helen is, indeed, doing Aphrodite's loving for her is surely suggested in the heated exchange between the two of them in book 3 of the *Iliad*, when Aphrodite, having lifted Paris from battlefield to bedchamber, now presumes to send Helen off to make love with him, the prospect of which Helen finds shameful. "Well, go to him yourself," she shouts.

You hover beside him!
Abandon the gods' high road and be a mortal!
Never set foot again on Mount Olympos, never!
You suffer for Paris, protect Paris, for eternity . . .
    until he makes you his wedded wife—
    that or his slave.
Not I, I'll never go back again.[26]

Unless Helen draws the line here, there will be no end to Aphrodite's desire nor to Helen's shame. After Paris's bed there will be another. This much Helen knows for sure about Aphrodite. "Where," she asks, "will you drive me next?

Off and away to other grand, luxurious cities,
out to Phrygia, out to Maeonia's tempting country?
Have you a favorite mortal man there too?[27]

There is no mistaking Helen's meaning here. Maeonia is tempting to Aphrodite not to Helen; and her next lover will again be Aphrodite's favorite, not hers. She sees Aphrodite in everything she, Helen, is made to do; and so, presumably, does Aphrodite. Helen is, as it were, possessed. What this means, among other things, is that Helen has no choice. Like Aphrodite, she *is* desire. Helen can no more resist the power that defines her than can others resist her.

There, in the beginning, when Aphrodite rose from the waves and the bright foam, were *Himeros* and *Erōs*, Desire and Love. Together, they "attended her [Aphrodite's] birth and accompanied her as she went to join the family of the gods."[28] Her other attendants include the Charites, or Graces, daughters of Zeus and personifications of loveliness, who are said in the *Iliad* to have woven Aphrodite's ambrosial robe.[29] Among their tasks or privileges is to give Aphrodite her baths and to anoint her with oil. Still another of Aphrodite's typical companions is "one who brooks no denial,"[30] Peitho, whom Walter Otto calls "the assistant and double of Aphrodite."[31] *Peitho* was, indeed, a cult name of Aphrodite at Pharsalus and Lesbos; and L. R. Farnell suggests that *Potnia* (Mistress) *Peitho* in Hesiod is probably a designation for Aphrodite herself.[32] In the iconographic tradition, Aphrodite, as well as Peitho, Eros, and Himeros, frequently accompanies Helen to assist in her seductions or abductions, and, when needed, to protect her from harm.[33] Beauty, grace, loveliness, and the longing, all-persuasive desire that they provoke: these are the accompaniments of Aphrodite and Helen. They go nearly everywhere together.

Although Aphrodite is occasionally honored as the patroness of married life and, in Sparta, appropriates even the name of Hera,[34] and, correspondingly, although Helen is on rare occasion portrayed as the most loyal of wives,[35] both Helen and Aphrodite most often represent *erōs*, the anarchic force of free love, the principle of spontaneously combustible passion, all but impossible to put out before it has run its chaotic course. "Blessed are those who sip the pleasures of Aphrodite slowly and with sublime good sense," sing the Chorus of young girls in the *Iphigenia at Aulis*, with Paris and Helen luridly on their minds:

> In her bed, peace of mind is a rare prize.
> Blessed is anyone who finds calm there,
> Where most are driven mad.
> Eros the hovering golden-haired boy with the bow
> Has but two arrows in his quiver.
> The one brings bliss.
> The other casts a net of confusion
> And chaotic pain.[36]

The Chorus go on to beg for themselves, singly, each in her own life, "a tame love that knows its place,"[37] very different from what Aphrodite had in mind for Paris and for her favorite Helen.

In case there might be misunderstanding on this point, the "chaotic pain" loosed by Aphrodite, the "snare-knitter,"[38] on hapless lovers is not the sentimental pain of the heartsick, the ephemeral gloom of those become unhappy in love. The arrows of Eros are all too often dipped in death. "With his venom," writes Sappho,

> Irresistible
> and bittersweet
> that loosener
> of limbs, Love (*Erōs*)
> reptile-like
> strikes me down.[39]

The wounds inflicted by Eros, at Aphrodite's bidding, or at Helen's, are quite literal and lethal. The death they bring is the real thing.

"Hell to ships, hell to men, hell to cities"[40] is how the Chorus of the *Agamemnon* describes Helen, who sat by her loom at Troy and, like the Fates, wove the destinies of men, entangling them in doom.[41] The *Iliad* offers a brief glimpse of Helen in her *megaron*, her great chamber, embroidering into the wide web before her the struggles and deaths of Greeks and Trojans alike battling on her account.[42] The warp on her loom is, we are told, *porphyreēn,* a dark crimson, once the color of life but by now, among both the Achaeans and their foes, the color of death.[43] For her part, Aphrodite, whose cultic names[44] include *melainis,* the "dark one," *androphonos,* the "man-slaughterer," and *tymborychos,* the "grave-digger," finds appropriate company with Helen *rhigedanēs,*[45] "the one who chills and stiffens," and Helen *stygerē,*[46] "the one who brings the hated chill." This last epithet is one that Helen in fact assigns to herself when she confronts Aphrodite in book 3 of the *Iliad.* Its Indo-European root is *\*stug-,* "to be stiff," a root that in Homeric poetry is invariably associated with death.[47] This same root is found both in the verb *stygeō,* "to hate" or "to fear," and in *styx,* a common noun connoting both something hateful and something piercingly cold, which makes it a suitable name for the dread river of the world below.[48]

Finally, in the last book of the *Iliad,* when Helen speaks in tears before the corpse of Hector, laid out in a great carved bed, she pays tribute to the rare friendship he has offered to her, to the fact that "[t]here was no other in all the wide Troad who was kind to me, and my friend; all others shrank (*pephrikasin*) when they saw me."[49] The word used here to describe all but Hector's response to the sight of Helen—*phrissō*—means to bristle, to shiver, to shudder with fear. It is used when teeth chatter or when hairs stand on end. The truth of Helen must encompass, it seems, not only the bed of love but also the bed of death.

Helen is, indeed, an object of hate, perhaps *the* object of hate in archaic and classical Greek literature, a hate that appears to have touched her myriad counterparts, the women of Greece. "Good or bad, we're all thrown together," complains Creusa in Euripides' *Ion.* "We're an object of hate. It's our lot, what we were born for."[50] "Of all creatures who have breath and wit," adds Medea, "we women endure the most assaults."[51] It comes as no surprise, then, to find Helen all but encompassed by hate in the *Iliad.* When at last Helen, calling herself *stygerē,* frigid and loathsome as death itself, rebels against her own divine paradigm, against Aphrodite, telling her that if she wants to see Paris's needs met she can meet them herself, Aphrodite turns on Helen, fiercely and without pity:

> Don't provoke me, wretched girl.
> I might lose my temper
> And cut you loose.
> My frightful love for you
> Could easily turn to hate.

> You would die a miserable death
> Where I would leave you,
> Encased in hate
> Between Greeks and Trojans alike.[52]

So fiercely is Helen hated from every side, that her own self-hatred is sometimes overlooked. In book 6 of the *Iliad*, Helen confides in Hector, the closest she comes to a friend in Troy, and tells how she regrets not only her marriage with Paris but the fact that she was ever born at all.[53] It would require exceptional wit and venom to devise a more abusive epithet than that which she attaches to herself in that same conversation. "Nasty bitch evil-intriguing"[54] is Richmond Lattimore's rendering; but if we eschew the demands of poetry, attending to each of the three words in the original phrase, we might suggest "evil-spinning, blood-chilling dog." Once again the focus is on death, death of the most violent sort, battlefield death. Adjectives aside, she calls herself a *kyōn*, a dog, three times;[55] and, in the world of the *Iliad*, dogs are not pets but predators, scavengers, worrying the flesh from the bones of the dead. In the arms of Helen, men are, sooner or later, carrion.

In sum, although the commonplace association of both Helen and Aphrodite with erotic love is unchallengeable, the *erōs* they bring is often convergent with *eris* and *thanatos*, with violent conflict and death. It comes as no surprise, then, to find the myth and cult of Aphrodite occasionally mingled with that of Ares, god of war, as well as with that of Hermes, guide of the dead. Though Hephaestos's Homeric longing for Aphrodite is legend, it is most often the warlord Ares, astride his bronze war chariot,[56] who becomes her spouse, to whom Hesiod has her bear three offspring: two dread sons—Fear and Panic—and one daughter, Harmonia, the eventual bride of Kadmos.[57] Correspondingly, one of Helen's legendary spouses, her last, is Achilles, who is to violent force what she is to beauty: its fullest human embodiment. The divine marriage of Aphrodite and Ares may indeed be reflected in the marriage of Helen and Achilles, the two most godlike figures to be found among the *Iliad*'s mortal cast.

"Thanatos and Eros, Death and Desire," writes Jean-Pierre Vernant, "are neighbors."[58] In the *Theogony*, the birth of laughter-loving Aphrodite, whose allotted province is "the whisperings of girls; smiles; deceptions; sweet pleasure, intimacy, and tenderness,"[59] is followed by the birth of Night's fearsome brood, which includes hateful Doom (*Moros*), black Ker, and Thanatos. Thanatos, like his brother *Hypnos*, or Sleep, is masculine.

Indeed, they resemble each other; and neither is ever ugly in Greek art.[60] "There is nothing terrifying and even less that is monstrous about this figure of Thanatos," suggests Vernant, "whose role is not to kill but to receive the dead, to transport the one who has lost his (or her) life. . . . it is another feminine figure, Ker—black, grim, evil, horrible, execrable—who represents death as a maleficent force that sweeps down on humans to destroy them."[61] Thanatos is rarely personified in Greek literature; most often it is described as a mist, a cloud, or a veil, which comes down over the dead, separating light from darkness, life from death. *Ker* is more fatal and fearsome. "She is the poetic and private equivalent," writes Emily Vermeule, "of the corpse-ravagers of war, the birds and dogs" who hover over and roam about the battlefield.[62] In the *Ker*, we find still another image of Helen.

Helen's province, it seems, extends from bed to battlefield, and the oblivion she brings is not always sweet, not always a laughing matter. Sex and slaughter, making love and making war, are strangely analogous in the Greek poetic and iconic imagination. In Homer, there seem to be as many ways of killing, of murderously penetrating the flesh of a victim, as there are of loving, and more. In fact, the language and attendant images for these two realms—love and war—converge. The verb *damazō* (as also its equivalent *damnēmi*) spans a range of meanings from subjugation to slaughter to rape to seduction, and the "mingling" conveyed by *meignymi* may be that of lovers or that of warriors. Both kinds of couples grapple and cling and know a desperate, intense intimacy with few if any parallels anywhere else in human experience. Furthermore, both the love-act and the death-act are accompanied by "small talk"(*oaristys*)[63] and preceded by a form of play, a not-yet-violent contest soon to be raised to a higher power and decided or consummated on another plane. "Homer has a habit, at mocking moments," claims Vermeule,

> of treating enemies as lovers, fusing the effects of Eros and Thanatos. The *oaristus* of war, the manipulated bodies, the lily-white (thus feminine) fallen enemy stripped on the field with the spear lusting to taste him, the marriage with death. . . . it was a formal principle of Greek myth and literature that love and death were two aspects of the same power, as in the myth of Persephone or Helen of Troy.[64]

It is the convergence of *erōs* and *eris*, of eroticism and rivalry, moreover, that fires the *mythos* or plot line of the *Iliad*. In the Greek poetic and iconographic tradition, it is Helen's provocative beauty that both arms and disarms men, making them either raise or drop their swords. Greece flew to

arms over her, waged and endured for ten years a slaughterous war for
her, and then, as soon as Troy fell, nearly murdered the prize, the *cause
célèbre*, as it were. Seemingly without transition, love turned to hate; the
desire to possess became the desire to destroy, as if little or nothing truly
separated them. What saved Helen was her beauty.[65] Countless archaic
and classical vases, spanning several centuries, depicted more or less the
same scene: Greek warriors or Menelaos himself lowering or, more commonly, dropping their swords[66] when Helen exposed a bit of herself, her
shoulder or her shining face.[67] Even in an age such as ours of epidemic
cultural illiteracy, that Helen's face launched ships—warships, not yachts
or cruise liners—is a byword, so much so that philosophers and scien-
tists, concerned to define and quantify everything, even beauty, have proposed that the standard unit of beauty be a "milli-Helen," defined as the
beauty required to launch a single ship.[68] The poignant datum behind
such humor is the assumed measure-for-measure correspondence
between beauty and firepower. Clearly many things provoke contention
and violence—lethal violence—in Greek poetry. Men go to war over
crowns and cities, trade routes and cult places, as well as over an assort-
ment of insults and injuries. What presently concerns us is the tradition of
violence over women, notably beautiful women, the favored objects of
men's sexual desire and romantic attachment. In short, what concerns us
is the congruence of love and war.

If the Shield of Achilles forged by Hephaestos and envisioned by
Homer offers any map at all of the archaic Greek imagination, it would
seem that war and peace, though sharing the same cosmos, constitute
realms apart, and that love belongs to the realm of peace, not war. Surely
the arts of laughter-loving Aphrodite and of her favorite Helen belong as
far away from the arts of war as imagination might possibly place them.
Prominent among the peaceful arts of Aphrodite is the *Choros*, the dance
and song that she shares with the Nymphs, the Charites, the Muses, and
with her sister Artemis. Aphrodite's association with the *Choros* is a frequent theme in ancient Greek poetry, early and late,[69] and seems to derive
from her function as a fertility goddess.[70] In fact, Helen's abduction by
Theseus, which may have provided the narrative pattern for her later
abduction by Paris, is said to have occurred as she was dancing in the
temple of Artemis Orthia at Sparta.[71] Aphrodite too, we are told, was herself once snatched away from the *Choros* of Artemis.[72] Curiously, when
Aphrodite becomes the abductor and lifts Paris from the battlefield to his
bed, from war to love, she describes him to Helen not as a warrior but as a

dancer. "Come with me," urges Aphrodite. "He is in his chamber now, in the bed with its circled pattern, shining in his raiment and his own beauty; you would not think that he came from fighting against a man; you would think he was going rather to a dance, or rested and had been dancing lately."[73] Obviously, he is ready for love not war; and for the moment these are not to be confused.

Indeed, the contrast between the arts of war and those of love is often sharply highlighted. When Paris, at the opening of book 3 of the *Iliad*, slips back behind the front ranks,[74] shivering with fear at the mere sight of Menelaos, Hector shames him at once. "Evil Paris, beautiful, woman-crazy, cajoling,"[75] he calls him, for his not standing up to the warrior Menelaos. And what if he did hold his ground and fight? "The lyre would not help you then," adds Hector, mocking the would-be dancer, "nor the favours of Aphrodite, nor your locks, when you rolled in the dust, nor all your beauty."[76] Later, when Hector himself, the warrior's warrior, has been slain, and with him nearly every battle-fit man in Troy, Priam laments bitterly their loss. "All these," complains Priam, "Ares has killed, and all that are left to me are the disgraces, the liars and the dancers, champions of the chorus."[77] Unlike Priam, Alkinoös, king of the Phaiakians, does not disdain his people because they do not excel in feats of brutal strength, preferring feasts, music, dancing, changes of clothing, hot baths, and their beds. Instead, he calls upon them to entertain and to impress Odysseus, their guest, with what they do best. "Come then," he says, "you who among all the Phaiakians are the best dancers, do your dance, so that our guest, after he comes home to his own people, can tell them how far we surpass all others in our seamanship (for which the Phaiakians were widely renowned) and the speed of our feet and dancing and singing."[78] In these and other moments, it would seem that the arts and delights of Aphrodite have nothing in common with those of Ares; and yet, we know, they shared the same bed.

Long before Homer, in an oral and written epic tradition that likely exercised a profound influence on Greek poetry and thought, the arts of love were regarded as civilizing. In the *Gilgamesh*,[79] the wild-man Enkidu,[80] who is thought to have represented "primitive" man, man before cities and civilization, indeed "primordial" man, is not only first "civilized" but even first "humanized" by his love-making, for six days and seven nights, with Shamhat the *harimtu*,[81] the temple courtesan from the precinct of Inanna/Ishtar,[82] Aphrodite's Mesopotamian counterpart. Afterwards, it is this woman, Enkidu's first lover, who leads him from the wilds to the city, from savagery to civilization. What is clearly affirmed in the cult of Inanna/Ishtar, as well as in the cult of Aphrodite, is that sexual passion and the accompanying arts of love are as integral to culture as they are to nature and are shared by human beings not only with the animals but also with the gods.

Indeed, among the *mes*—the attributes and measures, the arts and prerogatives, of civilized life, which Inanna herself first brought to her holy city of Uruk—were the following: not only priesthood, godhood, and kingship, not only scepter, crown, staff, and throne, but "the colorful garment . . . the loosening of the hair . . . the binding of the hair . . . the art of lovemaking . . . the resounding musical instrument . . . the art of song . . . the rejoicing of the heart."[83] Admittedly, among the *mes* as well were the arts of war, "the art of the hero . . . the art of power . . . the kindling of strife . . . the plundering of cities." Even here, as in the Gilgamesh tradition, in the earliest literature known to us, the human heart is torn two ways. The conflict between hedonism and militarism lies deep within ancient Near Eastern literature,[84] constituting a vast fault line from Inanna to Aphrodite, from Enkidu to Paris, from Shamhat to Helen. The world encompassed by the *mes*, like the world hammered into Achilles' shield, like the bed of Aphrodite and Ares, contains an essential contradiction.

What concerns us here, however, is not simply the coexistence of love and war in society but rather their congruence in the figures of Aphrodite and Helen. When Aphrodite, on behalf of her son Aineias, enters the fray, the great Diomedes, "knowing her for a god without warcraft," wounds her in the palm and then tauntingly sends her on her way. Warlike Athene too mocks Aphrodite, suggesting that she "tore the tenderness of her hand on a golden pin's point" as she was pushing still another Greek woman toward some Trojan's bed. Zeus, smiling, makes the same point more kindly. "No, my child," he says, "not for you are the works of warfare. Rather concern yourself only with the lovely secrets of marriage (*himeroenta . . . erga gamoio*)."[85]

How, we might reasonably wonder, does this Aphrodite become the "man-slaughterer," and how does her familiar Helen become "hell to cities"? How do the arts of love provoke the arts of war? How do the goddess of desire and her most perfect image become the object of undiluted hate? This question lies at the center of our concerns here and throughout this study.

Aristotle, in the *Poetics*, traces the origin of poetry to the pleasure human beings find in the *mimēsis*, or "imaging," both of what delights and of what disturbs them.[86] Very early, Aristotle explains, before any of the actual poems or poets known to him, poetry divided into two currents: praise and blame. Corresponding to the most fundamental distinction in what exists prior to *mimēsis*, prior to language, the distinction between what evokes delight and what evokes distress, there are, according to Aristotle, two fundamental poetries: a poetry of celebration and a poetry of assault. Donald Ward, in his comparative study of early Indo-European poetry, finding these same two poetic currents in early Vedic, Celtic, Roman, and Germanic literatures, suggests a prior Indo-European tradition as their common source.[87] Interestingly, he notes that in the range of literatures under consideration the dog frequently occurs as a metaphor of slander and abuse.[88]

In classical Tamil literature, representing the pre-Indo-European culture of southeastern India, we find essentially the same two ancient currents defining the poetic tradition, divided between "*Akam* poems" and "*Puram* poems," poems of love and poems of war. Unlike the Greek practice, as Aristotle describes it, whereby a poet characteristically writes one or the other type of poem, in accord with his natural disposition, Tamil poets often write both. As in the Indo-European tradition, the Tamil poets were "the articulate bearers of honor and blame."[89] The "business of the bards," writes A. K. Ramanujan, was "to keep honor alive. . . . A legendary warrior is said to have bequeathed his skin to be made into the war drum of his tribe, to inspire later warriors every time it was sounded. The Tamil bards drummed on such drums of war."[90] The same bards, who companioned kings and their armies, sang of love and beauty, of intimacy and poignant stillness. There are moments, however, when the streams of *Akam* and *Puram* mingle, as in a poem entitled "A Leaf in Love and War." Ramanujan explains that the dark green leaves of the "chaste trees," the *nocci*, "were used by women in love as leaf skirts (made and given by their lovers), and as emblematic wreaths by warriors during a seige."[91] In the words and in the central image of this poem, we stare down into a truth neither simply bright nor simply dark; and we find a clue to Helen.

> The chaste trees, dark-clustered,
> blend with the land
> that knows no dryness;
> the colors on the leaves
> mob the eyes.
>> We've seen those leaves

> on jeweled women,
> on their mounds
> of love.
> Now the chaste wreath lies slashed
> on the ground, so changed, so mixed
> with blood, the vulture snatches it
> with its beak,
> thinking it raw meat.
>> We see this too
>> just because a young man
>> in love with war
>> wore it for glory.[92]

Under the centripetal influence of poetic imagination, the sublimity of love and the savagery of war find a common emblem and therein reflect each other. There is something right in the wrongness of their proximity. Their convergence seems more than a coincidence. It is as if they belong together. Freud, in reviewing a pamphlet by Karl Abel entitled "Über den Gegensinn der Urworte" (The Antithetical Sense of Primal Words), began by saying that he Freud had already noticed but not yet understood the fact that "dreams show a special tendency to reduce two opposites to a unity or to represent them as one thing." He pointed out that for dreams "the word 'No' does not seem to exist."[93] Dreams, as images, both are and are not what they are. The dream world is, after all, a world of images. Freud had already learned from and followed the lead of ancient dream interpreters in assuming that any element in a dream might mean its opposite. Now, from Abel's philological studies, Freud said he was astonished to have learned that "this habit of the dream-work to which I refer exactly tallies with a peculiarity of the oldest languages known to us."[94]

In ancient Egyptian, Freud learned, many essential words had two meanings, the one being the very opposite of the other, such as "strong" and "weak" or "light" and "darkness" or "command" and "obey." Even more extraordinary to Freud's mind was that the Egyptians often took two contrary elements and united them to form a single compound, whose meaning was then derived solely from one of its constituent elements, the other being swallowed altogether. Thus, "oldyoung" meant simply "young" and "farnear" meant simply "near." Another curiosity of this ancient tongue was that oftentimes the sense of a word could be reversed by reversing the order of its sounds. And all this in Egypt, which, he concurred with Abel, "was anything but a home of nonsense."[95]

Additionally, Freud accepted Abel's further claim that the originally contradictory meanings of many essential words extend from Egyptian more widely throughout Semitic and Indo-European languages. For Freud, the implications were clear. Abel's philological theories and data corroborated his own work with dreams. Freud found the fact that the language of dreams and the oldest languages on earth display elements of the same syntax to be "a confirmation of our [his] supposition in regard to the regressive, archaic character of thought-expression in dreams."[96]

For us, in our search for Helen, it is less clear what we have found here. However, if the oldest roots of the oldest words, as well as dreams, often reveal contradiction, then we may be closer to, rather than farther from, the meaning of Helen, when we uncover contradiction in her. If the earliest practitioners of written language "used to entrust two most inimical thoughts to be borne by one and the same sound, and used to combine in a sort of insoluble union what was mutually most intensely opposed,"[97] and if in our dreams, thousands of years later, we still do the same thing, then perhaps contradiction lies at the core of more than Helen. She may be no more than an image of the contradiction at the core of things.

Every image, as we have seen, is composed of contradiction. Every image both *is* and *is not* what it is. Every image, therefore, reflects the state of *becoming*, the state of finitude, the state of everything and everyone poised between being and non-being. When that state becomes conscious, it is called "mortality," the condition of a living, breathing contradiction, which is what we have found Helen to be. Here, in the world of images, she, in whom war and peace, love and hate converge, comes as no surprise.

Helen is too real, however, to be explained. She is simply to be seen, now here, now there, now in this light, now in that. In each of her moments and facets, she reveals always more than we thought and always less than is.

Rene Girard, for whom "violence is always mingled with desire,"[98] would tell the story of Helen in a different way. The greater the desire, the greater the violence. How could the most lengendarily desirable woman in the world *not* be the cause of its legendarily most violent war? Furthermore, if Helen is the object or victim of what Girard calls "mimetic rivalry," then it is no wonder that she is both hated and loved. "Mimetic rivalry," after all, does not arise over a woman when two men happen to desire her but rather when one man desires her solely because he sees that another man already desires her.[99] The woman's desirability, then, is not intrinsic but is assigned to her by men. Like an item on auction, she acquires incalculable value the moment she becomes, for no reason proper to her, the object of fierce bidding.

In point of fact, all desire, according to Girard—and, for that matter, Plato—is at its core a desire for *being*. Man [*sic*], however, not knowing what *being* is or where to look for it, defines it in practice as "something he himself lacks and which some other person seems to possess. The subject thus looks to that other person to inform him of what he should desire in order to acquire that being."[100] All desire, then, is infinite, essentially blind, and eventually mimetic. Unable to quench the desire that consumes us or to discern the object whose attainment would satisfy us, we turn to others whom we perceive to be as desirous, and imagine not to be as unknowing, as ourselves. If we cannot define the essentially desirable, at least we can detect the actually desired and assume that, if it is already desired, it must be desirable. In fact, the more it is already desired, the more desirable it must be.[101]

Few would deny that mimetic rivalry is at work in the *Iliad*; for the ultimate object of that rivalry is *kydos*, which Emile Beneviste defines as "the talisman of supremacy."[102] Unless one is seen, one will never be sung; and unless one is sung, one will never be remembered. *Kydos* brings *kleos*. Glory (shining before the eyes of others) brings fame (surviving on the tongues of others). Clearly, heroes require poets and poets require heroes. Great deeds are forgotten unless they are sung, and without great deeds to sing there would be no songs. Ordinarily, the way that any warrior becomes seen in battle is by doing something big, something great, so that all or most eyes fall on him even as he shines. Then, after the battle, if he survives in the flesh as well as in song, the hero will be awarded a prize, a shining object to enhance his *ousia*, his net worthiness, his essential visibility. Just as glory is gained in battle (wherein men are despoiled of their lives), goods are gotten after the battle (when dead men are despoiled of their possessions). Shining deeds are rewarded with correspondingly shining objects. The latter are fitting tokens of the former. Anyone ought to be able to see, after the battle as well as during it, who is "best among the Greeks"; for he will have in his possession the finest *geras* or prize of honor, the most shining object of desire.

In the Greek war of wars and the subsequent song of songs, the most shining object of desire was not a bronze tripod or a team of horses or a shield or a jeweled crown or even a city; rather, it was a woman: shining (*argeie*) Helen, the most perfect mortal image of golden (*chrysee*) Aphrodite. In fact, the *eris* shaping the *Iliad* may be said to be twofold: the strife or rivalry between Menelaos and Paris over Helen and the strife or rivalry between Agamemnon and Achilles over fair-cheeked Briseis, who like Helen is said to be "in the likeness of golden Aphrodite."[103] Friedrich would expand this even further. "Three catalyses of honor," he argues, "unleash much of the force that drives the epic."[104] The first of these is the abduction or seizure of Helen; the second is the seizure of Chryses; and the third is the seizure of Briseis. In the end, however, not even the least of the victors will be without his prize, which is to say without his woman. Nestor's words reach out to the entire Greek host to provoke analogous desire and anger, and to anticipate their consummation: "Therefore let no man be urgent to take the way homeward until after he has lain in bed with the wife of a Trojan to avenge Helen's longing to escape and her lamentations."[105] If there is to be enough violence to make a great war, there must be enough rage and lust and women to go around. Any man, from the best to the least of the Achaeans, if he is to be willing to kill or to die, must have Helen herself or, at worst, some poor image of her as incitement to his war effort.

The taking of the city of Troy is never seen directly in the *Iliad*, only foreseen, imaginatively. When Hector is slain and the Greeks swarm around his corpse and take their turns with it, the ravaging of the city becomes all but immediately visible. It is as near as the Greeks decide it to be. From within the walls, the sight of Hector despoiled becomes, in a moment of communal *eikasia*, the sight of the city despoiled. Hecuba tears her hair from her head and throws off her veil. Andromache too uncovers her head, casting to one side the encircling veil that was a gift to her from Aphrodite on the day of her wedding. The scene they enact will soon be familiar: son and husband slain, mother and wife unveiled. Wailing and lamentation fill the city. Any doubt that we are witnessing the fall of Troy is dismissed when the poet comments: "It was most like what would have happened, if all lowering Ilion had been burning top to bottom in fire."[106]

The violation of the city of Troy and the violation of its women become imaginatively one in the scene described above. In reality they will be moments apart. The metaphor alive in these images is linguistically embedded in the single word *krēdemna*, which means both a city's battlements and women's veils.[107] It is all of these *krēdemna* that will soon come down together, when women and city alike are defiled in a free-for-all of *eris* and *erōs*.

Outside of the formal Greek tradition, in that greater consortium of cultures that made up the East Mediterranean world of the Bronze Age, we find the same phenomenon, the same convergence of *erōs* and *eris* celebrated in song. In fact, this theme of violence or the threat of violence provoked by rivalry over a beautiful and beloved woman, although noticeably absent from the older literatures of the ancient Near East, came to pervade the tales and epic literature emergent from the Mycenaean/Amarnian age,[108] as well as the oldest epics of the Indian subcontinent.[109] For example, in the Hebrew patriarchal narratives of Genesis, we find three distinct episodes telling essentially the same story:[110] The husband of a remarkably beautiful woman, fearing that his wife's desirousness might put him at risk as they travel through foreign lands, passes himself off as her brother instead of her spouse. This subterfuge, quite predictably, leads to the irresistible sister-wife's being taken to the house and the bed of the resident ruler, from which she is eventually retrieved. In the first instance of this story, Genesis 12:10–20, the object of desire and rivalry is Sarai,[111] the beloved, compellingly beautiful wife of Abram and now the temporary possession of Pharaoh. In the end, Pharaoh is more than eager and relieved, however, to see Sarai gone; for she has brought not passion but plague to him and to his house.

The closest ancient East Mediterranean counterpart to, and perhaps even model for, the story of Helen seems to be the *Epic of Kirta* (perhaps *Keret* or *Kret*, as only the consonants—*Krt*—are written in the original text). *Kirta* is a story from Ugarit (modern Ras Shamra), a once-prosperous Canaanite city-state located on the northern coast of Syria, which fell prey to the Sea Peoples near the end of the Bronze Age. Once thought to have been a Mycenaean colony, Semitic Ugarit was surely frequented by Mycenaean ships and was, along with nearby Cyprus, a focal point for contact between Greeks and the diverse peoples of Egypt and the Near East. Admittedly, the evidence for any direct influence of Kirta on the Greek tradition is circumstantial. All the same, the parallels between them are striking and serve to extend our awareness of the genre to which the Greek story of Helen belongs.

Kirta, a hero-king of ancient Canaan, his house in ruin, is approached by the great god El, the Father of Men, and asked: "Why are you weeping, Kirta, why does the Gracious One, the Lad of El, shed tears? / Does he want to rule like the Bull, his father, or to have power like the Father of Men?"[112] Like Paris, Kirta receives divine offers of kingship and of power but longs for something else. Kirta wants sons, descendants—and not from just anyone. He wants sons from Hurriya, the beautiful daughter of the king of Udm, seven days' journey from the house of Kirta. At once, he raises a massive force of men. No one—not the blind nor the sick nor the newlywed—no one in his kingdom is exempt from the call to arms. Like a plague of locusts the army of Kirta arrives in and proceeds to devastate the land of Udm, whose king, Pabil, attempts to sue for peace. With lavish gifts—silver, gold, slaves, horses, and more—the king of Udm would buy off Kirta and his army; but Kirta's response is more to the point than Pabil's largesse:

> Why should I want silver and gleaming gold,
>     a controlling share in a mine,
> and perpetual slaves, three horses,
>     a chariot from the stable, servants?
> Give me rather what is not in my house:
>     give me the Lady Hurriya,
>     the fairest of your first-born:
> her fairness is like Anat's,
>     her beauty is like Astarte's,
> her eyebrows are lapis lazuli,
>     her eyes are jeweled bowls.[113]

Despite lacunae in the text, it is clear that Kirta wins the beautiful Hurriya for his wife and that, with the blessing of El, she bears him numerous sons and daughters. Once again his house flourishes.[114]

Hurriya, like Helen, is a woman prized above all other treasures. She brings new life and fresh prosperity to a despoiled house. In her fairness and beauty, Hurriya is likened to Anat and Astarte, two manifestations of the Syrian goddess of erotic love and war, a goddess closely resembling, among others, Sumerian Inanna, Semitic Ishtar, and Greek Aphrodite. This Syrian goddess, whom we will refer to simply as Astarte, is mythically and cultically associated with fertility, trees, birds, and the sea, all of which are equally significant for Aphrodite and her mortal emanation, Helen. We are told by Philo of Byblos that the Phoenicians themselves identified Astarte with Aphrodite and that when Greeks heard the Syrian myth of a goddess of love hatched from an egg fallen from the sky into the river Euphrates, it was natural that they would think of Helen.[115] Furthermore, Astarte's temples, like those of Ishtar, were centers of sacred prostitution, a practice found, though only rarely so, in the cult places of Aphrodite.[116] The survival rather than the scarcity of this quite un-Greek practice in Greek temples would seem most relevant, providing one more strand in the cord joining Aphrodite to the ancient Near East. In fact, the bond between Aphrodite and the Orient, as the Greeks understood the term, is inseverable.[117] And what is true of Aphrodite is rarely false of Helen.

Now, if we are to reveal still deeper strata in the stories of Aphrodite and Helen, we must consider again and afresh the theme of rape and abduction. Until now, we have considered this theme under the rubric of epic poetry, wherein *erōs* and *eris*, erotic love and deadly conflict, fuse. Our concern, in part, has been to lay bare the romanticization of violence and the sublimation of greed into erotic desire, which so clearly mark the poetic tradition emergent from the Bronze Age, not only in Greece but throughout the ancient East Mediterranean world and beyond. Now, if we peel away this layer, as it were, we find still another and older layer, preserved in the poetic tradition and reenacted in ritual. Here the concern is not with the *erōs* of sex, nor with the *eris* of sexual rivalry. These belong to history, the web of stories woven by the actions and the passions of mortals who are born to live and die only once and briefly, while our focus now is on the cosmos and its endless story, retold and reenacted in the daily cycle of the sun's rising and setting and in the yearly cycle of the earth's birth, death, and rebirth, cycles that inspired and shaped countless ancient myths and rituals, among them those involving rape or abduction.

That the human life cycle mimics or mirrors the greater cycle of life that encompasses it is a truth pervading ancient myth and ritual. Indeed, it is a truth not yet wholly lost on us. Each year the earth grows fat and flourishes with fresh life and then dies, languishing until it is made soft and moist again, seeded with new life. In most of the varied mythologies of the ancient East Mediterranean world, it is the male sky-god who in the spring rain showers the female earth with his wet seed, filling her with the new life which she will bring to fruition. This sacred and essential event is celebrated in myriad ancient myths, songs, and rituals and nowhere more beautifully than in a fragment from the lost drama *Danaides* of Aeschylus:

> Now the pure Heaven yearns to pierce the Earth;
> Now Earth is taken with longing for her marriage.
> The rains showering from the mating Sky
> Fill her with life, and she gives birth, for man,
> To flocks of sheep and to the life-giving wheat.
> And from that liquid exultation springs,
> Perfect, the time of peace. In this I share.[118]

Frequently, in ancient cities, it was the king in his priestly or even divine capacity, who with his temple consort reenacted and thereby served to reassure the *hieros gamos,* the sacred mating of Heaven and Earth, without which life would cease forever. In this light, sexual intercourse is each time a sacrament, a potent ritual provocation and celebration of the forces that rouse the world from death to life. In this same light, Aphrodite, the goddess of *erōs,* and with her the pan-erotic Helen, are goddesses of regeneration, inspiring sexual activity on, as it were, a cosmic scale. Aphrodite's exciting influence, it should be noted, is not confined to human circles, as we learn in this scene from one of her hymns:

> And she came to Ida with its many springs,
> the mother of animals. She went right up
> the mountain to the sheepfolds. Behind her
> moved grey wolves, fawning on her, and
> bright-eyed lions, bears, and quick, insatiable
> panthers. When she saw them she felt joy in
> her heart, and she put longing in their breasts,
> and immediately they all went into the valley
> in twos to sleep with each other.[119]

Both in her role as surrogate for Aphrodite and in her own right, Helen possesses an *ex officio* relationship to sex and fertility. Thus, it is altogether appropriate that she should have multiple spouses. Tradition assigns her at least five: Theseus, Menelaos, Paris, Deïphobos, and lastly Achilles.[120] Interestingly, Achilles' placement on this list of Helen's mates resulted in his being nicknamed *Pemptos* or "number five" on the island of Crete.[121] Long before her multiple associations with Greek heroes, however, Helen was herself worshiped in the Peloponnese. Erected on a site known to have been occupied by the late Mycenaean period,[122] the temple at Therapnai, though it was and is traditionally referred to as the *Menelaion,*[123] quite likely first belonged to Helen and her cult. Female figurines found on the temple site at Therapnai, some *phi*-shaped and others mounted on horseback, resemble objects found at the temple of Artemis Orthia,[124] with whom Aphrodite and thus Helen are associated.[125] It has been argued that even Helen's name, as would befit a vegetation goddess, is derived from either the word for baskets carried in the festivals of Artemis and Demeter or a word meaning "shoot" or "sprig," and possibly from both.[126] Reference has already been made to the legendary hanging of Helen on Rhodes, where Helen bears the cult name *Helenē Dendritis,* "Helen of the Trees," reflecting an ancient fertility ritual associated with Helen not only on Rhodes but also at Dendra, near Sparta.[127] This ritual involved the hanging of figurines of the moon-goddess, with whom Helen is likewise closely identified, from the boughs of orchard trees as fertility charms. Ariadne, who may be seen as Helen's counterpart in Minoan Crete,[128] is also associated with the moon, is abducted by Theseus, and said to have died hanging from a tree. Clearly, in the web of myth and ritual woven tightly around the figures of Aphrodite and Helen, the strands of death and life, violence and grace, despair and regeneration are not to be plied apart easily or perhaps at all.

A large share of Helen's claim upon the title of fertility goddess lies in her repeated abductions;[129] and abduction or rape is often linked in myth and ritual not only with the resurgence of life but also with the waning and eclipse of life. By one account, with myriad ancient variants, the earth, the great mother of all living creatures, loses her will, as it were, to live and to let live, when her beloved daughter is taken off to the world below, often to be the bride of the lord of the underworld. Not until the child is retrieved and restored to her mother, not until a deal is struck with the chthonic powers to allow the child to remain in the world above, in the land of the living, for half of every year, does the great mother's period of lethal mourning come to an end with the renewal of all living things. Thus, the two polar extremes of life and death, childbirth and mourning, remain forever feminine preserves, the *temenoi,* the sacred precincts as it were, of woman, preeminently the great goddess of many names and faces, Aphrodite for one, with Helen as her avatar.

Abduction, then, in the myths and rituals retelling and reenacting the earth's cyclical birth, death, and regeneration, is a bivalent image. It is as close to decay as it is to fruition. Abduction is full of *erōs,* the irresistible pull of life. It is also full of *thanatos,* the equally irresistible gravity of death. In fact, with Hades as abductor and his victim as his bride, *erōs* and *thanatos* collapse into each other and become one. The frenzy of life and of love and of death, marriage bed and death bed, womb and tomb, become all but indistinguishable. Thus Helen, invariably the bride of mortals, is all the same closely associated with death, the "other abduction." *Erōs* has *thanatos* as an overtone; when the one note is struck, the other is heard, even if faintly. It is, in a word, unavoidable. This would explain, in Euripides' *Helen,* the otherwise odd introduction of the story of "the mountain mother of the gods"[130] and her lost girl at precisely that point in Helen's story when she is being abducted or, from her perspective, retrieved from Egypt. It is as though Helen and Menelaos strike one note and the Chorus hear and resonate to another.

The truth may be that they are somehow the same note; for the world of myth, like that of music, is mysteriously cyclical. The cries of love and of birth and of death would seem to be a mere octave or two apart from each other. Our human ears, curved by mortality, hear them nearly as one.

In the story of the great mother and her *korē*,[131] the child "whose name may not be spoken"—a story inseparable from that of Demeter and Persephone, brought to cultic life in the mysterious rites at Eleusis—the mountain mother of the gods, "wild with worry and longing," searched for her daughter "torn from the soft grip of the other girls, as they danced the circling choruses." Then, when her search failed, the mother cast herself down on the cold earth and brought an end to all life, the price the world would have to pay for her daughter's violent, untimely end.

> So she brought blight upon the barren earth,
> Making the soil sterile, unyielding to any fruit.
> Total was the ruin she brought to the race of men.
> For the sheep and the cattle she provided nothing,
> No fresh, leafy fodder, no curling green tendrils.
> Cities lost their means of life.
> The gods went without their offerings.
> The altar flames went out.
> And with a mother's endless grief,
> Bitter for her daughter lost and gone.
> She sealed shut the earth's springs.
> The glistening streams ran dry.

As it happens, and appropriately so, it was Aphrodite, "loveliest of all the blessed ones," who first went to the side of the mourning mother and stirred her to life again. It was she

> Who took in her hand the skin-taut tambourine,
> Rimmed with brazen castanets.
> And soon her clamor reached the depths of hell,
> Where a smile broke across the goddess-mother's face,
> As she took up the blaring flute,
> And in the wildness of it all,
> Rediscovered joy.

In sum, abduction can and does mean at the same time both abduction from life into death and abduction from death into life. The circle described here is both the circle of life and the circle of death; and Helen, together with Aphrodite, is as yet mysteriously at its center. There is still another cycle of abduction and retrieval, told in myth and enacted in ritual, to which Helen and Aphrodite are utterly central. In this cycle, it is the goddess who does the abducting. Aphrodite, unlike Helen, is never herself raped, never abducted. In matters of love, she is the procuress, the agent force. The *Theogony* tells how Aphrodite once abducted Phaethon, Dawn's resplendent, godlike son, when he was a mere boy.[132] Later, as a ploy in her seduction of Anchises, related in her first Homeric Hymn, Aphrodite pretends to have been abducted by Apollo from the circle of girls dancing to Artemis and brought by force to the house of Anchises as the victim of Apollo's designs rather than the perpetrator of her own. Finally, when Anchises finds her out, she cites Eos's abduction of Tithonos as a precedent for what she has just done. In fact, Eos has a number of abductions to her name.[133] Here, in these stories of Aphrodite and Eos, we possess clues to another, celestial dimension of Helen's world, too vast to reveal fully here.[134] Instead, we must make do with the simplest of maps.

That Aphrodite, like Eos or Dawn, may also be a celestial goddess is already suggested in her name. If we accept, with Ernest Maass and Vittore Pisani, that the two essential elements of the name *Aphroditē* are *aphros* ("foam") and *ditē* ("bright"), then we appear to have a name pointing in two directions: to the bright sky above and to the dark sea below.[135] One bridge between them and Aphrodite, of course, would be the foam that formed around the genitals of the sky-god when they were hurled into the sea, whence emerged Aphrodite. But there is another possibility. One occurrence of *aphros*, a word rare in epic, is to describe the river Okeanos, forever circling the cosmos.[136] Its reach is from east to west, from the heavens to the underworld. *Helios*, the Sun, in its rising and setting, emerges from and plunges into Okeanos. In its bright foam, the ambiguity of Aphrodite's birth—from sky or from sea—may well be resolved; for Okeanos is both.[137]

While Aphrodite and Eos share, with others, the epithet *dia* ("shining" or "bright," related to the Indo-European word for "sky," *\*dyēus*, from which the name of Zeus is derived) Helen is called *argeiē*, which on the face of it means "Argive," that is, "from Argos," known for its horses. The dilemma here is that Homeric Helen is not from Argos, unless the meaning of Argos here is derived from the adjective *argos*, meaning "shining" or "bright," in which case Helen *argeiē* would be "bright Helen," from Argos, the "place of light."[138] Suddenly, heroic saga becomes transparent to celestial myth. Abducted from Argos, Helen is taken far from the light into a place of darkness, from which she must be retrieved. Her *nostos*, or "homecoming," to Argos will be a return to the place of brilliance, the place of horses, "the place of life and light."[139]

If we wish to gaze at the celestial brilliance of Aphrodite and Eos, reflected in Helen, then we must consider another celestial figure who will unlock for us the mysteries of Argos, the place of light and life. I have in mind the Vedic Dawn Goddess, Uṣas,[140] the direct counterpart of Greek Eos and Aphrodite. Uṣas, the Vedic embodiment of loveliness and charm, shares with Aphrodite and Eos the following elements:

> red, rosy colors, bathing in and emergence from water, cosmetics and golden ornaments, display of the body, particularly the breast, smiling, singing, dancing with and being attended by young maidens, multiple lovers and (at least the suggestion of) erotic affairs, the mixing and combining of multiple roles in sex and kinship (including maternal ones), patronage of paths and routes, motion, the sources of fertility and creation, control over living creatures, and association with the cosmic ambiguities of light and darkness, life and death.[141]

Perhaps most importantly, Uṣas, alone of all the gods and goddesses in Vedic Sanskrit, is given the title "child of god" or "child of the sky," shared by Aphrodite and Helen.[142]

In the light and shadow cast by sky-born Uṣas, daughter of the Sky and sister of Night, we see many things. We see that the *choros* of Aphrodite refers not only to a dance or to a group of dancers but to a dancing-place, the place of the sun's rising.[143] It is a place of peace and love and life, the home of the goddess of light, the bedchamber of the goddess of love, the dance-circle where goddesses of life dance the world to its flowering. No wonder that Paris, abducted by Aphrodite and brought to the bed of love, looked in his shining beauty as though he was just about to enter or had just left this place. Like Uṣas, Eos traverses the sky with the Sun, *Helios*, her brother, rising from the waters of Okeanos at dawn and plunging into the same waters at sunset.[144] To her lovers, her unwitting mortal companions, she brings both shining beauty and dark death.[145]

Helen too belongs there, with her lovers, at the edge of the world, where darkness and light, past and future, west and east, death and life meet. From there, after all, beyond Okeanos in the West, from a grove tended by the singing Hesperides, came the golden apple, sealing so many fates with her own. In Helen is reflected not only Uṣas, but Helen's even more direct Vedic counterpart, Sūryā, the Sun Princess, daughter of the Sun God and his bride Uṣas, cognate with Helios and Eos. In her cir-cuiting of the sky, Sūryā is accompanied by the Ásvins, the shining Horsemen, identified with the Morning and Evening Stars.[146] In the Vedic hymns, they are called "the Retrievers," rescuing her each day from dark-ness. The one precedes her at dawn out of the darkness of night and the other follows her at sunset into that same darkness. The Ásvins' sexual relationship with Sūryā is ambiguous. Sometimes they are her suitors, who give her to her bridegroom Soma, the moon, the sacred plant and its fiery, life-giving juice.[147] Indeed, the marriage of Sūryā and Soma is the divine prototype of all human marriages.[148] Sūryā's immortality, how-ever, left her with time for many lovers and husbands,[149] including both of the radiant Ásvins.[150]

The correspondences between Sūryā and Helen, as between the Ásvins and the Dioskouroi, Kastor and Polydeukes, are both numerous and remarkably close-fitting. Even the shades of difference between the two Vedic brothers are discernible in their Greek counterparts,[151] as well as in the twin sons of the Ásvins, who are among the five husbands of Drau-padi, Helen's counterpart in the *Mahabharata*.[152] Furthermore, the Ásvins are likened to swans,[153] depicted as celestial birds[154] or as riding in a sky-chariot drawn by swans,[155] reflecting the legendary birth of the Diosk-ouroi from a swan's or goose's egg[156] as well as their frequent iconic association with those birds.[157] Finally, of course, the Ásvins and the Dioskouroi are reflected in Helen's various legendary suitors, husbands, and retrievers, most notably Theseus and Pirithous, and Agamemnon and Menelaos.

Like Sūryā, the Vedic Sun Princess, bright, shining Helen moves in an endless orbit through darkness into light and through light into darkness. Light and darkness, the world above and the world below, love and war, life and death: Helen belongs to each of these, equally. Hers is not just a pretty face; it is dreadful too. The many Helens come down to two, as dif-ferent and inseparable as day and night.

# 3

# *The Duality of Helen*

The many facets and faces of Helen have come down to two. The one is bright, provoking desire and joy. The other is dark, provoking hatred and grief. The relationship and balance between these two, however, remains to be examined. To minds like the Greeks', noted for critical reasoning, committed to ratio and proportion, unresolved dualism is no better than an unanswered question. Besides, the poetic and political traditions of archaic and classical Greece make it manifestly clear that men were at peace neither with Helen in particular nor with women in general.[1]

Indeed, outside the artistic *temenos* of those poems and pots in which Helen's bared face or breasts made warriors drop their swords and surrender to her loveliness, Helen's spectacular beauty provided her with little or no protection against the insults of centuries. Helen-bashing was an accepted poetic pastime. However desirous Helen was renowned to be, she was mostly an object of contempt. Add to this phenomenon the demonstrably profound and rarely denied misogyny of the Greek tradition, and it is a short leap to some rather disturbing conclusions regarding male ambivalence, or the lack thereof, toward Helen and her countless, more ordinary images, the women of Greece. We will avoid that leap for now, however, and take instead what may appear to be an unwarranted detour. We will consider the figure of Pandora, the first woman of Hesiod; and from her we will find our way back—a short distance—to Helen. Our own eventual and peculiar defense of Helen will be seen to depend on what we discover from Pandora and on the relevance of those discoveries to Helen's case. For now all that is needed is the benefit of whatever doubt this detour might instill.

   The composition of the *Theogony* and of *Works and Days,* attributed to a supposed Boeotian farmer-poet by the name of Hesiod, is commonly assigned to the late eighth or early seventh century.[2] To confine these works, however, to the pen or stylus of a single man and to a narrow chink of all but lost time is to overlook several salient realities. The works of Hesiod, like those of Homer, represent both the terminus of a vast oral tradition and the source of a vast written tradition. Their debts to the past as well as their authority over the future are incalculable. Since we are unable to hear a past we cannot read, the words of Homer and Hesiod appear to have emerged from a silent void resembling that of the first verses of Genesis. Indeed, what we know as Greek literature was first conjured into existence by the voices of Homer and Hesiod. We cannot afford to forget, however, those countless other anonymous voices of uncertain origin and age, who like underground rivers fed the first visible streams of archaic Greek poetry.[3] They are the true Muses to whom both Homer and Hesiod were so outspokenly grateful.

   All this is to say that when we read Hesiod we cannot really know whose voice we hear nor precisely whence it comes. The alphabet, like a cloak thrown over a ghost, makes merely spoken words visible; yet we cannot see through that cloak, behind the written word, to the oral past which is lost in its own preservation. The more we learn about that past from other sources, however, the older and more vast it becomes, a fact that we will soon confront in the figure of Pandora.

   The *Theogony* is an account of origins, preeminently the origins of those divine beings who compose and preside over the cosmos. It is also a narrative of divine history, tracing the succession of regimes seen to have culminated in the reign of Olympian Zeus. The narrative of Zeus's rise to power and of the consolidation of his regime is doubtless rooted in an earlier array of succession myths, which circulated throughout the ancient Near East. The proportion of Hesiod's debt owed to each tradition and the itinerary of each transmission are matters of wide and likely irresolvable disagreement. The likeliest principal influences on Hesiod's account of the succession from Ouranos to Kronos to Zeus, together with Zeus's collateral struggles with the Titans, with Prometheus, and with Typhoeus, would seem to be the Hittite versions of the Hurrian Kumarbi[4] and Ullikummi[5] myths as well as the Babylonian *Enuma Elish.*[6] M. L. West suggests that a hellenized version of such Oriental material reached Hesiod via Crete and Delphi, whereas P. Walcot traces its transmission, particularly that of the *Enuma Elish,* from Al Mina in northern Syria to

Euboea, and from there to Boeotia, the reputed homeland of Hesiod and a center of cultural influence in the archaic period.[7]

The *Theogony*, like most theological works, is no example of sublimely unbiased metaphysics. Instead, it is highly political. In it, the regime of Zeus and the reign of Olympian justice are celebrated as the achievement of the aeons, the arrival of celestial civilization. It is, one might say, Hesiod's version of "how the West was won." In the *Theogony*, Hesiod, a poet with "a burning passion for Zeus," offers "not just the story of the beginnings of the universe and the history of the gods" but "even more a resounding hymn of praise in honor of Zeus . . . relating the exploits of the king of the gods, as just as he is terrible."[8] It is most like the hymns to Yahweh attributed to David or the *Enuma Elish*, which sings the praises of the divine warrior-king Marduk. In each instance, there is a fusion of absolute authority, martial glory, and what promises to be justice. In each instance, too, there is the clear subordination of female to male, presented as an evolution from the old order to the new, and from savage, even theriomorphic, ways to resplendent anthropomorphism.[9] When the divine becomes so transparent to the human, it is little wonder that the human is seen to resemble the divine.

The *Theogony* may be the oldest Greek literature we possess; in any event, it addresses the oldest of times and of concerns, human concerns. For while humanity may appear quite peripheral to the *Theogony*, the opposite is the case. Indeed, "Hesiod's cosmos is human—or at least protohuman—before it is a cosmos, and the *Theogony* is the story of its progressive humanization."[10] In other words, Hesiod's account of origins traces the development of a world that becomes progressively familiar with time, progressively human and progressively Greek.

The origin of peculiar immediate interest to us, in our defense of Helen, is not surprisingly the origin of women, the first woman, who is called the *"kalon kakon."*[11] In fact, it is this very name that draws us to the *Theogony*. Comprised of two adjectives—*kalon* meaning "beautiful" and *kakon* meaning "evil"—it is essentially dualistic. Paradigmatic Woman, which we may assume this first woman to be, is, it seems, a living oxymoron, a living contradiction, which is precisely what we have already found Helen to be. Perhaps the faithless Helen has been faithful at least to her origins as a woman; and it would appear that Hesiod has provided, in *kalon kakon*, her definitive epithet. The truth is that he has provided much more.

Out of any context, *kalon kakon* would be irresolvably ambiguous. It

could mean "beautiful evil" or "evil beauty" or "beauty-evil." We would
have no clear indication as to which of woman's elements is substantive
and which only modifying. We could not know whether woman, in being
called *kalon kakon*, was being called: (a) essentially beautiful though qualifiedly evil; or (b) essentially evil though qualifiedly beautiful; or (c) essentially both evil and beautiful. In this tangle of words there lie profound
differences, which Hesiod for his own purposes sorts out for us. When he
is through, there is no ambiguity left. In the context provided by Hesiod,
it is *kakon* that defines the substance or essence of woman. Repeatedly,
*kakon* is made to stand alone, stripped of *kalon*. The truth of woman is
stripped of pretense, and woman is revealed as unambiguously evil:
"Thunderous Zeus made women to be a *kakon* for mortal men";[12] "he
fashioned this *kakon* for men to make them pay for the theft of fire."[13]
What then, has become of the *kalon*, the beauty of woman?

Before responding to this question directly, we must consider the fuller
context within which the story of the *kalon kakon* occurs. Woman, as stated
above, is made and presented to man in retaliation for the theft of fire; but
that theft by Prometheus, son of Iapetos, was provoked by Zeus's withdrawal of fire from mankind in retaliation for Prometheus's earlier theft
of the finest sacrificial portions. In the perpetration of both thefts,
Prometheus proved himself more clever than Zeus, using his *doliē
technē*,[14] his "deceptive skill," to outwit the king of the gods. In the first
instance, Prometheus wrapped the meat and fatty portions of the sacrificial ox in the victim's inedible hide and stomach and then wrapped the
bare bones in glistening fat, knowing that Zeus would mistakenly insist
on the latter as his prerogative. In the second instance, Prometheus concealed living embers in a hollow fennel stalk, enabling him to elude
Zeus's embargo and to return fire to mankind. The theme is unmistakable. Skill or craft (*technē*) is set to work in creating a ruse (*dolon*) which
even a reputedly intelligent godhead would fall for. Poetic justice, much
less Olympian justice, requires, however, that the tables be turned. In
falling twice for the same *dolon*, Zeus has to have learned, or remembered, something. Enter woman; but not yet.

The words *technē*, *doliē*, and *dolon* occur repeatedly in Hesiod's account
of Prometheus's twin offenses, which lead up to Zeus's retaliation in
kind.[15] But these are not their first appearances in the *Theogony*. There is
an older and equally significant Hesiodic history to these words and the
deeds they describe. When the hate of Kronos for his father peaked and
Kronos plotted with his mother Gaia against Ouranos, she thought up for
the two of them an "evil deception" (*doliēn . . . kakēn . . . technēn*),[16] which

West translates "a nasty trick,"[17] an understatement to be sure. Later, when Kronos learned from Gaia and Ouranos that he too would be undone by his own child and began to swallow methodically his wife's children as they dropped from her womb, further *technē*[18] did the trick. Zeus was hidden away in a rock cave; and a massive rock was wrapped in swaddling clothes. Kronos, of course, went for the *dolon* and swallowed the rock-baby, just as Zeus in due course would swallow the bundle of bones, and as man, the last in a line of dupes, would take woman home with him.

It is this same word—*dolon*—that resolves the ambiguity of woman and puts her seeming contradictions in perspective; for woman, once she is properly adorned, veiled, and crowned, is called a *dolon*,[19] a "trick," a "baited trap." It is eminently true of woman, as fashioned and fitted out by the gods, that what you see is not what you get, which makes her a fitting rebuttal for the glistening bag of bones foisted upon Zeus. The difference between woman's beauty and her evil is the difference between appearance and reality.[20] Robed in silver, modestly veiled, garlanded with flowers, and crowned with gold, woman is a *thauma*,[21] a "wonder to behold." Gods and men, mortals and immortals, are filled with awe at the sight of her. Unlike the gods, however, men are defenseless against her charms. Woman is a "lure" before which men are "without resistance."[22] She is, in short, the irresistible bride whom men will be unable not to take home with them. But when they do, when they remove the veils, the robes, the flowers, all the cosmetic evasions given her by the gods, when they rapidly exhaust her superficial charms, then men will find out that they have taken into their homes and their lives a *pēma mega*,[23] a great misery, a great pit into which all of their toilsome efforts will be quite futilely poured.

Before considering this woman, man's *pēma mega*, in still further detail, we would do well once again to open wide the scope of our considerations to encompass the history within which this moment, the moment of woman's creation and man's ruin, occurs. More precisely, the moment I have in mind begins with the sacrifice gone wrong at Mekone and ends with humanity's, even Prometheus's, consequent misery. Brief insubordination results in lasting subordination, with a vengeance to be remembered. This moment is framed by two statements: first,

> It was just as men and gods were in crisis (*ekrinonto*) at Mekone that he [Prometheus] cunningly cut up a great ox, apportioning it in such a way as to seduce Zeus into making a big mistake;[24]

and second,

> Thus it is impossible to mislead or to elude the mind of Zeus.[25]

The issue here is clearly sovereignty. What has happened before, one would imagine, could happen again. In a line of ultimately unstable regimes, the stability of Zeus's regime is theoretically and practically open to question. That there is indeed a crisis, something remaining to be decided, is made evident by the two stunning challenges to Zeus's wit and rule soon offered by Prometheus in the name of humankind. In fact, all four sons of Iapetos and Klymene—Atlas, Menoitios, Prometheus, and Epimetheus—are minor trouble from the start. Coeval with Zeus, they represent a rival line of descent from Ouranos and Gaia, which, if allied with unruly mankind, could spell major trouble. Indeed, their very names—"the Endurer," "the Endeavorer," "the Forethinker" (one with creative imagination, seeing things before they exist or happen), and "the Afterthinker" (one who sees things only after they exist or happen)—suggest that these figures represent larger-than-life human paradigms, magic mirrors, in which men may see themselves and their possibilities blown large. Most troublesome is Prometheus, who seems determined to bring Zeus down and to elevate the status of humankind by giving them creative imagination, defiant wit, and divine fire, in short all that is needed to make them like gods.[26] With Prometheus as a model[27] and benefactor, humankind may embrace ambitions which they have yet to imagine, much less act on.

Apparently, at Mekone in Sikyon, all this—the imminent contest between humankind and Zeus—was to be decided. In the act of animal sacrifice,[28] the central ritual act of Greek religion, the essential order of the cosmos would be affirmed and entrenched. The primacy of gods over men and of men over beasts would be made ritually visible and politically secure. The cornerstone of Greek piety and Olympian politics would be laid. For all this to be, however, the sacrifice must be duly performed, which was what Prometheus neither had in mind nor did. The humiliating failure of the *krisis*, the critical test of Zeus's sovereignty, prompted Zeus to take the more extreme measure of withholding from men any access to divine firepower or transformative force, without which men would soon be virtual animals, shivering in caves and eating their meat raw. Then, thwarted a second time, Zeus devised his final solution: woman. Woman would guarantee that man, with or without fire, had offered his last threat to the sovereignty of Zeus. She would be living testimony to the truth that "it is impossible to mislead or to elude the mind of Zeus." As an added bonus, she would make man suffer for ever having imagined otherwise.

Essentially the same account of the First Woman, man's *pēma mega*, the exquisitely tied fly—momentary splendor and then all hook—is to be found in Hesiod's *Works and Days*. The context for that account is, however, a good deal more mundane than the framework of the *Theogony*. While in the *Theogony* the human story was only beginning, humankind is mostly old history in *Works and Days*. Four ages of man have come and gone, each a good deal worse than the one before;[29] and Hesiod finds himself in the fifth, wishing he were anywhere else. Strife defines every relationship; virtue is rewarded with misery, and so is everything else. Yet it was not always so. Men once lived without toil and without pain. Like fruit they ripened in the sun of the god's blessings; and then, when full, they dropped from life, as from a tree, quietly in their sleep. Hesiod's account of the fall of man begs the question Why? Why and from where so much misery? The answer is again woman, the source of all of man's woes.[30]

Although in *Works and Days* the First Woman has a name, a name of great significance (*Pandōra*), she is presented in very much the same terms as in the *Theogony*. She is bait set by the gods for men, who with pounding enthusiasm throw themselves upon her, expecting to embrace bliss and discovering, in retrospect, that they have swallowed their doom. It is no wonder that her first husband is named Epimetheus, that is, "After-thought"—one who learns the truth, the essential evil of woman, only later, on the morning after. She is given the awesome exterior of a god-dess;[31] the *ēthos* or inner character of a sneak thief; and the *noos*, the heart and mind, of a *kyōn*, a dog, a predatory scavenger who waits for men to fall and then picks clean their bones.[32] Her face, the focus of her appearance, is immortal, provoking immortal thoughts; her soul, invisible at first yet revealed implacably in all she does, is the deadly handiwork of Argos-slaying Hermes, the guide of souls lost to the world below.[33] Woman is like a gleaming gold cup brimming with poison, with honey smeared around its lip: lovely to behold, sweet to the lips, and lethal to the last drop.

Woman, adorned by the gods with every beauty and grace, burdens man with all that is hideous and devouring in his new condition. Woman, the recipient of all that is bright, is the giver of all that is dark. Indeed, both of these claims are conveyed in her name, *Pandōra*, which means at the same time both the "All-gifted" and the "All-giver." Like her other,

impersonal name, *kalon kakon,* this new name suggests an essential ambiguity which Hesiod is quick to interpret and so to resolve. Hesiod's comment on the naming of woman tells the whole story. She is called
Pandora, he informs us, because "all those who dwell on Olympos gave
each one to her a gift, a grief for men who strive and toil."[34] Pandora, "all-
gifted" with every *kalon* is the "all-giver" of every *kakon.* All of the divine
largesse which she embodies has only one purpose: human misery.

Pandora, then, is indeed the recipient of the gifts of all the gods. She is
not, however, their final recipient; for these gifts are intended ultimately
and primarily for men, to provide for their endless torment. First there
are the cosmetic gifts, Pandora's various charms and adornments, which
serve to ensnare men; then there are the dark contents of Pandora's jar,
released forever among men when Pandora removes its lid. Toil, disease,
pain, care, old age—all of the *myria lygra,*[35] the innumerable miseries that
make up man's condition—pour from the jar of Pandora the "All-giver,"
the giver of all grief.

The transparent meaning of this text has been obscured over recent
centuries by the substitution of "box" for "jar," a decisive change of
image attributed to the sixteenth-century monk Erasmus, who mistrans-
lated the original Greek word *pithos* with Latin *pyxis.*[36] A *pithos* is an often
huge earthenware jar used to store and to preserve wine or oil or other
foodstuffs.[37] Womb-like in shape, it is also a symbol for the earth, the
mother of all. In early Helladic burials, the pithos frequently served as a
coffin.[38] After the corpse was folded into fetal position and inserted into
the pithos, honey was often poured over the dead as a preservative;[39] and
then the lid was sealed in place. The womb-like shape of the pithos, the
fetal position of the corpse, and the sweet nourishing fluid surrounding it
all suggest birth as well as death—in other words, the presence of hope,
the hope of regeneration, which like the hope in Pandora's jar remains in
the pithos until the end of time.

In this context we may recall the story of Glaukos, who as a child fell
into a pithos full of honey and disappeared.[40] When Polyeidus, com-
manded by Minos to find the boy, descended into the labyrinthine palace
and came upon an owl,[41] he knew the boy to be dead and soon found him
head down in a pithos of honey. Minos's next demand was for the regeneration of his son from the pithos, which Polyeidus was enabled to
accomplish through the magical properties of an herb, which a serpent[42]
happened to be carrying in its mouth to its own dead mate.[43] While this
story contains multiple images integral to our concerns here, our present
focus is upon the pithos, the symbol and locus of both death and rebirth.

The implications of the pithos for the story of Pandora are immediately clear and telling. Pandora's gifts are released not from some box she holds but from her own womb. Her fault lies not in her curiosity but in her being. She is constitutionally deceptive and essentially lethal; for when she opens the lid of the pithos and gives birth, she brings death as well. Death, Hesiod makes clear, comes soon and miserably, after a toil-some life. The lid of Pandora's pithos is opened first in the act of love, to which men are drawn by her irresistible charms; and then the lid is opened again to give birth either to men who will live out short miserable lives or to her own unique progeny, the separate race of women, who will extend the human plague indefinitely. At the end of the day, as it were, the lid is opened a last time to receive the dead, exhausted by life.[44]

Pandora herself, it would appear, *is* the pithos, from which dismal, pro-lific mankind issues forth and to which men return, either to bury their desires for a moment or to be buried forever. This image of woman as pithos is very old indeed, the inheritance and not the creation of Hesiod.[45] From the Neolithic period onward, over four thousand years before Hesiod, earthenware vessels—some large and wide-mouthed for storage and others in a range of shapes for a variety of uses—were frequently shaped or painted to suggest their identity with woman or womb. In addition to bearing the face, the breasts, the vagina, and other anatomical features, these pots were commonly painted or inscribed with emblems, images, and what may be interpreted as a symbolic script, all together making unmistakable the intimate association of woman with life, death, and regeneration.[46]

It is also true that Pandora *is not* the pithos, which Hesiod mentions as an object apparently separate from Pandora herself, the woman. Imagina-tively one, they are literally two, disconnected, estranged. What is more, a profound, pervasive estrangement may be discerned within the entire account of Pandora, from her creation to her deployment. Like her pithos, assuming for the moment its earthenware composition, Pandora is fash-ioned from clay, moistened with water.[47] Commissioned by Zeus, she is the handiwork of Hephaestos. Her beginning, then, is uniquely un-natural. She is the work not of nature (*physis*) but of craft (*technē*). Although the entire race of women and, from this day forth, all men are to issue from a womb, either hers or that of one of her daughters, Pandora herself comes into being not from the belly of a woman but from the hands of a man.[48]

There is a double humiliation and reversal here: first, that woman, the womb of all humankind, should be fashioned from clay, literally like a pot; and second, that the potter should be a man. In Hesiod's account, man has somehow come into being long before and without woman; it is woman who is the afterthought, derivative and secondary. At the very least, this violates unmolested common sense. Admittedly, the emergence of the first human being presents a challenge to any imagination, ancient or modern; but already with the second and the third human being, a clear pattern presents itself. Nothing is observed more universally than that every human being comes from woman. The existence of women before men is a mystery, while the existence of men before women is a contradiction, which is precisely what Hesiod intends.

The inseparable bond between woman and the unfolding of life is embedded in the word *physis,* a word encompassing the entire order of nature and yet referring quite specifically to the female *genitalia,*[49] the lips of Pandora's jar. In Hesiod, what spills from these lips is not so much joy and life as misery and death.[50] Sex, something apparently new and overwhelming to Epimetheus, disrupts the harmonious order of things. Woman, herself a contrivance, overturns nature, irrevocably. Because of her, men can no longer appear and disappear inexplicably, like flowers. Instead, they must be born and must die. No thought, if we enter Hesiod's imagination, is to him stranger and more unsettling. We are mistaken, however, if we suppose his imagination to be innocent and primitive, the product of clueless wonder. He knows what he is doing, and why. His is not the original account of such matters; rather, his is a conscious denial of that account, an effort to articulate its demise. He is a man not with a silly idea but with a powerful ideology, which at the same time happens to be silly.

Hesiod is not alone, of course, in his overturning of the self-evident order of things in which woman and womb are the natural—that is, genital—source of man. In the J, or Yahwist, account of creation, composed during the reign of Solomon and thus the older of the two creation accounts in Genesis, man is created first to a deathless, god-like existence; and woman is the afterthought, a by-product of man.[51] Soon, almost inevitably it seems, she brings sex, laborious birth from the womb, a life of labor, and certain death. Similarly, Enkidu, Adam's Mesopotamian counterpart, is torn from idyllic nature by woman, the seductress, whose irresistible charms leave him weakened and marked for death, a death whose universal claim Gilgamesh sees reflected in his dying friend's eyes. Amidst the diverse complexity of these and other ancient accounts of the first man and woman, we may perceive a common thread in the assertion that it is woman, an unwitting interloper into the original scheme of things, who disturbs the natural order, bringing sex, strife, suffering, and death.

The second form of humiliation and reversal inflicted upon woman by Hesiod is related to the first. She is made to be the one fashioned from clay and not the fashioner—the pot, as it were, and not the potter. Contrary to Hesiod's account, however, woman seems to have been the first to work with clay, whether as creatrix or as simple potter. "The art of pottery," writes Robert Briffault, "is a feminine invention; the original potter was a woman. Among all primitive peoples the ceramic art is found in the hands of woman, and only under the influence of advanced culture does it become a man's occupation."[52] This original association of woman with pottery is reflected in those early creation myths wherein it is woman who fashions man from clay. In perhaps the earliest of these,[53] already current in the third millennium, the birth-goddess Nammu, the primeval sea, "the mother who gave birth to all the gods," mixes the first mortal clay and, together with Earth-mother Ninmah and the goddesses of birth, fashions the first human beings. Compared with these goddesses, the likes of Greek Hephaestos and Egyptian Khnum are newcomers to the art of pottery, much less to the fashioning of human life.

A striking feature of these myths of female creativity is the conflation of nature and craft, sexuality and ceramics, in the fashioning of humankind. The potters are birth-and-womb-goddesses, mothers all. Thus, in *Atrahasis*, the first mortals—nips of clay fashioned into human form by birth-goddesses—step forth nine months later from a "womb." Womb and kiln, it seems, are one, as are flesh and clay. To say with the same breath that all life comes from earth and that all life comes from woman is not yet a contradiction but a truth, reflected in the art and imagery of clay, softened with water and impregnated with form. In a world of images, pithos, woman, womb, and earth are one.

Hesiod works with these same images, disfiguring them until they reflect only shame. The poet too is a potter of sorts; and it is, after all, Hesiod who shapes Pandora and her pithos on his poetic wheel. His Pandora, the mother of all living, is not only less than divine but less than human. Prehistoric and ancient potters and artists, in their creation of female figurines and "pot-ladies," as we shall see in the next chapter, commonly emphasized woman's genitals and breasts, her mysterious fonts of life and nurture; and, when they gave the lower torso exaggerated proportions, it was to provide space for the fullness of life contained therein. Hesiod, on the other hand, in his depiction of Pandora and of the separate race of women who are her daughters, is all but obsessed with the female *gastēr*, the belly.[54] For him, it might be said, the belly is the *physis* of woman.

Zeus's preoccupation with "bellies" is not surprising in context; for bellies have been a theme and a problem in the *Theogony* long before the appearance of woman. In fact, the succession myth in which Zeus takes the ultimate place involves a succession of "bellies." When the offspring of Gaia and Ouranos prove frightful and loathsome to their father, he hides them away at birth in Gaia's *keuthmōn*[55] her "hiding place" or "hole," the chthonic equivalent of a *gastēr*. Later, when Kronos has filled his father's shoes and begins doing away with his own children, he takes no chances. He swallows them himself, which works well until he consumes an indigestible boulder wrapped in swaddling clothes. We remember the scheme; but now we sharpen our focus on two words crucial to the account of it. While the stone-baby passes into the *nēdys*[56] (meaning any of the body's cavities: belly, bowels, or womb) of Kronos, the flesh-and-ichor baby Zeus passes into a dark cave deep within the sacred *keuthos*[57] (the same word as *keuthmōn*), or "hiding place," of Gaia or Earth, wherein Ouranos once upon a time confined his unwanted progeny. The womb of Earth, once a place of peril, has become, it seems, a place of refuge. The next relevant belly is Zeus's own, which he hopes to fill with the sacrificial feast at Mekone. Clearly his outrage over being given a bag of bones wrapped in slabs of fat and his ensuing outburst have to do not only with wounded pride but also with an empty stomach, which brings us back to the belly of woman, created as a curse to repay man in kind for a spoiled feast and for stolen fire.

Ever since the revenge of Zeus, men's days are long and hard, full of labor. Meanwhile, like bees, or bellies with heads, women stay at home in their hives, waiting to consume the fruit of others'—namely, men's—labors.[58] Woman is reduced by Hesiod to her belly; and the belly, the *gastēr*, is seen as a symbol of lazy, insensitive, insatiable demand.[59] Like a living, bottomless pithos, woman swallows the labors and the very life of her mate. On the other hand, the full force of the synecdoche by which woman is her belly, as well as its close connection with the pithos of Pandora, are lost unless we recall that *gastēr* means not only "belly" but also "womb." Women's demands are not confined to food. Her sexual demands, and their consequences, are likewise consuming. Defined by compulsive desire, woman hungers for both food and sex; and, in return, she produces only more hungry mouths and wombs and, admittedly, male offspring—her sole justification—who will in turn and all too soon inherit the misery of their fathers. In short, Epimetheus and every man after him, to use a familiar colloquialism, can say legitimately of his spouse that "she will be the death of me."

The ultimately lethal and bottomless *gastēr* or pithos that is woman is, admittedly, only an image of and a prelude to that all-consuming chasm or hole, the dark *keuthmōn* of goddess Earth, certain to swallow from first to last every child of woman. Pandora, the first mortal woman, is but an image and agent of Gaia, the first divine woman. Thus, when Pandora removes the lid from her pithos, we may imagine her opening the gates of Tartaros, "a place of decay, at the end of the vast earth."[60] Indeed, Hesiod, in his description of Tartaros[61] in the *Theogony*, seems to think of it as a great storage jar.[62] This same thought clearly guided the painter of a fifth-century *lekythos* or funerary vase on which Hermes *psychopompos*, guide to the world below, is depicted standing next to a giant pithos, half-buried in the earth, from which come forth in flight the winged spirits of the dead.[63]

Pandora is not, then, the first female to be reduced to and indentified with her all-consuming "hole." Nor is she the first female to be the living source of misery and grief. In the beginning, according to the *Theogony*, there was Chaos, which in Greek means dark "Abyss" or "Chasm" without any connotation of confusion or disarray;[64] and there was Gaia, the "Mother of All,"[65] the first Pandora or "All-giver," the foundation of all.[66] These two, Gaia and Chaos, simply come to be—like the primordial hillock emerging from the waters of chaos in Egyptian myth[67]—and from them proceeds all that ever is; but this line of descent and its early products prove mostly unacceptable in poetic retrospect. Besides, nothing about mortal men—their origins and history—is revealed in this account, a matter to which Hesiod turns in *Works and Days*. There, before presenting his own version of man's story, however, he alludes to an account of divine and human origins quite different from his own and makes the following offer:

> If you like, I will summarize another tale
> for you, well and skillfully—mind you take
> it in—telling how gods and mortal men have
> come from the same starting-point.[68]

Possibly he has no takers. For whatever reason, Hesiod says no more here of this common source of all divine and human being, perhaps because he has already told that tale in the *Theogony*.

That Earth, emergent from watery Chaos, is the common source of all beings—human, divine, and otherwise—is confirmed on the golden diadem fashioned by Hephaestos for the first woman. On this wondrous object, we are told, there are wrought many images presenting to the eye "all the awesome creatures spawned by sea and earth."[69] There is telling irony in this crown's being placed on the head of woman, from whose fertile depths shall pour out *myria lygra,* all the innumerable ills of humankind. Queen of grief, woman shall repeat within time what took place before time, before Kronos, before the erotic lineage that led to Zeus. At first, we recall, Chaos brought forth Erebos, the darkness of the world below, and black Nyx, night. From feminine Nyx came forth an ominous brood[70] including Death, Pain, the Fates, the Destinies, Nemesis, hateful Age, and Eris or strife. Daughter Eris, in turn, spawned progeny[71] every bit as dark as those of her mother Night, progeny that include Quarrels, Labor, Famine, Lies, Murder, Wars, Anarchy, and Ruin. All of these, we know, have found their way into the pithos, the belly-womb, of Pandora, the mortal image of that dark, primeval chasm from which everything we know and dread has come.

At the same time, Gaia produced her own firstborn, Sky, "as an equal to herself,"[72] and soon, under the novel influence of Eros, the "limb-weakener,"[73] Earth and Sky mated and produced Kronos and his siblings, all so monstrous and hateful to Ouranos that he refused them entry into the light, keeping them hidden away in Gaia's "secret hole." Groaning with distress, Gaia schemed with her son to release her brood from the tyranny of Ouranos. Their scheme and its outcome are already familiar to us; yet it is well to have certain details fresh before our eyes. According to plan, as Ouranos, quickened with desire, spread himself over Gaia, Kronos, with a jagged flint sickle, sliced away his father's genitals, hurling them into the sea. The fertile blood of Ouranos sprayed Gaia with the seed of Giants and of the Furies, while the sea boiled up and from its foam there emerged the goddess Cypris or Aphrodite, accompanied by Eros and *Himeros,* or Desire. When, after the act, the hated sons were released into the light, Ouranos named them Titans and said that vengeance would follow them, a vengeance whose trail led all the way to Pandora.

There are quite evidently too many distinct fibers here to weave now into our account of woman and of the feminine origin of evil. With only a few in place, however, the pattern of the whole becomes clear. Long before Pandora releases from her womb the full plague of toil and pain and death, which humans know as their condition, Gaia and Nyx, female Earth and Night, have released into the cosmos the paradigms, as it were, of Pandora's "gifts." From the "hole," the dark, mysterious cavity, the *gastēr*, the belly-womb of woman, divine and human, imagined as a great pithos or jar, pour out all those bitter realities under which the divine and human orders, the cosmos and the polis, languish. Not until the female *gastēr* is replaced by its male counterpart will the pollution of woman be lifted from the family of the gods and from the race of men. The last great birth of the *Theogony*, the birth of Athena from Zeus marks precisely that event in the divine order. In fact, the entire movement of the *Theogony*, the narrative of the orign of the gods, may be seen as a progression, a triumphal ascent as Hesiod would have it, from the female womb of Gaia to the male womb of Zeus, and so from savage nature to Olympian civility.

After Zeus has proved himself supreme in cosmic combat, he becomes king and lord of the gods. Hesiod's one-sentence account of this moment provides all we need to assess the dynamics of the scene.[74] Like Marduk of Babylon and Yahweh of Israel, but unlike several other divine warrior-kings who "win some and lose some," Zeus has swept the field of rivals.[75] His power is incontestable. Gaia, who has retained her realism if little else, knows that hers and anyone else's independent claims to primacy are memories now, nothing more. Zeus, we are told, is elevated into place by acclamation, but not spontaneously; for Hesiod adds the intriguing detail that behind the proclamation of Zeus's sovereignty by the divine assembly lie Gaia's *phradmosynēsin*, her "cunning maneuvers."[76] She is not so far behind the scenes or the times to escape his notice. If nothing else, she is a survivor.

Conquest alone does not make kings. Proper sovereignty requires not only prowess in battle but preeminence in the council of the gods.[77] The arts of war must be complemented by the arts of peace. For a king to rule both in time of peace and in time of war, his word must prevail as surely as does his sword. In the *Enuma Elish*, the warrior king Marduk, triumphant in battle, is confirmed in his kingship by the full pantheon.[78] Having slain Tiamat, Marduk forms the ordered cosmos from her chaotic matter; and, in response, the other gods bestow upon him the "Fifty Names," encompassing all of their own proper powers and prerogatives. He is now not only the one who "performed miracles in the battle with Tiamat," but is "profound in wisdom, skilled in understanding."[79] His sovereignty is whole and complete.[80]

We find this very same pattern replicated in the *Theogony*. After the last of his dynastic battles, Zeus, triumphant over Ouranos, Titans, and Typhoeus, restores order to the cosmos; but his will not be a lasting order unless he can complete his sovereignty with wit, cunning, and wisdom. This he accomplishes with the "swallowing" of Metis, the goddess of cunning and wise counsel, "who among all gods and mortals is wisest."[81] In short, he metabolizes all of her powers. Initially, of course, he makes her his wife, his first wife; but he seems to be aware that we are what we eat, not what we marry. Both his father and his grandfather were out-witted by their wives because they had failed to realize this. As a result, they married too soon and swallowed too late; mistakes he does not repeat.

Zeus, with timely advice from Ouranos and Gaia, works a unique vari-ation on the succession and swallowing themes, appropriating his own eminently clever wife's powers and plots before it is too late not to suc-cumb to them. "By marrying, mastering, and swallowing Metis," write Marcel Detienne and Jean-Pierre Vernant, "he becomes more than simply a monarch: he becomes Sovereignty itself."[82] Then, after putting away mother and daughter, pregnant Metis and unborn Athena, deep within his *nēdys*[83] (meaning any bodily cavity: mouth, belly, or womb) Zeus takes, as his second wife, Themis. Like Egyptian *Maat* or the Mesopota-mian *mes*, Themis is the embodiment of all that is right and just in the societies of mortals and immortals. Unlike Metis, Themis, it seems, need not be swallowed in order to be at his disposal. It is enough for her to be at his side. Of all the gods, surely she is the one who can be trusted. Their six daughters—the *Horai* (the "Watchful Ones": Order, Justice, and Peace) and the *Moirai* (the "Fates": the Spinner, the Allotter, and the Unyielding One)—take after their mother and serve their father, perfectly comple-menting his inhuman force and his unprincipled cunning. Now the reign of Zeus promises to be both secure and just, unable either to be over-thrown from without or to be corrupted from within.

Zeus, in swallowing Metis, not only reverses the succession of un-witting, unstable regimes beginning with Ouranos, but reverses as well the primacy of female fecundity beginning with Gaia. Hesiod's insistence that Zeus does so with the advice and consent of both Ouranos and Gaia[84] may resemble the charade in which consent is elicited from sacrificial ani-mals just prior to their demise. Regardless, their apparent concurrence in this most radical of overturnings confers upon it both a certain legitimacy and a seeming continuity with the past, neither of which it could claim for itself.

Already first in "firepower," now—with Themis at his side, Metis in his head, and Athena in his "womb"—Zeus has consolidated in himself every essential power and prerogative in the universe. For the moment, we focus on fecundity; for this is perhaps his most strange and radical acquisition. Nothing, it was suggested earlier, is observed more universally than that every human being, and for that matter every anthropomorphic divine being, comes from woman. Zeus, by absorbing pregnant Metis, fetus and all, and taking the unborn Athena into his own male womb, from which she will soon be born, overturns the most inalienable claim of woman and severs her defining bond with nature and with life. With the parthenogenetic birth of Athena from the head of Zeus, history has a new beginning, in which woman plays no essential role. Not only is she powerless in the formulation of *nomos* (custom and law), but now she is irrelevant to the unfolding of *physis*, or nature. Like *Pandora*, every woman is an afterthought—and an unfortunate one at that.

There are, as one might expect, alternative accounts of Athena's origins.[85] One such account, preserved iconically, is found on a pithos dating from approximately 700 B.C.E., whose neck is "decorated with a picture of a winged goddess, who sits with outstretched arms on a throne; from her head there springs another winged figure, armed with a helmet, a spear, and perhaps a thunderbolt."[86] Walcot argues that there is only one possible interpretation of this scene: the birth of Athena from a goddess, presumably Metis. There is indeed a tradition according to which Metis not only conceived Athena but gave birth to her as well.[87] Regardless, by any account the female womb did not go out of service. Even Hesiod's Zeus continued to employ the wombs of his wives and of other women. In giving birth himself, he apparently intended to establish a principle, not a practice.

In the human order, men have been, so far, unsuccessful in finding a male replacement for Pandora and her womb. In the Greek world, this failure was not for lack of will or desire. Indeed, "the dream of a purely paternal heredity never ceased to haunt the Greek imagination."[88] Greek poetry is resonant with the voices of men who long for a world exorcised of women, a world in which men by themselves are capable of producing their own sons. Insofar as the divine order, as imagined by men, reflects the human order, as experienced by men, Zeus's two parthenogenetic successes, that is, Athena born from his head and Dionysos born from his fatty thigh, may reflect directly the failures of men at the same endeavor. Here, misogyny may be seen to conspire with the love of men for men; for when men make love to men, their seed often finds its way to the head and to the thighs, the would-be "wombs" of Zeus. Fantasy, likewise, finds its way to poetry and to being born as myth.

Apart from these moments of fantasy, Gaia and Pandora, Earth and Woman, remain the mothers of all that lives. Pandora is to the human order and the race of men what Gaia is to the divine order and the race of gods. Pandora is "Gaia in human form,"[89] "a kind of Gaia reborn, symbol of the power of the female, displaced from the divine onto the human realm."[90] The power of Gaia and Pandora, focused on the *gastēr*, is in Hesiod's revisionist mythology, however, no longer primarily the power of fecundity and life, but rather the power of hunger and death. The homology between Gaia and Pandora (and, by extension, between Helen and Gaia) is indeed close and complex. In fact, the virtual identity of Gaia and Pandora has long been widely accepted and rarely questioned.[91] The remaining question for us here concerns the bond, if any, between Helen and Pandora and, by extension, between Helen and Gaia.

The most obvious, indisputable bond between Helen and Pandora lies in the fact that Pandora is the first woman, the mother of the separate *genos* or race of women, and Helen is thereby her distant daughter. When we consider that Hesiod describes that race as *oloion*,[92] which means at the same time both "deadly" and "lost," we may go further and propose that Helen is the most notorious of Pandora's daughters. Helen, then, may be seen as Pandora's avatar or emanantion, her image, which in turn recalls Helen's relationship with Aphrodite, and appropriately so; for Aphrodite is as close to the figure of Pandora as she is to the figure of Helen. After all, Pandora and Helen possess in common the divinely compelling *charis*, the outward loveliness or simply "charm," of Aphrodite. It is Aphrodite's gift to them both. Furthermore, in *Works and Days*, Pandora is accompanied by *Potnia Peitho*, mistress Persuasion, who, as we have already seen, is the virtual "double"[93] of Aphrodite, perhaps even a designation for Aphrodite herself.[94] This same Peitho, whom Sappho regards as a "cheat" and as "Aphrodite's daughter,"[95] is at the same time a frequent "vase-companion" of Helen. In fact, in ancient iconography, it is frequently Aphrodite and Peitho together who accompany Helen to ensure either Helen's elopement with Paris or her reconciliation with Menelaos.[96] Additionally, two other cosmetic benefactors of Pandora, Hephaestos and Athena, have equally close associations, respectively, with Helen, the weaver of tapestries, and with Aphrodite, the heartthrob of Hephaestos.

What is most telling, however, is that in the Greek poetic tradition Pandora and Helen manifest the same profound duality and suffer the same resolution of that duality in the consistent disfavor in which they find themselves. Pandora and Helen are virtually defined by the contradiction between their outward loveliness and their inward perversity, the disparity between their apparent charm and their essential fatality. Both are misleading and mischievous, not by virtue of anything they say or do but by virtue of what they are: in a word, "women"; and, in the words of the seventh-century iambic poet Semonides, women represent "the greatest *kakon* or evil Zeus has made."[97] Woman's *noos* or mind and heart, the seat of her perversity, was made by Zeus "apart" and "in the beginning."[98] Zeus creates woman from the inside out, while men discover woman from the outside in. In other words, Zeus begins with the essential reality, while men start with the appearances. The intended and actual result is that women—Pandora, Helen, and "all the other tribes of women"[99]—are desired by men, briefly, and then forever hated. In no more time than it takes for men to pass from illusion to reality, women pass from being objects of desire to being objects of loathing.

> Yes, women are the greatest evil Zeus has made.
> If someone who has a woman imagines her useful
> To him, she will prove all the more evil.
> A man's good spirits never last a whole day
> When the day includes a woman . . .
> Yes, women are the greatest evil Zeus has made,
> And men are bound to them, hand and foot,
> With impossible knots tied by god.
> It is no wonder that Hades waits at the door
> For men at each others' throats
> Over women.[100]

The only reason, presumably, why Pandora was not fought over was that she had, for all we know, only two possible suitors, Prometheus and Epimetheus, and one of them could see beyond the *prima nox.*

The consortium of Helen, Pandora, and Gaia is, at root, the timeless consortium of women. If Pandora is Gaia in human form, then Helen is Pandora in person. And all three are familiar with golden Aphrodite, who in the *Theogony,* alone among all the deities eventually composing the Olympian household of Zeus, spans the aeons separating the regime of Zeus from the regime of Ouranos. Thus, in Greek chronology, Aphrodite links the time of origins with the present; for although she belongs to the first generation of gods, Aphrodite finds her way into the Olympic pantheon and to Helen's side. And Helen—the living image of Gaia, Aphrodite, and Pandora—is, at least potentially, all women.

Lineage among images and emanations is, admittedly, a tenuous reality traced in leaps as often as in close, careful steps. Some would find any movement now from Helen to Gaia to be a leap, while others would consider it a modest, even obvious, step. Perhaps, once again, Aphrodite provides a common bond and a bit of light here. Aphrodite's communality with Pandora and with Helen is already clear; and her bond with Gaia should become, momentarily, a shade more evident.

According to Herodotus, the very oldest temple of Aphrodite was her temple in Ascalon, Syria.[101] It was from there, he said, that her cult was carried to Cyprus and to Cythera, which coincides with what has been said already of her Near Eastern roots. What is more, Aphrodite's cult name in the temple of Ascalon was *Ourania*, "Queen of Heaven," a name and a cult denounced in the prophetic writings of Jeremiah[102] and possibly her earliest title among the Greeks, a title suggesting her association with Ouranos. The cult of Aphrodite *Ourania* is widely attested among Hellenic communities, and her most illustrious cult image was carved of ivory and gold for her by Pheidias for her shrine at Olympia. How close the name *Ourania* brings Aphrodite to Gaia, who mothered, mated with, and helped to unman Ouranos, is surely a matter for speculation and debate; but at the least it is one more gesture back to the earliest times, to the time of origin. The name *Ourania* is for us a heuristic clue to the meaning of Aphrodite, Pandora, and Helen, the meaning of Woman. It points us in the direction of, if not directly to, Gaia, the Mother of All.

The worship of Gaia, Earth, was aboriginal to the earliest Hellenic tribes. To her belonged the mysterious powers of life and of death and of regeneration, of dreams and of prophecies. Incarnate as a serpent, she brought healing, vision, and rebirth. Hesiod, we know, lamented the steady decline in the status and condition of men from the first to the fifth age, wherein he found himself, full of complaints; but we also know that his complaints, though legitimate, overlook the far more drastic decline of women, human and divine. Gaia, the first woman, the first mother, shared the denigration of her human daughters. Even so, in the *Oresteia* of Aeschylus, which heralds the final Olympian eclipse of the feminine, celebrating male ascendancy in cosmos and polis alike, Gaia is not forgotten. At the earth's navel, in the holy precinct of Delphi, the Pythia, the serpent-priestess, pays Gaia peculiar deference. "Of all the gods," she says in the opening lines of the *Eumenides*, "I pray to Gaia first."[103]

Aphrodite, Pandora, and Helen, as well as their myriad imaginative counterparts such as Demeter,[104] Ariadne, and Korē, like emanations from a single source, point us back to the first woman, the first mother, the first *pithos*, the first font of life and of death and of regeneration. They point us to a time beyond the specific traditions of Greece, before the familiar voices of Greek poetry construe Mother Earth and the mortal mothers who imitate her[105] as devouring and deceitful beings, loved too soon and loathed too late. We may catch a glimpse of that first feminine power and presence, the true mother of Helen, in the *Hymn to Gaia:*

> The Mother of us all,
> the oldest of all,
> hard,
>> splendid as rock
>
> Whatever there is of the land
>> it is she
>>> who nourishes it,
>> it is the Earth [Gaia]
>>> that I sing
>
> Whoever you are,
> howsoever you come
>> across her sacred ground
>> you of the sea,
>> you that fly,
> it is she
>> who nourishes you
> she,
>> out of her treasures
>>> Beautiful children
>>> beautiful harvests
>>>> are achieved from you
>>> The giving of life itself,
>>> the taking of it back
>>> to or from
>>>> any man
>>>>> are yours . . . .[106]

Here too, unless I am mistaken, we glimpse the reality of Helen, a reality that Euripides too must have glimpsed; for, as we shall see, he sought eventually to disclose it.

# 4

# The First Helen

"Only one woman exists in the world," writes Nikos Kazantzakis, "one woman with countless faces."[1] One woman, we might add, with countless names. Among them: "Helen." Helen, together with Aphrodite and Pandora, has brought us, by way of many turns, to Gaia, the Mother of All, the divine *Pandora* or "All-Giver." Even "Gaia," however, is only one name for, one image of, the first woman, the first source of all things. Here, in search of the "original" woman, of whom Helen, Aphrodite, Pandora, and Gaia are remote reflections, we must leave written texts behind and let the stones, as it were, speak of her; which they may be said to do. In fact, to be precisely honest, stones mostly mumble; and, as a consequence, archaeologists, heavy with parasites from other disciplines, must employ both science and art in equal measure to bring their finds to full voice. Fortunately, for those who would understand Helen, the science and art of archaeology have begun to retell the story of woman as image with seeming precision and vivid imagination from the "beginning"; and the central figure in this emerging story is that of the Great Goddess, the Mother of All, arguably the first Helen.

The "beginning" that concerns us here is not the beginning of matter, nor of life, but rather the beginning of Helen's world, the world of images, which may be traced to the Upper Paleolithic (ca. 35,000–9,000 B.C.E.), when, for all we know, the human eye and hand first conspired to fashion lasting symbols and images. Indeed, it seems that during this "revolutionary" period there occurred "a virtual explosion of symbolic behavior"[2] to which we are the current heirs. Whether the earliest Ice Age paintings and carvings mark a revolution in thought is, of course, indeterminable; for ideas, language, and stories, so long as they are only spoken, inwardly or outwardly, leave no trace. The imaginative life first unveiled by Paleolithic art may be far older than we suspect.[3]

With the Upper Paleolithic now the declared beginning of our story of Helen, we might reasonably despair of finding a finite way back to classical Greece and so to the end of our story. Admittedly, we are already beyond any question of simple closure. We will never know Helen, never even catalogue, much less comprehend, her images. Her world is too vast; and yet it is continuous with our own. We have no choice but to make some provisional sense of it; and, if a world can be made to "fit" onto a map, then Helen can be made to "fit" into a story. Indeed, it is a similar sleight of hand that we find evidenced on the walls of the caves where our story begins. Meaning, then or now, must be imagined, reduced to human scale, created in defiant communion with realities we never fully comprehend.

Every image is part observation and part creation. History too can claim no more than this for the stories it tells. Archaeologists and historians construct the past neither from thin air nor from pure fact. Everything they find mumbles something to them; but they must decide for themselves what all the voices they hear are finally saying. The inevitable outcome is a multiplicity of accounts, often irreconcilably divergent, one from another. The account offered here is no exception.

"The Upper Paleolithic," writes D. H. Trump, "saw the replacement of Neanderthalers by fully modern men."[4] Indeed, Upper Paleolithic art, considered together with burial remains from the same period,[5] reveals a keenly observant and profoundly reflective human consciousness, more like than unlike our own, appreciative of life and aware of death. More specifically, the palette of images and symbols created by Paleolithic art, "based upon the recognition of a single life-giving principle,"[6] clearly envisioned as feminine, constitutes the undeniable source of the symbolic language of the Neolithic cultures of Europe and of the Near East. "Indeed," comments Marija Gimbutas, "what is striking is not the metamorphosis of the symbols over the millennia but rather the continuity from Paleolithic times on. The major aspects of the Goddess of the Neolithic . . . can all be traced back to the period when the first sculptures of bone, ivory, or stone appeared around 25,000 B.C. and their symbols . . . to an even earlier time."[7] One such symbol, the vulva,[8] often abstracted into a downward-pointing triangle, is ubiquitous in Paleolithic art and similarly pervasive in the later Neolithic symbolic system.

The primary "texts" telling us of the prehistoric Great Goddess, the first "Helen," are tens of thousands of nameless, speechless figurines,[9] made from bone, ivory, stone, or clay, and found in caves, cult places, and graves throughout Europe, the Near East, and beyond. The earliest such figurines begin to appear around 25,000 B.C.E., though our focus here will be on a much later period, from the early Neolithic onwards to the late Bronze Age. The peculiar contexts in which these figurines are found, the occasional accompanying carvings, frescoes, or ritual objects, as well as the virtual language[10] with which they are inscribed, are all sufficiently of a pattern to permit coherent, if provisional, interpretation. The story they help to tell, although open to question and refinement in myriad details, is well documented and has about it, even now, the ring of truth.

The first, most noticeable aspect of these figurines is that they nearly all represent women; in fact, fewer than five percent are male. They are nearly always nude[11] and, while often abstracted and lacking in detail, the breasts and pubic triangle are, as a rule, clearly indicated, if not exaggerated. These figures are commonly ample and rotund, embodying the peculiar fullness of woman, the bearer and nourisher of life. These figures, in the words of Vincent Scully, "generally regarded as images of the earth mother [are] certainly, despite differences in style and possibly in intent, carved as the child knows the mother, all breasts, hips, and *mons Veneris*, full and round, with the head often inclined forward."[12] Indeed, the feminine emphases of these statues correspond to what we know of the peculiar sacredness of mounds, mountains, caves, and, of course, menhirs in Neolithic cult. Whether or not, and to what degree, the male role in the generation of life was recognized, a question to which we shall return, the earth and woman were imagined to be the source of all living things and of life itself. And no wonder. Woman and earth, in accord with their own cycles, flower and grow fat and produce from their deep hollows the wondrous fruit of life.

In addition to those figures of the Goddess which are swollen with life, there are many others, often carved from bone, which are mostly long and lean, with arms folded stiffly across the belly. Commonly found in graves, these sculptures are usually white, the Neolithic color of death.[13] The Goddess, it seems, presides over not only life but death as well. Apart from her anthropomorphic form in these stiff nude sculptures, she is often figured zoomorphically as a predator, or a harbinger of death. Thus she takes such forms as vulture, owl, raven, hawk, boar, dog, or cuckoo. Her soil not only grows fat and throws up new life but also grows cold and hard and swallows the dead.[14]

The consciousness and cult of woman as earth and of earth as mother were quite clearly both lunar and chthonic. The moon in its aspects and the earth in its seasons revealed the cyclical movement of life itself from fullness to diminishment and from diminishment to fullness. The moon waxes and wanes; the earth flourishes and dies. Then, from the darkened sky and the blighted earth comes renewal, the rebirth of light and of life. The Great Goddess, the feminine source of all that is, was never simply a fertility goddess, never simply the "Mother of All"; rather, as suggested in the name *Pandora,* she was the "Giver of All." And the "All" which she was seen to give included death as well as life, diminishment as well as increase. Even if *Gaia* and *Chthon* represent, which they may not, two divorced aspects of earth—earth as furrows ploughed for fresh life and earth as graves dug up to consume the dead[15]—no such divorce is apparent in Neolithic art and cult. The Great Goddess, the pure parthenogenetic source of Nature—a Nature that both enlivens and destroys—encompasses night as well as day, death as well as life. She is at once the "All-giver" and the "All-gifted"; for she both gives and receives back again all that lives and dies.

The one Goddess, then, has at least several faces, several manifestations. Like the moon, always in motion, she has many aspects. She may be a mere sliver of a child, a young girl about to bloom into a woman, or a withered crone[16] all but vanished from sight. She may appear in multiple human, animal, or hybrid forms, or she may be figured solely in symbols. "The Goddess in all her manifestations was the symbol of the unity of all life in Nature. Her power was in water and stone, in tomb and cave, in animals and birds, snakes and fish, trees and flowers."[17] She produces life, wields death, and from death brings forth life again. Imaged as, or associated with, for example, a snake, a bird, a frog, a butterfly, and a uterine-shaped hedgehog, she presides over the mysterious transformations that earth and its creatures undergo in their cyclical births, deaths, and returns. Her womb is also a tomb, frequently depicted as an egg, the cosmic egg, from whose dark, hidden stillness issues the regeneration of all things.

Where there is life, there is death; and where there is death, there is regeneration. What is perhaps most striking here in the art and associated cult of the Neolithic Goddess is the unity, the wholeness of vision which sees death to be as natural as life and sees regeneration to be no more mysterious than birth. This unity is particularly manifest in the many, ubiquitous symbols of continuous, irrepressible life found in, or associated with, tombs—symbols that include spirals, trees, columns of life, serpents, aqueous meanders, butterflies, wombs, vulvas, pubic triangles, "ships of renewal," and lunar cycles. In sum, the

> celebration of life is the leading motif in Old European ideology and art.
> There is no stagnation; life energy is constantly moving as a serpent, spiral,
> or whirl . . . there was no simple death, only death and regeneration. And
> this was the key to the hymn of life reflected in this art.[18]

In offering or considering such an account of the Great Goddess, it is both easy and convenient to forget that all of these words are ours. The images and symbols that provoke our words and stories are themselves stone-silent, forever so.[19] Even if we accept that "the Neolithic and certainly the Chalcolithic Old Europeans had developed their own linear script for the expression of their deepest beliefs concerning the worship of the goddess,"[20] that script, pictorial not phonetic in character, furnishes images, not words. Any current endeavors to read that script are likely nearer to alchemy than to science, which makes all the more surprising and persuasive the virtual consensus among scholars regarding the universal primacy of the feminine in the Paleolithic and Neolithic religious imagination. No one has stated the core of this consensus more simply and boldly than J. J. Bachofen, who said that "all these phenomena disclose the same law: the more primordial the people, the more the feminine nature principle will dominate religious life."[21]

In an earlier chapter, reference was made to the broad consortium of Bronze Age cultures spanning the Mediterranean from Italy to Egypt and the Near East and reaching perhaps as far as India. That, we suggested, was the world of Hellenic Helen, the vast cultural expanse from which her myriad archaic and classical images emerged. Now, as we consider the prehistoric Helen, the "original" Helen, we confront a similarly vast expanse and an equally broad consortium of peoples, united in its reverence for her. "To suppose that the great cultures in the eastern Mediterranean area and in the Near East were separated from each other, in the beginning, by the broadest of gulfs," writes A. W. Persson, "is an interpretation wholly at variance with the facts. On the contrary, it has been clearly enough established that we have to deal, in this region, with an original or basic if not uniform culture, so widely diffused that we may call it *Afrasian*."[22]

"This region," as Persson defined it a half-century ago, included everything from southern Italy to Egypt to the Tigris-Euphrates and Indus valleys, "perhaps as far as China in the east, and certainly . . . a large part of the African continent." In sum, Persson suggests that we must "take account of cultural relations of a most intimate nature between eastern and western lands in prehistoric times," for "the Afrasian culture world" was, in his view, "the chief seminal influence behind the great cultures which were to follow,"[23] including, of course, the Minoan-Mycenaean culture, the womb from which ancient Greece, in due course, emerged.

Well before Persson, Sir John Marshall, the Director-General of British Archaeology in India in the 1920s, described the newly discovered Indus civilization as "part and parcel of that greater civilization which during the Chalcolithic Age extended across the broad Afrasian belt, and (as) intimately related to other branches of that civilization in Western Persia and Mesopotamia." It was his conclusion that during the Chalcolithic Age the vast stretches of land and peoples from the Indus to western Asia and to the Nile were "united by common bonds of culture . . . with ramifications as far west as Thessaly and Southern Italy, and as far east, perhaps, as the Chinese Provinces of Honan and Chihli." Despite the manifest diversity of races, languages, customs, and cults embraced by so vast a net, Marshall argued that, for all their differences, the prehistoric cultures of Southern Europe and *Afrasia* shared "a fundamental unity of ideas," including, he suggested, religious ideas.[24]

One of the common bonds, then, uniting India with western Asia, Egypt, and the Mediterranean was surely the cult of the Great Goddess. In a more or less unbroken line from the cities of the Indus Valley to Baluchistan across western Asia to Mesopotamia, Egypt, Anatolia, Crete, Greece, and southern Europe there have been found recognizably kindred female cult figurines, images of the Great Goddess. Various theories have been put forth regarding the geographic origin of this cult, southeastern Anatolia being perhaps the most widely nominated candidate;[25] but, if the cult of the Great Goddess had at any time a true motherhouse, its location has yet to be convincingly disclosed. India, so far as I know, has never been considered the source of this cult and yet it has been claimed, soundly, that "in no country in the world has the worship of the Divine Mother been from time immemorial so deep-rooted and ubiquitous as in India."[26] The truth is that the symbols and images of the Goddess lie everywhere too deep to trace still further to some common point of emanation. Dig deeply enough anywhere, it seems, and—like the water that was among her central symbols and embodiments—she is found. Each river and spring, even every well, may have a name of its own; but the water issuing from them is somehow one, sharing a single hidden, inaccessible source. So too, the mistress of the earth and its waters is everywhere one, as old and original as images get.

This "oneness" of the prehistoric Great Goddess is, as we might imagine, an elusive and complex issue, which will receive only relatively brief mention here, not because it is a slight matter. Needless to say the images and symbols of the Goddess are from the beginning many and diverse, which provokes the question whether they might represent not one but many, diverse deities. Later, once the names of the Goddess are inscribed and not merely invoked, the same question can be documented with a vengeance. Eventually, as written myths and stories emerge from what was for us a silent prehistoric past, the question itself plunges into irrelevance, as distinct divine personalities appear and speak for themselves. Polytheism, arguably present all along, rears it unmistakable heads.

It is perhaps inevitable, in the Western tradition, that this question of the oneness of the Goddess should be articulated in terms of monotheism,[27] the standard measure of divine unity. The measure itself is, however, deeply problematic, and possibly beside the point. Within the Christian tradition, for example, the existence of the divine Trinity may be seen to obviate any simple claim to monotheism. Even in doctrinal theory, much less in devotional practice, the threeness and the oneness of the Christian God present an open question, despite the efforts of the early church councils to close it. Furthermore, if we excluded from our consideration or simply failed to ponder—as an overwhelming plurality of Christians have always done—the dogmatic decrees and theological speculations of clerical Christendom; and, instead, if we observed over the centuries the sacred art, the public cult, and the personal devotions of Christians, I doubt that "monotheism" would spring to mind to describe what we had witnessed. This is not at all to deny that Christians worship, roughly, one God. It is, of course, the "roughly" that both describes experience and offends dogma. Monotheism, it may be argued, is a figment of dogma, too rigid and literal to accommodate the very reality it seeks to acknowledge.[28]

With reference to the common tendency "to bring all representations of a female deity into a comprehensive formula and to apply them to one goddess only," Martin Nilsson claims that "analogy and the fascinating name of the Great Mother determine the views of most scholars."[29] Leaving aside the matter of fascination, which is doubtless present though questionably determinative, there is no denying that analogy is integral to any widely perceived unity in the myriad figurines, images, symbols, myths, and cults attributed to a Great Goddess. Analogy or image, by which we see one thing in another, plainly lies at the heart of the matter, a fact that Nilsson apparently takes to be discrediting. Literally myriad, the Great Goddess, if she is one, is so only in the imagination. In a world of images, there is no higher realm in which to dwell.

Any simple assertion of the primacy and original unity of the Great Goddess must be complicated in due course by the entry of her male counterpart or companion. But not quite yet. Until the connection between sexual intercourse and the generation of life was discovered,[30] life, we may assume, appeared to spring with gracious regularity from the earth, from she-animals, and from women. In the Paleolithic period, there was from all evidence no father-god, presumably because there were, for all anyone knew, no fathers. "There is no trace," writes Gimbutas, "of a father figure in any of the Paleolithic periods. The life-creating power seems to have been of the Great Goddess alone."[31] Even in the Neolithic "the male element, man and animal, represented spontaneous and life-stimulating—but not life-generating—powers."[32] Life was, without any apparent qualification, from woman.[33] The earth and woman, who according to Socrates in the *Menexenus* of Plato imitates the earth in conceiving and in giving birth,[34] bring forth their first children from themselves. Or so it must have seemed; for among the earliest myths of the Great Mother are those that tell how she created all life parthenogenetically from the fertile darkness deep within herself. Thus, in Sumer, Nammu, the great *apzu* or abyss, brings forth *Anki*, the universe, comprised of the divine sky (*An*) and the divine earth (*Ki*). In Egypt, Net or Neith, who emerges from the predynastic era as "the personification of the eternal female principle of life which was self sustaining and self-existent and was secret and unknown and all-pervading,"[35] rises from the primeval waters to create the world. And, in Greece, it is wide-breasted Gaia who first ascends from Chaos and produces from herself Sky, Mountains, and Sea.

The unwitting partnership of male and female in the early reproduction of life finds curious recognition in a wide range of hermaphroditic images from the Paleolithic and Neolithic periods. Female figurines with extended phallic necks and heads, for example, are commonplace in the Neolithic.[36] Others are still more ambiguous in their gender: figures with male sexual organs and female breasts. One quite remarkable sculpture, found on Cyprus and dated ca. 3000 B.C.E., is that of a seated figure, which viewed from the back presents a precise image of the male genitalia and viewed from either above or below reveals female genitalia.[37] It may be that the bisexual Aphrodite depicted on a relief plaque from Perachora[38] is a much later reflection of the same tradition; if so, it provides one more strand in the cord connecting Helen with the Goddess. Finally, while all of these images may be seen as tokens of profound confusion, they may also be seen as expressive of an acknowledged complementarity of male and female power.[39] We may witness in them, as well, a harmony that was all too soon lost.

In the *Theogony* of Hesiod, as we have seen already, Eros, who assures that future generations will be the result of heterosexual reproduction, emerged from primordial Chaos second, at an unspecified interval, after Gaia, the parthenogenetic source of all first life. At what point in prehistory Eros's presence, the presence of erotic desire, became consciously associated with the desire for offspring must remain likewise unspecified.[40] Clearly, with the Neolithic development of settled agriculture and, even more, of animal husbandry, the discovery in question was only a matter of time.[41] Or, if it had dawned earlier, it was now more fully understood and widely recognized.

An eventual cultic and mythic repercussion of this discovery was the appearance of a male consort for the Goddess, oftentimes her son or her brother, united with her in a *hieros gamos,* or sacred sexual union,[42] which assured for their entire domain the continued flourishing of life, vegetal, animal, and human. The most widely dispersed theriomorphic embodiment of this male god was the bull,[43] the principal sacrificial animal in the cultic dramas of creation and the appropriate mate for a Goddess commonly figured as a cow. In the yearly ritual reenactment of the nuptials of the Goddess with her young consort and of his subsequent death and rebirth, the annual cycle of fruition, decay, and renewal in nature was reflected and reassured in its course. The names of these goddesses and their young "year-gods" are many, dispersed widely throughout the Mediterranean and the Near East—Inanna and Dumuzi, Isis and Horus, Anat and Baal, Rhea and Zeus,[44] to mention only a few—but among them a single narrative pattern endures: a son, brother, or, in any event, a younger and lesser male,[45] is introduced to share the bed and/or the throne of the Goddess[46]—only to perish as do all of Earth's *kouroi,* whether young men or vegetal "shoots"[47]—and, in due course, to be restored to life. This pattern, transparent to the yearly round of the seasons, provided the mythic and cultic core of the religion of Minoan Crete, a religion that in turn, appropriated as it was by Mycenaean Greece, deeply influenced later Greek religion.

It may be argued that from this core—the Goddess and her youthful consort, a divine "duality in unity"[48]—there proliferated a host of gods and goddesses, who took on lives, cults, and myths of their own.[49] Thus *Britomartis*, "the sweet virgin"; *Diktynna*, "she who is worshiped on Mount Dikte"; *Eileithyia*, "she who comes"; *Aridela*, "the very visible one"; *Pasiphae*, "the one visible to all"; *Europa*, "the wide- or dark-glancing one"; *Ariadne*, "the very holy one"; *Hera*, "the lady"; and even *Helene*, "the shining one,"[50] may all have originated as cult names or invocations of the one Goddess. Similarly, *Glaukos*, "the gleaming one" or "the grey-blue one," and *Hyakinthos*, "the wild hyacinth, that is, bluebell" or "the blue one," although absorbed into later Greek myth as distinct personalities, may well echo early cult names of the Cretan boy-god, eventually identified with Zeus, who, in turn, as the "Zeus of Nysa,"[51] becomes *Dio-Nysos*, who frequently takes the form of a bull. Similar patterns may be found in the Near East, where *Adonis* and *Baal* are essentially synonyms, meaning "Lord" or "Master"[52] and referring to the increasingly dominant consort of the Goddess. While we may wish to avoid any extreme assertion of an original monotheism—becoming, in stages, dualistic and trinitarian—there are sound reasons to wonder how many members of the later Greek and Near Eastern pantheons may not be traceable to far simpler, more focused origins. It is time, however, to remind ourselves that our principal concern here is with Helen, "the shining one," and with her origins, which lie clearly in the lap of the Mother of All, to whom, "full circle," we now return.

All beings—all that comes to be and ceases to be—belong to the largesse of the Goddess, the cosmic Creatrix and Regeneratrix, whose vulva and breasts are not from the beginning construed as objects of sexual desire nor of violent male rivalry.[53] Instead, they are seen to produce and to nourish every living thing. *Erōs* and *eris*, sex and strife, are as yet beside the cosmic point. Woman is not yet the possession or prize of men; still less is she the loathed carrier of human misery and death. Even though the Goddess, provoking neither desire nor strife, is not literally an Aphrodite nor a Helen, she has left recognizable traces of herself in both. The prehistoric "All-giver," the first image we have of Woman, is clearly the giver, the source, of Aphrodite and of Helen and of their myriad kith and kin. Despite the thousands of years and the catastrophic events that divided the Neolithic from the Iron Age, the paradigmatic women, human and divine, depicted in the Greek poetic tradition, retain discernible aspects of the Goddess, which serve to collapse for a brief, imaginative moment the silent, prehistoric gulf stretching between them.

Indeed, certain homologies are evident between Helen, on the one hand, and the Goddess in her multiple manifestations, on the other. These become clear in considering, even briefly, two central images, emblems, or associations that they have in common: the bird and the tree. First, there is the bird, a figure already present in the art of the Upper Paleolithic and eventually the most common zoomorphic manifestation of the Goddess. In fact, hybrid depictions of an anthropomorphic goddess with pronounced breasts and the beaked head of a bird are common occurrences in the Aegean and Mediterranean world as late as the second millennium B.C.E. Some of the clearest and most striking of these images appear on seals from Minoan Crete, dating from the late palatial period. We may add to this bird identity of the Goddess her close association with water, preeminently the primordial waters, from which ordered earth and life first and forever emerge. The Goddess, as avian Creatrix, may be imagined to hover over the watery chaos at the beginning of all things, spanning heaven and earth, an image that summons at once the *Theogony*, Genesis, and the all-but-universal ancient myth telling of a sacred waterbird who laid the cosmic egg.[54] This image summons too the story of another waterbird, another egg, and another goddess: the story of Helen's origin from a divine swan and her birth from an egg.[55]

The "other" divine bird, the bird of prey and of death, also has echoes in the story of Helen; for Helen, like the Goddess, is a sure source of death. The owl, the Egyptian hieroglyph for death, commonly stands for this aspect of the Goddess. The owl, at the same time, was thought to convey wisdom and prophecy, which may account for its association, many millennia later, with Athena and Helen, both known as seeresses.[56] Also associated with images of the owl is the labyrinth, the mysterious abode and magically regenerative womb of the Goddess, who often appears in the form of a bird. The most famous labyrinth of all was, of course, the one said to have been designed by Daedalus for Minos and for his daughter, Ariadne, "the very holy one," herself perhaps the "Mistress of the Labyrinth" as well as a legendary princess. As with Helen, Ariadne's prehistoric cult long precedes her "historic" reputation. By some accounts, as we have seen already, Helen shares the same dark death—death by hanging—with Ariadne, who may prove to be her closest link with the Goddess. Indeed, Helen and Ariadne are nearly doubles. Each, as a young girl, is abducted by Theseus—stories that are not easily unraveled, one from the other.[57] Yet it is in their deaths that they are truly one; for it is there, dangling from the limbs of trees, that they reveal their common origins in a tree cult whose roots plunge into the past beyond sight.

The tree, the second central image, emblem, and association linking Helen—*Helenē Dendritis*, "Helen of the Tree"—with the Goddess, was an object of cult throughout the Eurasian expanse for many thousands of years. The tree is the focal symbol of vegetative life, the gift of the Goddess. It encompasses her domains and embodies her largesse. Its roots reach down into the underworld, drinking the waters below; and its branches climb into the sky, all but touching the waters above. Thus it is the common home of both the chthonian serpent and the celestial bird, two primordial forms of the Goddess. The cult tree, the tree of life, is indeed the home and even the body of the Goddess. It is the first sign of life, the first token of her presence.

In the Sumerian tale "The *Huluppu*-Tree," one of the earliest recorded tales of the earth's beginnings, we read:

> In the first days, in the very first days,
> In the first nights, in the very first nights,
> In the first years, in the very first years,
> In the first days when everything needed
>     was brought into being . . .
> At that time, a tree, a single tree, a *huluppu*-tree
> Was planted by the banks of the Euphrates.[58]

It was the Goddess Inanna, we are told, who brought this tree to Uruk, planted it in her holy garden, and tended it with her own hand. In its roots the serpent made its nest. In its branches, the *Anzu*-bird (a lion-headed eagle) set its young. And in its trunk the dark maid Lilith made her home. From its wood were carved the bed and the throne of the Goddess. When she made love in that bed with Dumuzi, "the wild bull," "plants grew high by their side. Grains grew high by their side. Gardens flourished luxuriantly."[59]

In Egypt, too, the tree is both the home and the body of the Goddess. Egyptian art abounds with images of the Goddess as tree, giving birth to the sun, suckling the king, nourishing the souls of the dead. Nut, the Sky-mother, friend and protector of the dead, is closely associated with the sycamore. Emerging from its trunk amidst its central limbs, she pours out life-giving waters over the dead. Elsewhere, in the *Book of the Dead*, the Sun-god is said to rise each dawn from between two sycamores standing at the eastern gate of heaven.[60] Hathor too, in the form of a tree, gives birth to the sun; and Isis, depicted as a tree with breasts, nourishes the young pharaoh and thus all of Egypt. Finally, in death, the king is encased in the body of the goddess Nut, carved from a tree, where he will await rebirth, as did Osiris, around whose corpse once grew a tamarisk tree.[61]

There would seem to be little symbolic space between the tree and the pillar. After all, the first pillars were merely hewn trees. Thus the asherah, a cult symbol reverenced in Israelite religion at least from the time of the judges to shortly before the fall of the southern kingdom, was a wooden pole or pillar representing a tree.[62] "What is an asherah?" we read in the Mishnah. The answer: "Any tree which is an idol. Rabbi Simeon says: Any tree which is worshipped."[63] Among the ancient Canaanites, the tree symbolized the fruitful, nurturing Goddess and indicated her presence. In fact, on certain Late Bronze Age Canaanite figurines, trees or branches have been found etched between the navel and pubic triangle.[64] Similarly, in Mesopotamia, the sacred tree and pillar were clearly an acknowledged focus of numinous power. And, in India, the pipal tree (*ficus religiosa*), depicted already on Chalcolithic seals from the Indus Valley, remains even today an object of worship. This is the *bhodi*-tree, the "tree of wisdom," beneath whose shade the Buddha is said to have attained enlightenment. It was once the dwelling, the place of appearance, of a tree goddess. Indeed, "at both Mohenjo-daro and Harappa two forms of tree-worship (are) represented; one in which the tree itself is worshiped in its natural form, the other in which the tree spirit is personified and endowed with human shape and human attributes."[65] Indeed, the tree—planted in the soil, hewn into a wooden pole or pillar, or represented in stone—was a universal object of cultic reverence,[66] the home and body of the Goddess, the giver and receiver of all life and its blessings.

On Crete, insular and relatively remote, the "old ways" of the Goddess and her cult flourished as long as anywhere else, probably longer, well into the second millennium, long enough to influence profoundly the religion of Greece and thus to help shape the figure of Helen. Here, in the religion of Minoan Crete, two images integral to the person of Helen converge: the bird and the tree. In the Minoan tree cult, of which we catch revealing glimpses from scenes carved on numerous signet rings and seals, the bird, preminently the dove, is a frequently present figure and doubtless represents the epiphany of the Goddess.[67] Nilsson points out that trees and their boughs were not merely accessories to the cult, nor simply the abode of the deity, but were themselves the direct object of what is here a true tree cult. "They are adored and venerated," he writes, "with ecstatic rites and dances, and their holy branches touched and shaken."[68] And "the real divinity of the tree cult" was the Great Goddess, "from the beginning a universal deity, the goddess of nature herself, like the Great Goddess in Asia Minor, Syria, and Egypt."[69] In Crete, as elsewhere, this Goddess, the source of life and regeneration, had, as we have seen already, many cult names and epithets, among them quite likely *Ariadne*, "the very holy one," and possibly *Helenē*, "the shining one."

In any event, the bonds between Ariadne and Helen are many and close, some of which we have traced already. Both, it seems, represent quite ancient nature goddesses, widely venerated on the islands of the southern Aegean; and both are said to have died hanging from trees, further indication of their close association with a tree cult. Both—as though they were not only timeless chthonic deities but once mere girls, irresistible in the never-to-return moment of perfect youth—were said to have been abducted by Theseus. Finally, both Ariadne and Helen, sometimes so close as to be nearly lost in each other's reflection, similarly pale before Aphrodite. We are already accustomed to seeing Helen as a, or rather *the*, mortal glimmer of Aphrodite; and Ariadne too assumes an eventually close yet subordinate posture toward Aphrodite. Thus Ariadne's own cult on the island of Delos[70] seems to have yielded to the cult of Aphrodite; and, on Cyprus,[71] the grove in which a tomb belonging to Ariadne is said to lie is called the grove of Ariadne Aphrodite. Finally, it has been argued that the Cretan name *Ariadne*, "the very holy one," represented an early Hellenic epithet for Aphrodite herself.[72] In sum, the cult of the Great Goddess, recognizably one, for all its metamorphoses, from the Upper Paleolithic to the Neolithic to the Chalcolithic periods, was preserved on Crete well into the Bronze Age, leaving a deep impression on the figure of Helen, so deep that Helen may herself be said to be partly of Minoan origin. In this light, we are enabled to see in Helen not only Ariadne but "the very holy one" whom Ariadne reflects, the Great Goddess, the First Woman.

From "the beginning," the beginning of images, the first episode of Helen's story, Woman has been both divine and human, each one always somehow the image of the other. Inasmuch, then, as the divine and the human, heaven and the household, tend to reflect each other, we may rightly wonder what the society, the human society, of the Goddess might have been like. It goes without saying that any comments here, or elsewhere, addressed to this question must be grandly tentative. Indeed, the closer we approach "the beginning," the closer we come to watery chaos, devoid of any solid footing. Or, if "chaos" is too extreme a name for the reigning principle in the realm we are about to enter, at the very least we may say that controversy reigns therein.

The immediate controversy I have in mind found early, extreme articulation in the last century as two noted European jurists, Sir A. Maine and J. J. Bachofen, offered starkly opposing views on the origins and development of human society. Whereas Maine, in *Primitive Law* (1851), asserted that the original unit of society was the patriarchal family—a view that found highly influential support in Edward Westermarck's *History of Human Marriage* (1891)—J. J. Bachofen, in *Das Mutterrecht* (1861), argued that patriarchy, or *Vaterrecht*, was in fact a quite late development, long preceded by *Mutterrecht*, a form of human society in which kinship, property, status, and rights were traced from and conveyed through the mother. *Mutterrecht*, as Bachofen presents it, implies matrilinear descent, matrilocal marriage, and, in its full-fledged form, matriarchy, understood as the all-but-unqualified subordination of men to women. Actually, Bachofen's broad scheme depicted the development of human society in three stages—the tellurian, the lunar, and the solar—which correspond to three distinct sexual relationships between women and men: unregulated promiscuity, matriarchal marriage, and patriarchal marriage.[73]

Robert Briffault, in *The Mothers* (1927), added the weight of his voice and of his volumes (perhaps a million and a half words in all) to Bachofen's claim that before patriarchy there existed a universal, primitive matriarchy. Furthermore, he argued that the movement from that original matriarchy to the subsequent patriarchy was correlated to the development of settled agriculture and to the emergence of private property. With extensive—indeed global—research, Briffault endeavored to show that marriage was everywhere originally matrilinear and matrilocal. Of course, Maine, Westermarck, Bachofen, and Briffault, had neither the first nor the last word on these matters. Rather, they provide a point of entry into a debate, as lively today as ever before, regarding the "original" shape of human society, in which there are few utterly safe assertions to be made.

Needless to say, it is especially precarious to assert anything at all about absolute beginnings or about universal stages. However, well before Maine and Westermarck, whose reliance on biblical "evidence" is particularly suspect, and now well after Briffault, two points were and are widely assumed and often well argued: first, that some form of matriarchy or mother-right, entailing at the least a matrilinear system of kinship, prevailed in prehistoric southeastern Europe and the Near East in the Neolithic and early Bronze ages; and, second, that, throughout the region in question, some form of patriarchy, entailing a rather thorough diminution of the rights and status of women, came to prevail more or less uniformly by the mid-second millennium.[74] Given the scope of our concerns, more than this might but need not be claimed here. A good deal more, however, may be suggested.

To account for the widespread change from matriarchy to patriarchy in southeastern Europe and beyond, most scholars introduce at once the Indo-Europeans, whose intrusive and pervasive influence is by now a commonplace. The "Indo-European Question" remains, however, just that, a question, a quite open question. Who they were, when and from where they came, what they caused and what they merely occasioned or witnessed are matters of enduring inquiry and debate. In short, there is little about the "Indo-Europeans," including their separate existence, that is not for someone a matter to be disputed.[75]

Many of the most deeply rooted differences of opinion regarding the Indo-Europeans may be traced to the discrepant assumptions, methods, and evidence employed by linguists, on the one hand, and by archaeologists, on the other. While linguists are quick to point out that pots do not equal people, archaeologists are equally ready to question any facile identification of words or word stems with distinct ethnic groups or cultures. For example, the proliferation of *kilims* and Persian carpets in the Upper East Side of Manhattan does not amount to proof of an Iranian migration, much less an invasion; neither, of course, does the introduction of *ciao* and *bon appetito* into the conversations of San Franciscans indicate a proportionate increase in the Italian population in the Bay Area. Words and artifacts change location and hands in many ways, a fact that is surely not lost on circumspect scholars. The problem, as Colin Renfrew sees it, is "that these two disciplines have not yet interacted very significantly one with another," or, more pointedly, "that there has hitherto been no valid methodology for matching the evidence obtained from the study of the languages themselves, that is from historical linguistics, with the material evidence of archaeology."[76]

Clearly, if we enter further into these disputes here, there will be no exit from them in the remaining course of this book. And yet the completion of our current discussion requires at the least a tentative sketch of the society of the Goddess and its demise. For our present purposes, we may narrow our focus to the society of Old Europe, Anatolia, and Crete, the proximate homeland of Helen of Argos, the Helen of Greek epic and dramatic poetry. Furthermore, we will confine ourselves mostly to one available account,[77] the closest we can come for the moment to a broadly consensual understanding of the unique character and the catastrophic

dissolution of the matriarchal or, perhaps more accurately though awk-
wardly, "gylanic"[78] civilization of the Goddess. With all appropriate pro-
visos and cautions in place, then, we return to our initial question
regarding what the society, the human society, of the Goddess might have
been like and what became of it.

First, it is notable and striking that, despite the unique cosmic sovereignty of the Goddess, there is no evidence of matriarchy, understood as
the female domination of men, in Old Europe. Instead, there is substantial evidence of equality between men and women in societies that were
most probably matrilinear and matrilocal. Evidence for equality, it should
be noted, frequently means the absence of evidence for inequality. Specifically, in Old European graves, there are no evident distinctions made,
along the lines either of sex or of class, in the mode or wealth of burial. In
short, "an equalitarian male-female society is demonstrated by the grave
equipment in practically all the known cemeteries of Old Europe."[79]
Additionally, it is reasonably clear that, while a division of labor existed
between the sexes, there was no corresponding ranking of the work or
worth of women over men or of men over women. And there is no evidence of slavery. The society of the Goddess appears to have been a
sedentary, agricultural society without any form of institutional inequality, without warriors and serfs, without masters and slaves, without dominant males and subservient females.

In selecting the sites for their communities, the Old Europeans, unlike
the Indo-Europeans who later supplanted them, chose locations not for
their strategic, military importance but rather "for their beautiful setting,
good water and soil, and availability of animal pastures."[80] They neither
seriously fortified their towns nor fashioned thrusting weapons—daggers, swords, or spears—suitable for warfare, which suggests that the
communities of Old Europe coexisted in peace, relatively unthreatened
from within and from without. The essential harmony of the civilizations
of Old Europe—harmony with each other and with their world—is
silently reflected in their art: their pottery, sculpture, frescoes, and
engravings vividly affirm and celebrate life. Always, in their images and
symbols, there is the eloquent absence of warriors, slaves, battle, and the
spoils of conquest; instead, there is the even more eloquent presence of
Nature, the largesse and being of the Goddess.

Contrary to earlier and still quite common conceptions, the agrarian
civilizations of Neolithic Europe and the Middle East were not primitive.
Their successes in agriculture and in the domestication of animals made

possible a stable prosperity, which, in turn, led to substantial population growth, technological specialization, and extensive trade, in part by sailing ship. They developed proficiency in a range of crafts, including copper and gold metallurgy for the sake of tools, ritual objects, and jewelry; and they produced quite compelling art. In fact, they seem even to have created an embryonic script. Recent excavations at such sites as Catal Hüyük and Hacilar in Turkey, and Jericho in Israel have dispelled the notion that urban civilization was born in the alluvial flood plain of Sumer at the dawn of the Bronze Age, demonstrating that prosperous urban centers existed well over a thousand years before the emergence of the Sumerian city-states and of the first Egyptian dynasty. In sum, human society did not leap from primitive, isolated, familial or tribal communities, focused on survival, to the fortress-cities of the Bronze Age, focused on plunder. Instead, there existed for several thousand years, in Europe and beyond, stable, prosperous, peaceful, egalitarian, Goddess-worshiping civilizations, some remote echo of which may possibly be heard in Hesiod's depiction of the first or "golden" age:

> Everything that is truly good was theirs.
> Graciously, the furrowed earth bore rich
> fruit for them, harvests beyond their efforts
> or their needs; [and their flocks flourished]
> [Dear to the blessed gods and] at peace with
> each other, they lived gentle lives, blessed
> from every side.[81]

In time, Hesiod relates, "the earth covered up this race,"[82] which would seem a euphemism for what happened to the towns and villages and people of Old Europe; for they fell prey, over several thousand years, to peoples altogether alien and hostile to the ways of Neolithic Europe. These invasive peoples, whose weapons were to them sacred objects and whose gods were warriors, descended upon Europe from the Eurasian steppe north of the Caspian and Black Seas. Traditionally, they have been called most commonly the "Aryans" or the "Indo-Europeans," though recently the name "Kurgans" has been suggested for the first three migratory "waves" or incursions of Proto-Indo-European peoples entering and sweeping across Europe from the mid-fifth to the late third millennium.[83] These first migratory invasions were followed, in the Greek world, by two more notorious ones, the Achaean and the Dorian,[84] which bear immediately upon the story of Helen, legendary bride of Menelaos and of Paris and prize of the Trojan War. The last surviving remnant of Old

Europe, as we have already considered, appears to have been the fortunately remote Minoan civilization of Crete, together with the related communities of Thera and the Cyclades, the last "high civilization" of the Goddess to succumb, in the mid-second millennium, to the weapon-wielding, horse-breeding Indo-Europeans.

As we shall see briefly but in some detail, the Kurgans, or Proto-Indo-Europeans, could barely have been more alien to the peoples whom they first confronted over six thousand years ago. Whereas the Neolithic peoples of Europe were settled agriculturalists, the Kurgans were seasonally migratory pastoralists. The ancient hostility of farmer and shepherd, eventually a common theme in the earliest literature of the Near East, may have had its most decisive beginning here. In this possibly first incident between them, however, it was "Abel," the shepherd, who killed "Cain," the farmer. The peaceful, sedentary peoples of Old Europe, whose defensive weapons would presumably have been their copper tools, were no match for heavily armed, nomadic Kurgan warriors, mounted in four-wheeled, horse-drawn carts. The result, in time, was the end of an age.

> Towns and villages disintegrated, magnificent painted pottery vanished; as did shrines, frescoes, sculptures, symbols, and script. The taste for beauty and the sophistication of style and execution withered. The use of vivid colors disappeared. . . . [This] dramatic upheaval is evidenced in the archaeological record. The abrupt cessation of painted pottery and figurines, disintegration of egalitarian townships, and termination of symbols and linear signs is concomitant with the sudden appearance of weapons and horses.[85]

Indeed, it seems to have been the lethal combination of horses and bronze metallurgy that assured the pace and scope of the Kurgans' conquests. Employing an innovative metallurgical technique, the alloying of arsenic and copper developed in Transcaucasia in the fifth millennium,[86] and drawing upon the rich copper resources of that same area, the Kurgans armed themselves with hardened bronze daggers, swords, halberds, maces, and battle-axes, which they left behind them in their graves. With the speed of the horse and the hard edge of their blades they made relatively short work of the unfortified and comparatively unarmed villages and towns in their path. The Kurgans replaced these settlements with hilltop citadels (*acropoleis*) eventually encased in massive stone fortification walls, wherein warrior chiefs kept relatively extravagant households, while their lessers lived nearby in small, subterranean dwellings.

Kurgan communities were markedly hierarchical along both sex and caste lines. Men were dominant over women and warrior chiefs ruled over their inferiors, the most inferior being their slaves. They were a violent people, not only toward others but toward themselves. We know all of this from the graves of their warrior chiefs, graves that culminated in the magnificent *tholos* tombs of Mycenaean royalty. In contrast to the simple pit graves of Old Europe, wherein the ratio of men to women is roughly equal, the more elaborate barrow tombs of the Kurgans belong almost exclusively to men, who were buried with extensive caches of weapons, some encrusted with gold and jewels. There is ample evidence, as well, of Kurgan chieftains' having been buried not only with their horses but also with their wives, suggesting the practice of *suttee*, the immolation of women as burial companions to their men. Kurgan graves have likewise yielded the bones of children and of numerous others, possibly servants or slaves, whose remains tell of their savage immolation. These are sometimes combined with the bones of slaughtered animals, all of which suggests that sacrifice, human and bestial, was a common element in the burial rite of warrior chiefs. "The possibility of coincidental deaths is overruled," writes Gimbutas, "by the frequency of these multiple burials. Generally, the male skeleton is buried with his gifts at one end of the cist grave, while two or more individuals are grouped at the other end."[87] With remarkable consistency, across a wide geographical area and span of time, this grisly scene was repeated in Kurgan royal graves; and, although the practice of *suttee* and of human sacrifice became less frequent and eventually ceased, the burial gifts of royal tombs remained quite similar into the late Bronze Age. These tombs, shrines of violent supremacy and death, were for the Kurgans their signature, their dark entry into the human record.

It is no surprise to find that the Kurgan gods, and those of their descendants, the later Indo-Europeans, were fitting patrons and paradigms for the violence by which the Kurgan chiefs and warriors lived and died. Their gods were solar sky-gods, celestial warriors, and hunters, seated in the luminous upper air from which come thunderous shafts of fire. In extant Kurgan engravings, their gods, when depicted anthropomorphically, commonly bear weapons—axes, halberds, daggers, and spears— emblems of their power and sovereignty. Otherwise the gods are abstractly manifest in their weapons alone, particularly the dagger and the double-edged battle-ax. Indeed, the words of the much later philosopher Heraclitus distill with precision what appears to have been the guiding principle of Kurgan society, human and divine: "violence [*polemos*, i.e., violent conflict] is the father and king of all."[88]

Women, human and divine, suffered a common fate at the hands of the Kurgans. The regimes of the Kurgans and of their descendants, whether on earth or in the sky above, were decidedly patriarchal, violently so. Women, if they were fortunate, became wives, often one of many; otherwise they could find themselves slaves, at the disposal, sexually and generally, of their masters. In life they were peripheral, except as victims, to the violent lives of fathers, brothers, husbands, and sons; and in death they were often made to lie, before their time, on the periphery of a father's or a husband's grave. Close at a man's side, in death perhaps as in life, lay not his wife but his weapons.

The Goddess, of course, in all of her manifestations and aspects, being divine, could not be made to die. Instead, in a term well worn by historians of religion, she was "demoted."[89] The first stage in her demotion was perhaps enacted when the Kurgan chiefs chose the crests of hills for their fortresses. Mounds and mountaintops, gentle rises in the earth as well as towering conical or pyramidal peaks, often clefted softly like breasts and containing, further down their slopes, deep, mysterious caves, all of these high and hollow places of the earth were sacred to the Goddess. They were her bodily presence and were alive with her power. The Old Europeans mostly dwelled in valleys, under the surrounding protection of Goddess Earth, their eternal Mother. Their vulnerability was at the same time their opening to her largesse. The Kurgan chiefs, for their part, mounted these very hills, occupied them, and made them symbols of their dominance and of the dominance of their gods.

In the next stage of her demotion, the Goddess was mythically divided and conquered. Her many faces and functions were substantially fractured into distinct identities. Her essential unity was dissipated and demeaned. Like "dirty money," each of her new identities was "laundered" through an acceptably male line. The Goddess became a bevy of divine "beauties," with few exceptions each the daughter and eventual wife or concubine of a god. In sum, she was sundered, disempowered, and eroticized. Eventually, the demotion proceeded further and some goddesses became whole or partly human. These became paradigms for the race of women, which brings us back, of course, to Pandora and Helen. As if obeying some concealed genetic code, each Indo-European pantheon takes shape along similar lines. Presiding over each is a high-king, a sky-god, governing his household and his world from a sacred acropolis on a northern mountain peak where earth and sky meet in confirmed patriarchy.

In Helen's world, this sky-god is high-thundering Zeus, who acquired and holds his sovereign place through violent force, focused in the jagged bolts of fire he wields and hurls. In the dynastic wars preceding his reign, Zeus established himself as a preeminent warrior, savage and effective; later, in the seemingly endless lull following his heroic feats, he established himself as a lover, or more precisely as a rapist *par excellence,* which should not be attributed to a divine excess of lust. Rape, after all, is not about lust but about power.

Below, as it were, in the human realm, women followed in the footsteps of the Goddess. They became possessions, booty, and sexual prey. What is more, they were blamed for the violence from which they suffered first and most. In saying this, we have returned full circle to Pandora and to Helen, beautiful and deadly, luring and lethal. Now we see, however, that they are but sherds from the sacred pithos that is Earth, long since shattered, fossils of the Goddess of many faces and names, the One, the All. Helen is, indeed, enclosed in violence and hate. One wave of Indo-Europeans, the Achaeans, built the fortress in which she was born and another wave, the Dorians, tore it down. She lived in a time steeped in chaos; and she was, as a woman, a daughter of Pandora, supposedly to blame for it all.

Helen was, undeniably, a scapegoat. Arguably, she still is. Behind every scapegoat there is a truth and, of course, a lie. These require to be sorted out and revealed, which is what Euripides undertook in the name of Helen. He is our final witness for the defense.

# 5

# The Truth of Helen

In the midst of the strife and misery of the fifth age, the age of the race of iron, when "men know no respite by day from wearying labor nor by night from perishing,"[1] Hesiod sought and, for his purposes, found the cause of men's distress: women, mythically distilled in the person of Pandora. Similarly, when confronted with the most profound disaster ever yet suffered by the city of Athens—the debacle in Sicily—Euripides, striving to account for that unprecedented calamity, turned to Helen, the epitome of women, the most notorious of Pandora's daughters. Between these two, however, between Hesiod and Euripides, there extends a wide moral gulf—the space between a hideous lie and an awkward truth—a space that requires now to be explored.

Euripides presented his *Helen* in the year 412 B.C.E., the year following the calamitous defeat of the Athenian forces in Sicily. In that same year, he is supposed to have written the epitaph for the Athenians who died in Sicilian waters or on Sicilian soil. His words for the dead are lost; but his words to the survivors—the *Helen*—survived. They offer lucid commentary on the fusion of *erōs* and *eris,* and on the attribution of both to women. The *Helen*—on the face of it a light romantic comedy about the reunion of Helen and Menelaos in Egypt after the fall of Troy—would seem to have been a singularly insensitive on-stage response to that darkest of Athenian off-stage tragedies. Yet, as we shall see, it was, whether in the best or worst of taste, a pitilessly truthful response. First, however, before considering the *Helen* in detail, we have several excursions to make.

Already, in the title and in the opening lines of this chapter, the word *truth* has occurred with what for some may be disturbing centrality and frequency. In an age such as ours, or Euripides' for that matter, an age as corrupt as it is refined, to speak of truth is often to provoke discomfort and scorn. Clearly, Euripidean drama provoked both; and so perhaps must any straightforward discussion of that drama. The theater of Dionysos[2] in Athens, the *theatron*, or "seeing-place," was, after all, as its name suggests, dedicated to sight; and sight, as Plato would confirm and as anyone knows, is twofold: inner and outer.[3] Correspondingly, the sights to be seen in the theater were, in broadest terms, twofold. On the one hand, there was the outer spectacle, comprised of actors, costumes, set, movement, and action. On the other hand, there was the reality behind these theatrical appearances, the inner spectacle of truth.

In other words, the theater was inevitably and by intent a world of images, a place where one sight led to another, where one reality revealed another. On the masked[4] face of it, actors brought timeless myth to timely enactment. Gods and heroes, or rather their images, appeared openly to the eyes of spectators delighting in the theatrical suspension of one reality for the sake of another. Donning the robes and masks of the likes of Klytemnestra, Apollo, Agamemnon, Odysseus, Polyphemos, and of course Helen, actors became what and who they were not. Men became women, gods, kings, heroes, monsters, and living legends. As walking, talking, breathing, and dying icons, they made the unseen visible.

While myth became visible in the ancient theater, it also became transparent to history. The *mythoi*, or "plots," enacted in ancient tragedy offered to its spectators no simple escape from the similarly tortuous stories enacted in their own lives. Those who came to the theater to peer into the mythic past were eventually confronted with the all-too-real present. Inevitably, they came to see themselves and their own stories imaged or reflected in the characters and the myths made visible before their eyes. In the theater of Dionysos, as in the cosmos it mirrors, there are in the end no spectators, only the spectacle in which all beings play their part. Voyeurism, as Pentheus discovered in the *Bakkhai*, is the ultimate illusion, an illusion that Greek drama serves not to promote but to shatter.

Euripides, in particular, often held up the mythic past as a mirror to the historical present. Thus, the Trojan War frequently served, in Euripidean drama, as a mythic paradigm for the war Euripides, a citizen warrior of Athens, knew best, the Peloponnesian War, which broke out in 431 and ended with the collapse and Spartan occupation of Athens in 404. His concern, however, was not merely to capture one outward spectacle in

the reflection of another. Rather, his concern was with seeing beyond outward spectacle to underlying truth, beyond appearance to reality, which
returns us full circle to the question of truth, what it might mean and
where it might reside. In addressing this question here, with immediate
reference to Euripides, we must bear in mind that Euripides was a playwright, not a metaphysician, and that plays themselves—not unlike the
active, public lives of those for whom they are written—are made up
mostly of words and actions. It comes as no surprise, then, that Euripides
the playwright concerned himself mostly with moral truth, the truth of
words and of deeds.

We may find a clue to what we seek in the word *alētheia*, which means
"truth" as opposed to "lie," and "reality" as opposed to "mere appearance." Our clue lies, more specifically, in the composition of this word
from the privative *a-* and the noun *lēthē*, which means "forgetting" or
"oblivion," from which the underworld river crossed at death receives its
name.[5] We may add to this mix the related verb *lanthanō*, which in the
active voice means "to escape notice" and in the middle and passive
voices means "to allow to escape notice" or "to forget." Manifest truth,
then, is something we have not let escape our notice, or something we
have managed to "un-forget." Ordinarily, without such effort, truth is
what we already know but do everything in our power, consciously or
unconsciously, to overlook. Truth must be mined, as it were, like ore,
pried loose from oblivion. Otherwise, it lies hidden, unseen and silent.

"The true character of things and of people (*physis*)," writes Heraclitus,
"is inclined toward concealment."[6] Whether or not we accept, in theory,
that some metaphysical *chōrismos*, or gulf, separates the seen from the
unseen, matter from mind, only the inexperienced deny that, in practice,
appearances often deceive and words dissemble as often as they divulge.
In the moral cosmos, the world of words and deeds, lies are likely to
eclipse truth, and appearances are likely to pass for reality. Here, at least,
the aphorism of Heraclitus rings true and, at the same time, defines the
challenge of the ancient playwright, a challenge to which Euripides
responded with singular wit and integrity, to bring the true character of
things and, particularly, of people from out of concealment.

In the theater, as elsewhere, "the true character of things and of people"
often hide behind words.[7] "How I wish," wrote Euripides, "that facts
could speak for themselves, so that they could not be misrepresented by
eloquence."[8] Instead, people with something to hide are commonly
inclined toward that peculiar concealment offered by clever words. "The

clever tongue I find hateful and malignant,"⁹ protests Agamemnon, presumably including his own, if he is honest. Euripidean drama is indeed
replete with "clever tongues" doing their best to conceal the truth of their
deeds. To cite several, there is Admetos, the would-be "victim," who
blames everyone but himself for his wife's death; there is Jason, who says
he abandoned his wife and sons "for their sakes"; and there is Polymestor, who laments how he was held "hostage" by the young boy he
murdered.

In each of these instances, and in many others, it is in an *agōn*, a struggle
or contest of words, that the truth is dragged out of concealment. In what
often resembles courtroom drama, facile stories unravel, masks slip, and
the truth comes out, always under pressure. Thus, when Admetos
decides to disown his father instead of his own misdeeds, Pheres blasts
him and the truth shakes loose. "Big words, boy!" he shouts at Admetos,
"the fact is, your time to die came and went; and you've still got your life.
All you had to do was murder your own wife!"¹⁰ As for Jason and the
case he would make for himself, Medea assures him that "one word is all
it will take to stretch you out flat."¹¹ Finally, when Polymestor is done
putting the best possible face on his crimes, Hecuba turns to Agamemnon, the presiding judge, and reminds him that "we would do wrong to
let a desperate man's loud words deafen us to the message of his
deeds."¹² There is nothing worse, she suggests, than rot wrapped in fin-
ery. Behind whatever veil of words, however finely woven, a rotten life
begins to smell and give itself away. Knowing this, Hecuba urges
Agamemnon to cover his ears to the craft of Polymestor's words and to
smell, as it were, the kind of man he is.

Nothing surpasses, however, the lie told by Agamemnon to his own
daughter in the *Iphigenia at Aulis,* when he says that he must, against his
will, sacrifice her to a higher will and purpose than his own, that of Hellas, Greece. "Hellas" wills her death; and who is he or she to deny Hellas
anything? Hers shall be the first blood spilt in a great war, innocent
blood, assuring victory. The truth, pried loose in Agamemnon's encounters with his brother and wife, is another matter. Agamemnon's ambition
has outstripped his abilities. He is no more in command of his army than
was Hippolytos in control of his horses; but he would rather murder his
own child than surrender his illusions, much less compromise his career.
So he invents "Hellas," as well as the "barbarians," whose very existence
is said to be an affront and a threat to her. In a word, he invents "patrio-
tism" to conceal the shabby, consuming self-interest of moral nonentities

like himself and his brother, and the mob flattering itself as an army. In undiluted bad faith, he invents a lie as big as the atrocity he is about to commit; and his daughter believes it. Her only alternative is to admit that her own father is about to murder her for nothing, or for his ambitions, which come to the same thing. With this lie—something seemingly big enough to die for—Agamemnon anesthetizes his girl before putting her under the knife. It is doubtful whether, in doing so, he is motivated by compassion. Anesthesia, after all, may be administered as much for the surgeon's convenience as for the patient's comfort.

While the *Iphigenia at Aulis,* produced posthumously, was Euripides' last word on war—the passions that drive it, the lies that accompany it, and the victims who endure it—it was not his first. Drawing the true character of war out of concealment, out from under the lies with which it likes to robe itself, was all but an obsession for Euripides; and surely it is no bold stroke to suggest that his many depictions of war were rooted in his own experience, both as a warrior in and as a witness to the internecine violence that consumed Athens and indeed all of Greece during the last three decades of his life. Theatrical convention prescribed that he set his plays in times, cities, and wars other than his own, which required imagination. Presumably, no more than this was required for his fellow-Athenians to see themselves, their city, and their great war reflected in his productions.

Together with war, it may be argued that the other profound preoccupation of Euripides was woman. In fact, women may be said to dominate what we possess of Euripides' work.[13] Admittedly, Euripides' women represent a broad diversity of race, rank, age, and character. Among them, there are Greeks and barbarians, queens and slaves, daughters and grandmothers, innocents and hags. But most of all, cutting across every category, there are victims, victims of violence, domestic, civic, and international, sometimes subtle, sometimes savage. And it is here, in the sufferings of women as victims, that the two master themes of Euripidean drama—war and woman—converge; for it is in war, though waged by men, that women suffer first and most. And yet, paradoxically, its cause is assigned to them or, by poetic proxy, to one of their number, who represents all women in their misery and in their guilt. In matters of *erōs* and *eris,* all roads lead to Helen.

The treatment of Helen in Euripidean drama is not uniformly sympathetic. In fact, she is mostly confronted there by the same wall of hate that she meets elsewhere in Greek poetry. Guilty without trial of *the* war, it is war's worst victims who despise her most. When, for example, Klytemnestra demands that Agamemnon tell her why he is about to murder their daughter, he is silent; so she must put words into his mouth:

> "So that Menelaos can get Helen back."
> A lovely, perfect girl for a rotten whore.
> No one can accuse you of driving a hard bargain!
> So we give what we love most
> for what we despise.[14]

Hecuba, at the other end of the same war, suffers a similar loss. Her daughter likewise is torn from her arms to summon the winds and so to expedite a venture from which she will know nothing but grief. She too believes she knows precisely where to cast blame. "Oh what I wouldn't give," she screams, "to see Helen in her stead. That one Spartan bitch, with her large luring eyes, dragged thriving Troy to ruin."[15] Iphigenia herself, by one account rescued by Artemis and wafted away to maintain a distant shrine, inquires years later of apparent strangers what ever happened to Helen. When told that she is safely home, in her old bed again, Iphigenia responds bitterly in the same tradition: "How I hate her. And so must all of Greece."[16] For all her years in exile, her words are still on the mark.

From these voices, only a slight sampling of the vocal hatred for Helen to be heard in Euripides' plays, we might easily conclude that Euripides himself was no friend of Helen. Here, of course, we must remember that none of these voices can be uncritically equated with the playwright's own. Invariably, they convey what "others" say—in other words Helen's reputation. Furthermore, we should note that Helen is not only an occasional character in Greek myth and drama but also a central image therein, perhaps *the* image of woman as victim and scapegoat, woman as the object of universal hate. "I know full well," says Phaedra, "that I am a woman, the object of everyone's hate."[17] Clearly, it is here, at the center of hate, that Helen and woman become one; and it is here too, I would suggest, that Euripides' *Helen* is conceived.

My claim is simply this: that Euripides is no more concerned with Helen than he is with the Trojan War. Rather, these are mere icons or images for what does concern him deeply: woman and war. In Greek myth and in the drama that enacted it, the Trojan War was *the* war and Helen was *the* woman, its reputed cause. In fact, however, *the* war for Euripides was the Peloponnesian War, not only because it was more immediate but also because it was so much greater, both in the scale of its events and in the depth of what it revealed.[18] It was the true character of this war that Euripides sought to bring out of concealment. It was Athens's not Agamemnon's lies that Euripides sought to un-tell. In short, it is the Peloponnesian War and its victims that form the dark matrix of the *Helen*, Euripides' clearest, most eloquent statement on woman and war, eroticism and violence. Before turning to the *Helen*, then, we must explore further its historical context and source.

The Peloponnesian War represented the most prolonged and savage conflict that the Mediterranean world had ever known. Fired by the central rivalry between Athens and Sparta, it spread easily to other mainland cities, to the islands, and to Asia Minor, until virtually all of the Greek world was plunged into civil war. Thucydides likened this war to the plague and chronicled with chilling precision its moral effect: the unweaving, thread by thread, of a civilization. Athens, as agent and eventually as victim, learned how tenuous is the human grip on humanity and how chaos is always at the door, lessons that we in our century have learned, and relearned, with a vengeance.[19]

The Athenian expedition against Sicily, launched in the sixteenth year since the outbreak of hostilities, reveals clearly both the source and the outcome of the Peloponnesian War. The source, because the Sicilian Expedition manifests more fully than any other single event the imperial vision and passion which brought about the war in the first place; and the outcome, because the Athenian forces in Sicily knew by the end, according to Thucydides, that they were fighting in Sicily the "battle of Athens."[20] Their total defeat in Sicily left Athenians with shredded hopes, just as triumph there would have decisively vindicated their quest for empire.

The quest for empire, the passion of *pleonexia*—the consuming desire for always more and other than what one already has—may be said to have driven and possessed Athens ever since the second repulsion of the Persians in 479. In fact, the roots of Athenian restlessness and ambition[21] must have run far deeper than the opportunity for empire which presented itself after the Persian defeat. Regardless, the opportunity was there and the Athenians seized it. Twice, in the first two decades of the fifth century, the Persian empire had invaded Greece with epic force and arrogance; and twice Athens had played the decisive hand in repelling that threat. In the battles of Marathon and Salamis, Athenian military prowess and moral preeminence were well established. Indeed, in the eyes of the Athenians and of many others, Athens had shown itself the "savior-city" of Greece, the leader, as it were, of the free world.

Not for long, however, was Athens content to be the "first among equals." Athens soon began abusing its moral and military leadership, pressuring its allies into postures of varying subordination. Athens's former partners against Persia were made over now into satellite states within an ideological-commercial-military empire envisioned and ruled by the radical Athenian democracy designed and set in place by Pericles. The "savior-city," the city that had preserved Greece from Persian barbarism, became the "tyrant-city," offering to one city after another its "friendship" or its fist.[22] The more immoral were its policies, the more self-righteous its rhetoric. The further it departed from its own past, the more it appealed to that past.

Of the many episodes in Athens's quest for empire, the Athenian misadventure in Sicily, wherein Athens played the "Persian" aggressor to an ironically "Athenian" Syracuse, was the most extreme and the most revealing. Already exhausted from sixteen years of war on numerous fronts, unable to secure its own territory much less to retain its grip on the empire, Athens all the same defiantly launched the greatest invasion force in Greek history, dwarfing forever the armada of Agamemnon against Troy. Myth was clearly in the making.

In his account of the Athenians' decision to launch this invasion, Thucydides describes their frenzy for it as a form of eroticism. "There came over everyone, all at once," he writes, "an *erōs* for the sailing."[23] As pointed out by W. Robert Connor,[24] this mention of *erōs* in conjunction with the movements of a great army recalls the fear-filled premonitions of Klytemnestra in the *Agamemnon*, wherein she prays:

> Let no *erōs* fall upon the army, so that,
> overwhelmed by the desire for more,
> they are provoked to violate what they
> should not.[25]

Thucydides, we see, was not the first to seize upon the bond between *erōs* and *eris* in order to understand and to confront the fever of war. In Euripides' *Iphigenia at Aulis*, we find Agamemnon making essentially the same connection between *erōs* and uncontainable violence, when he explains to his daughter, Iphigenia, the compulsion to which he and she must yield. "Some kind of Aphrodite," he says, "has frenzied the army, made them mad to set sail as soon as possible."[26] The passion, it seems, that launches great armadas and provokes men to bold violence, whether directed at Troy or at Sicily, is *erōs*, ultimately the *erōs* of empire. It is here, in the pursuit of absolute power, that *eris* and *erōs* find their final conjunction and consummation.

Thus Aristophanes, in the spring of 414, with the recent launching of the Sicilian expedition clearly in his mind, presented to the citizens of Athens his comedy of the *Birds*, which may be seen as an extended poetic parody of the eroticism of empire. In it, two Athenian gentlemen, Euelpides and Pisthetairos, weary of the bold, restless, mercurial ambition of the city of Athens, summed up in the words *polypragmosynē*[27] and *pleonexia*, set out to the countryside in search of the quiet life. Their longing for moderation and leisurely contentment must have been shared by many Athenians, if Alcibiades, in arguing for the Sicilian expedition, was forced to argue against any temptation to "the quiet life" (*hēsychia*)[28] and against any policy that would promote "inactivity" (*apragmosynē*)[29] as incompatible with the pursuit and retention of empire. Aristophanes' two would-be rustics, however, pose no even theoretical threat to the rhetoric of Alcibiades; for they no sooner quit the imperial city and take their first bucolic breaths than they hatch a scheme for the most ambitious empire of all, the empire of the birds.[30]

Their scheme is, as all great ideas tend to be, simple and, once articulated, obvious. It combines the metaphysics of the Greek cosmos with the *Realpolitik* of world commerce. After all, the two greatest trading partners in the ancient Greek cosmos are men and gods, separated by the vast expanse of the sky. Men are utterly dependent on the gods' good will, without whose blessing their crops will fail, their wars will miscarry, their ships will go down at sea, and so on; and the one act that assures the good will of the gods is ritual sacrifice, often the sacrifice of a bird. The gods, on the other hand, are inhumanly consumed with the two great hungers attributed to the bellies of women—the hunger for food and the hunger for sex—and both involve the gods with mortals. If the gods' needs are to be satisfied, then, the airways must be always open between heaven and earth. The sweet smoke, the divine portion, of sacrificial meals must be free to rise to them from below; and they, in turn, must be free to descend on erotic errands to their mortal favorites. The plan of Pisthetairos is, in short, to control the cosmic air lanes and to levy a tax on all commerce through them, on all sacrifice being lifted to the gods and on all erotic descents from above.[31]

Pisthetairos reminds the birds that they are by design the natural rulers of the skies and, in fact, the primordial rulers of the cosmos.[32] All that remains is for them to assert their rule. Pisthetairos directs them to construct the longest wall ever raised and so to cordon off the regime of Zeus from the realm of mortals, sky from earth, until both recognize the supremacy of the new imperial city, the City of the Birds. Soon the gods sue for peace, offering to the birds the scepter of Zeus and to Pisthetairos a bride named *Basileia*, "Dominion" or "Empire." The *Birds* ends with their ecstatic nuptials. "Reach me your hand, dear bride," Pisthetairos sings to Empire:

> Now take me by the wings,
> oh my lovely,
>       my sweet,
> and let me lift you up,
> and soar beside you
> through the buoyant air.[33]

And so the quest for empire is consummated in the celestial bed of love.

*Erōs* does not enter the *Birds* for the first time, however, with the entry of the bride *Basileia*; for the eroticism of the entire work is quite unmistakable. "No other play of Aristophanes," writes William Arrowsmith, "not even *Lysistrata*, is so pervaded, so saturated by the language of desire. *Erōs, erastēs, epithymia, pothos*—over and over again the note of desire is struck, given constant visual dimension and the stress that only great poetry can confer."[34] The most blatant visual dimension given to the energy of desire was likely in the "wings"[35] worn not only by the birds but eventually by Pisthetairos and Euelpides. The defining characteristic of *Erōs*, after all, is that he is winged, as are the *erastai* or lovers of Cloud-cuckooland. His wings, however, are divine; and theirs are, like themselves, merely mortal. Paraphrasing Pindar, the wings of Pisthetairos and Euelpides are in brief delight exalted, only to droop groundwards again, shaken by a backward doom. Indeed, comments Arrowsmith:

> what to mortal eyes is the mysterious shimmering figure of winged Eros, is to the gods merely a curious natural phenomenon. In love, in the erect phallos, human flesh rises on its own, defies gravity; it reaches for the skies. The erect phallos is a winged phallos, and the figure of the winged phallos is of great iconographic antiquity....[36]

Here, in the *Birds*, Arrowsmith concludes, the use of the comic phallus must have been as generous as it was purposeful. The homology of the birds' wings and of the men's theatrical phalluses, and the uses to which they must have been put in performance, surely created from the outset a text parallel to the one we read today, a running erotic commentary, as it were, on the innumerable sexual allusions in the text and, of course, on

the sexuality of flying. Indeed, the walling off of the male sky from the
female earth, the core of the birds' strategy, creates a cosmic sexual tension which pervades the play until it is released in the *hieros gamos*, the
sacred nuptials, of Pisthetairos and *Basileia* or Empire in the final scene of
the play. This same tension, reduced to human proportions, runs through
the *Lysistrata*, wherein the women of Athens and Sparta conspire to bring
the Peloponnesian War to an abrupt end by denying sex to their husbands until the men lay down their arms. Once again, the link between
*erōs* and *eris* proves unbreakable and complex. The men decide to make
love not war. Why these two—*erōs* and *eris*—should be so alike, so inter-
changeable, remains the enigma into which we must delve still further.

Admittedly, the brilliant complexity and turbulence of the *Birds* cannot
be reduced to a single idea. Even so, very near the source and center of
that complexity and turbulence we can expect to find *Erōs*, born like
Helen from an egg. We do well to begin in the beginning. "There was
Chaos at first," sings the Chorus of birds,

> and Night and Space
> > and Tartaros.
> There was no Earth.
> > No Heaven was.
> > > But sable-winged Night
> laid her wind-egg there
> > in the boundless lap
> > > of infinite Dark.
> And from that egg,
> > in the seasons' revolving,
> > > Love (*Erōs*) was born,
> the graceful, the golden,
> > the whirlwind Love
> > > on gleaming wings.
> And there in the waste
> > of Tartaros,
> > > Love with Chaos lay
> and hatched the Birds.[37]

The birds, we learn from their own song, are born from the union of
Chaos and Desire. Presumably, Cloudcuckooland too, the empire city of
the birds, is a hybrid, a turbulent fusion of longing and nothingness. This
is its irresistible attraction for Pisthetairos and Euelpides, and for the
string of restless Athenians who soon follow them there. Its rarefied air is
what they breathe best. Indeed, in the genealogy of the birds, the first-

born of Eros, we find the clue to "winged man," the mortal avatar of Desire, a creature of chaos, consumed with desire. "Men too, like birds," writes Arrowsmith, "are chaos-creatures, hybrids of earth and heaven; and if the heavenly part—*technē* guided by intellect—is tempted to think itself divine, the swamp of its origins always reclaims it."[38]

When the leader of the Chorus of birds asks the Hoopoe who these strangers are, why they have come, and what it is they hope to get from the birds, the Hoopoe responds simply:

> Their motive is love (*Erōs*),
> Love is the burden of all their words.
> Love of your life
> and Love of you,
> to live with you
> in Love always. . . .[39]

The Love, the *Erōs*, best read as "desire," which possesses these two cosmic colonists, however, is timelessly coupled with "gaping" Chaos, whose very name[40] describes both a habit that all but discredits birds, and the inner abyss with which mortals must cope. Human desire and human chaos are drawn, as it were, to the same bed.

In Platonic terms, human beings live in a state of constant becoming, an essentially unstable condition comprised of "Being" and of "Non-being." Thus, like images, "shadows in time, flickering dreams," human beings always both "are" and "are not." It is no wonder that, wittingly or unwittingly, they live in their imagination, the common source of their desperation and of their delight. In the same tradition, centuries later, Thomas Hobbes, a wrapt student of Greek philosophy and history, and in fact a translator of Thucydides, wrote:

> Felicity is a continuall progresse of the desire,
> from one object to another; the attaining of the
> former, being still but the way to the later . . .
> So that in the first place, I put for a generall
> inclination of all mankind, a perpetuall and
> restlesse desire of Power after power, that
> ceaseth onely in Death.[41]

To speak at all of "Felicity" in these terms is, of course, profoundly problematic. Whether for Aristophanes, Plato, Hobbes, or Hegel, the negativity inherent in finite beings propels them into a state of absolute unrest, in which any power or control they attain is a passing illusion.

Their desire is infinite and everything corresponding to it, its every conceivable object, including themselves, proves finite. They are so many doomed gods, living out the lasting contradiction generated when *Erōs* and *Chaos* first threw themselves together in blind abandon. Here we find the source of endemic human *eris*, the notorious "war of all against all," which Hobbes sees as our natural strifeful state.

As Hobbes has made clear—though no clearer than did Thucydides or Aristophanes or Plato or Augustine or Nietzsche—it is power, absolute power, that Faustian man craves so ravenously as the antidote to his powerlessness. Constitutionally out of control, his thirst for control is seemingly insatiable, as is his rage when he fails to attain it. This, I would suggest, is the metaphysical source of *eris*, the "other face" of *erōs*, broken when it would break, tamed when it would tame.[42] *Eris is erōs*, chaotically jealous over every elusive power. Its fondest and most despised object is what never fails to elude it: "god." "What is god?," sings the Chorus of the *Helen*, "What is not god?"

> What lies in between?
> What man can say
>      he has reached the edges of existence,
> No matter where he may have been?
> What man has gazed upon god,
> Witnessed the wild confusion
>      at the core of things,
> The contradictions, the unexpected twists of fate,
> And returned to tell the tale?[43]

God, the shimmering object of human *erōs*, the dark object of human *eris*, has many names. Among them is *Basileia*, Empire. Also among them and, in the Greek poetic imagination, perhaps even first among them is Helen. "Helen," writes William Arrowsmith, is "the erotic figure of imperialism incarnate . . . the greatest single metaphor or symbol of . . . political Eros . . . the ultimate love-object of imperial *pleonexia*." "Men love Helen," he continues, "hunger for her with consuming passion, because she is the image of absolute power, of satisfied desire."[44] It is time to return explicitly to Helen and to her consummate poet, Euripides.

What is it, we ask one last time, that *erōs* and *eris*, sexuality and violence, have in common? In considering this question already we have seen that it emerges from a profoundly androcentric and misogynistic tradition and that the *erōs* and *eris*, the eroticism and warfare, in question are man's, not woman's.[45] Consequently, we ought to reformulate our question slightly to read: What is it that male *erōs* and male *eris* have in common? What is the precise point of their convergence? Euripides gives us his, if not *the*, answer to this question in the *Helen*, an answer altogether consistent with that of his colleague Aristophanes. In a word, his answer is: fantasy. The *Helen* is, surely, Euripides' ultimate statement on the politics of erotic fantasy; for Helen—the epitome of woman in the Greek tradition—is indeed the ultimate fantasy.

The *Helen* of Euripides is an ancient study in de-mythologization, in this case the myth of empire and of woman. In the play's first moment, Helen's prologue, Euripides provides a hint of what he is about to undertake: the plying apart of myth, understood as fantasy, from reality, understood as truth. Helen tells first the story of the house of Proteus in Egypt, where she finds herself; next she tells her own story:

> As for me, my home is well-known . . . Sparta.
> My father . . . Tyndareos.
> Oh yes, people tell a story about Zeus . . .
> > how he once feathered himself
> > into the likeness of a swan,
> > feigned flight from a pursuing eagle,
> > lit upon my mother Leda,
> > and won his way with her.
> It may have happened that way,
> > or it may not have.
> Either way,
> > my name is Helen,
> > and my story a long list of woes.[46]

The identity of one's father, a common uncertainty, rarely entails, it would seem, greater consequences than in the case of Helen. The ambiguity of her lineage spans divinity and mortality, myth and reality. Helen, however, acts as if very little is at stake here. In defiance, surely, of her audience, she passes off paternity as an irrelevance.

Later, however, the line between myth and reality matters more to her, when she encounters a shipwrecked survivor of the Trojan War, a Greek, her first source of news in twenty years. She asks him, among other things, about her two brothers, the twins Kastor and Pollux:

HELEN

What of Tyndareos' twin sons?
Are they dead or alive?

TEUKROS
You hear both.

HELEN
Well, which do you hear more?
God, I have suffered enough already!

TEUKROS
One story is that they've become gods,
    made into stars to circuit the night sky.

HELEN
*That* story makes me glad.
But you say there is another version . . .

TEUKROS
There is . . . that they slit their own throats
    and bled out their lives . . .
    victims to their sister's shame.
I've wept enough already.[47]

Here, when it is drawn between life and death, the line between myth and reality, between fantasy and truth, begins to matter; but how much it matters remains to be revealed.

Helen herself, after all, is the ultimate myth to be de-mythologized; for just as there are two alleged fathers for Helen and two alleged fates for her brothers—one fantastic and one real—so there are two alleged Helens: the fantasy Helen and the real Helen. The one went to Troy and the other didn't. This is the premise from which the *Helen* proceeds; nothing essentially new to the tradition,[48] but a shocking realization for anyone in any age to confront, anyone who has suffered an all-too-real Troy for the sake of an imaginary Helen. The contemporary poet Seferis captures the pain of this ancient and timeless realization:

        And at Troy?
    At Troy, nothing: just a phantom image.
    The gods wanted it so.
    And Paris, Paris lay with a shadow
            as though it were a solid being;
    and for ten whole years
            we slaughtered ourselves for Helen.

    Great suffering descended on Greece,
    So many bodies thrown

into the jaws of the sea, the jaws of the earth
so many souls
fed to millstones like grain.
And the rivers swelling, blood in their silt,
all for a linen undulation, a bit of cloud,
a butterfly's flicker, a swan's down,
an empty tunic—all for Helen.[49]

For the original audience of Euripides' *Helen*, absorbing the aftershocks of Sicily, there could have been little ambiguity regarding the real identity of Troy or of "the greatest Armada in history,"[50] launched against it by an ever-boastful Menelaos. Euripides' fellow-Athenians had watched in recent months with grief and horror the few survivors' return to Athens and listened to their stories, just as they now watched Teukros, Menelaos, and his old servant enter the orchestra, war-weary and sea-drowned, nearly. There is little reasonable doubt, however, that they identified not with Menelaos's joy but with the old servant's despair when they learned that Helen had never run off with Paris, never betrayed her husband, never even seen the walls of Troy. For Menelaos—oblivious, pompous, and so privileged as to be immune from life's harshest blows—Helen's account of how only a phantom of her eloped with Paris to Troy is sweet music. For the old servant, to say nothing of the countless dead, for whom a life lost is a life lost, her words bring bitter confusion. We are now at the dark center of the *Helen*.

OLD SERVANT

Menelaos, help me to share your happiness.
I can see for myself *that* you're happy,
    yet I can't for the life of me figure out *why* . . .
This woman . . . wasn't she the one . . . who . . .
    I mean . . . didn't she mete out our misery in Troy?

MENELAOS

No, not she. The gods made fools of us.
All we ever had of her was a pathetic effigy,
    modeled out of thin air.

OLD SERVANT

Wait . . . let me get this straight.
What do you mean?
That we went through all of that . . .
    for nothing more than a puff of air?[51]

Here is where myth and reality, as well as comedy and tragedy, like the two Helens, part ways. The old servant over long years has labored at Menelaos's side in every struggle, fought at his side in every fray. Though a slave, he has companioned Menelaos everywhere, through everything; but no longer. Menelaos sloughs twenty grim years and tens of thousands of hideous deaths as if they were a day's dirt. His insensitivity is divine, made understandable only by the immortality that is eventually bestowed upon him. On that note, he becomes irrelevant, part of the endless divine comedy. Fantasy springs eternal; but life does not. Set off against immortal comedy is human tragedy,[52] embodied in the old servant, who has squandered the only life he has for a fantasy. For him there is no consolation. Neither is there any for his audience.

Sicily, Empire, Helen: they are all one. The consummate fantasy. Just as Helen, absolute woman, is the ultimate power of *erōs*, the woman worth any struggle, the woman with whom one never wearies, ages, or dies, so Empire, absolute power, is the ultimate provoker of violence, whose goal is unlimited, always receding, like the horizon. Helen and Empire set fires that never burn themselves out. Not so with the lives fed to them, fed to fantasy. They simply go up in smoke.

Always there are the two Helens, the fantasy and the reality. Telling them apart is the challenge faced in any moment of truth, such as the *Helen* of Euripides. In the *Helen*, Teukros spews on the real Helen his rage against the fantasy Helen; and the real Helen calls him on it. "Tell me why *I* deserve your hate," she demands, "for what *she* did to you." To which he responds:

> You're right . . . I'm wrong.
> I had no business loosing my anger on you.
> I'll tell you something.
> I'm not the only one who hates that woman.
> I don't know anyone who doesn't.
> But to *you* I owe an apology . . .
> Forgive me, Lady.[53]

Teukros, "a worn and weary Greek . . . one of thousands,"[54] must, like all the others, find another object for his rage and his hate. In words recalled from Klytemnestra's earlier outburst in defense of her sister, he has been "barking up the wrong tree."

And what of Helen's legendary beauty, the supposed source of so much doom to men, their ships, and their cities? In the *Helen* we hear her own account: "My beauty is my hell."[55] If women provoke violence, they are the first to suffer from it. Now, in the dark light cast by the *Helen*, it seems more fair to say that women—like the earth they imitate—serve, or are made to serve, as a catalyst for fantasy; and fantasy provokes violence, from which women and the earth are made, ironically, to suffer most.

Another perhaps more candid word for "fantasy" is "lie"; for a fantasy is an untruth. And for those for whom the most critical line of all is that between truth and untruth, between reality and illusion, the fantasy Helen represents a paradigmatic untruth or lie. It was as such that Plato understood it. In Plato's critical eyes, the poets—Homer and Hesiod chief among them—were liars, conjurers of illusion; and he was out to break their spell. Helen and Pandora—woman—eroticized and hated, in a word "fantasized," was among their alleged creations. Such lies are pollutions from which one must be cleansed. Socrates, in the *Phaedrus*, speaks of such a cleansing. "For those who have gone wrong in the stories they tell," he explains,

> there exists a way towards purification and atonement. Stesichoros knew of it, Homer did not. For when, in return for slandering Helen, Stesichoros was deprived of his sight, he was not, like Homer, oblivious of the reason for his blindness. As a learned man he knew where he had gone wrong and wrote these lines (addressed to Helen): "There is no truth, nor reality, to the story (told of you). You never stepped foot in those well-oared ships, never went to towering Troy."[56]

This, of course, is the famous recantation of Stesichoros, the poet who lost his sight because he lied about Helen. The truth is that every lie brings blindness, as Plato suggests in his reference to the blindness of Homer; and blindness of the soul is contagious. For that reason liars are enemies of the truth and of those who would pursue it. This is surely how Plato regarded them. There is a saying among Native Americans of the Pacific Northwest that anyone who puts before my eyes something, anything, that prevents me from seeing as far as my eyes are meant to see is my enemy. Plato could easily have written this saying; and did, in his own words, over and over.

The first stage of cleansing, therefore, is recantation. The words of Teukros above might serve as a formula for this. In short, the lie must be untold. Thus the Greeks were forced *in* the *Helen*, if not *by* the *Helen*, to admit that all they ever had of Helen was a figment, a puff of air, a fantasy. Perhaps that is all the Greek poetic tradition too ever had of Helen— or of Pandora, for that matter. After all, according to Hesiod, when the gods set about to fashion the first woman, Pandora, they created not a woman, a real being, but a likeness (*ikelon*),[57] an image or an idea (*eidos*).[58] Like the surrogate Helen fashioned by Hermes, Pandora is a phantom, a figure of someone's imagination. If we read these texts with a fundamentalist squint, it is in each case the gods above, intent on punishing humankind, who are responsible for the fantasy. Already in the sixth century, however, Xenophanes, himself a deeply religious man, suggested that it was time to let the gods off the hook for men's creations. If horses or lions had hands to draw with, he argued, they would draw their gods as horses or lions.[59] Our gods, the ones we possess and train like household pets, are indeed our creations; and their creations are therefore our handiwork "once removed," once removed from awareness and acknowledgment. The fantasy of Helen and Pandora and their myriad daughters must be allowed to come home to roost. The Kurgans, the Achaeans, and the Dorians played their part; and the poets who followed them surely played theirs.

Poets need heroes and heroes need poets. Great deeds are forgotten unless sung; and without great deeds there is nothing to sing. The conquest of Neolithic Europe was a great deed, if scale matters; and it always has. Broken into myriad episodes, it was a deed the poets surely sang. By the same criterion, the conquest of the Goddess and of her daughters was a great deed; and the poets sang it too. However many verses there are to their songs, Helen remains the refrain.

An enduring irony of history, not lost on Homer, is that poets outlive heroes; and songs outlive deeds. The word *is* more powerful than the sword. If not face to face, one to one, pen to gun, then always in retrospect. Only the imagination controls aeons. Ideas, words, stories—true or false it doesn't seem to matter—make history; and the alphabet, not bronze, allowed man to grip history as he has. If there is any threat to that grip, it comes not from Antiope but from Sappho, not from the Amazon but from the poet. The Chorus of women in the *Medea* reveal that they know all this, as they know well their oppression, when they sing:

> The rivers, sanctioned in their course,
> Turn and flow back upon their sources.
> The scheme of things is reversed.
> Men prove liars in their thoughts,
> While the gods keep an unbroken trust.
> The scandal that is my life
> Stories will remold into a thing of honor.

Worth returns to the race of women.
Abuse no longer clings to them.

The muses who gave the ancient bards
Their songs of my unfaithfulness,
May they go mute.
Our thoughts, our side of things,
Have never been sung.
Awesome Apollo, master of song,
Kept from our fingers
The magic of the lyre.
If he hadn't, the other sex
Would have our answer by now.
An aeon is a long time,
Long enough for the whole truth
To come out.[60]

Hope, the last of Pandora's gifts, is released; and Helen, I submit, is innocent of the charges against her.

# *Conclusion*

In an extended cycle of poems published under the general title of *Maria Nephele*, the contemporary Greek poet Odysseus Elytis speaks through two voices: Maria Nephele's and the Antiphonist's. The latter is allegedly the poet's own. It is this voice which, in a poem entitled "Helen," says of the fictive character Maria Nephele:

> When she says "I'll sleep with this man"
> she means that she'll kill History once again.
> One should see then what enthusiasm seizes the birds.
>
> On the other hand in her way
> she perpetuates the nature of the olive tree.
> According to the moment she becomes
> now silvery now dark blue.
>
> That's why adversaries keep
> marching to war — look:
> some with their social theories
> many others merely brandishing flowers.
>
> Each era with its Helen.[1]

Umbilically tied to Earth and its cycles, woman, we are led to believe, continues to live in fickle oblivion and remains the unwitting cause of war. Each time she makes love, she kills the past, strangling it with forgetfulness; she lives only for the immediacy of the moment. On such immediacy, Albert Camus, writing not about woman but about himself, once commented: "brief emotions, devoid of the long echo that memory gives. The sensitivity of dogs is like that."[2] The phenomenon is familiar; but most often it is attributed, whether with admiration or with contempt, to the nature of woman, in this instance named Maria Nephele. *Nephele*, we should note, means "cloud"; metaphorically, in ancient poetry, it means the dark cloud of death. Death, bestiality, sensual oblivion, and beauteous charm: these stalk women through history like the Furies. As for the infamous forgetfulness of women in bed, Andromache, a slave in the house of the man who slew her own beloved husband, provided a response which has yet to lose any of its sting:

> What they say is
>> that all any man has to do
>> to make a woman lose her aversion for his bed
>> is to show her a good time for one night.
> I would spit from my sight
>> that woman who would throw off the man
>> whose bed she used to share,
>> and resume the ways of love with another.
> Even a young filly, torn from her running-mate,
>> balks at being yoked with another.
> Yet it is a dumb brute beast,
>> born without wit
>> and without a glimmer of our nature.[3]

Closer to the truth is that men go to the beds of women seeking forgetfulness, expecting it, projecting it; but it lies in men, not in the cloud, the fantasy they think of as woman. Woman is not the forgetful one but the forgotten one. It is not women who have killed history.

When history is murdered and the past is forgotten, a great many things are lost. This volume has focused on two: the humanity and the divinity of woman. Both come to a focus in Helen, the most notorious woman of the ancient world, equally human and divine, woman incarnate and eternal. Eventually, she yielded her titles, as it were, to Eve and to Mary, the second Eve. But that is another story, or rather another part of the same story, too long to tell here.

As for Helen's numberless daughters, their humanity, so commonly denied in ancient times, has been freshly forgotten countless times throughout the ensuing centuries. Not until the Council of Trent, for example, decreed in the mid-sixteenth century that women indeed have human souls, was the metaphysical status of women securely defined within Roman Catholicism; moral and political status, we know, is another matter.

The aim of this study has been to contribute to the process of unforgetting the past. If, as Heidegger understands it, history is the repetition of the possible, then history may be all we need to retrieve what is lost. I suspect, however, that we will need a good deal more. Imagination, humor, forgiveness, and common sense will do us no likely harm. Finally, whatever else this retelling of the story of Helen—the story of woman, human and divine—has evoked in the reader, it has evoked in me, throughout, a deep sorrow. Consequently, I would like to share with the reader, in closing, a brief list of "remedies" for sorrow. I myself discovered them many years ago in what seemed to me at the time a most unlikely place, at least as unlikely as their location here: *delectatio, fletus, compassio amicorum, contemplatio veritatis, somnus, et balnea.*[4]

APPENDIX

# History and Imagination

It has already been said and assumed that the history of Helen cannot be known or appreciated without imagination; for to enter her realm is to enter a world of images. Entry to her world requires imagination, in theory and in practice. This fact, in turn, calls for some discussion of imagination, which has a history of its own.

It is merely a matter of convention that histories should proceed from the past toward the present, from origins to endpoint, as if our mind, like our digestive tract, moves everything along in one fixed direction. Histories are, after all, the work of memory; and memory begins in the present. From there memory reaches out to the past. No wonder the ancient Greeks thought of the past as spread out before them and of the future as always to their backs; for it is the past that we face and the future that faces us. Always we see the past, not the future. The future comes at us from our blind side, the chosen approach of Fate.

History—the word itself, if we look to its roots—means, quite simply, "story." The story of imagination is a story beyond telling, here or anywhere. What I propose, instead, is only an episode, one that begins with Hobbes and ends with Gilgamesh. In other words, the episode sketched here begins before imagination's end and ends before imagination's beginning. Hobbes, after all, did not kill the human imagination. He only tried. And the human imagination was alive, to be sure, in the Paleolithic caves of Africa, Australia, and Europe tens of thousands of years before Uruk's most famous king lost his peace of mind. Regardless, the span of time between Hobbes and Gilgamesh will suffice to stretch our own imaginations and may allow the larger story to be glimpsed.

It is my own conviction that the history of imagination is at the same time the history of human being. It is, I believe, imagination, more than anything else, that strikes the human spark. Whether I am right or wrong about this, in the matter of imagination the stakes are as high as they ever get.

It was the late poet John Berryman who once said that when the human mind dies it exudes rich critical prose. To this I would add that when the human imagination dies the mind turns literal, which brings us to Thomas Hobbes, our point of departure; for what I am calling "literal-mindedness" involves a conception of language epitomized by Thomas Hobbes in his discussion "Of Speech" in *Leviathan*,[1] a conception that went on to shape not only the entirety of the *Leviathan* but a great wedge of European and American thought as well, in more ways than we can count or consider here.

Although the *Leviathan* comprises three parts, it may be argued that the core of that work is contained in the first two parts: "Of Man" and "Of Commonwealth." It may be argued further that Hobbes's understanding of Man, as distinct from god and beast, is centered in his understanding of speech. In part 1, chapter 4, entitled "Of Speech,"[2] Hobbes acknowledges the importance of the discoveries of writing and of mechanized printing, but insists that "the most noble and profitable invention of all other, was that of SPEECH, consisting of *names* or *appellations,* and their connexion" by which he means the primal sense-making activity of the paradigmatic Man, Adam, who names and thus defines the elements and entities of his world. Actual Man, however, unlike biblical Adam, is plural, a fact not lost on Hobbes, who in recognizing the plurality of humankind acknowledges the plurality of speech. The essential human and therefore linguistic problem emergent from the acknowledgment of such plurality is this: How do human beings come to share the same speech? How do human beings come to make fundamental sense in common?

Hobbes's response to this question provides the key not only to his understanding "Of Man" but also to his understanding "Of Commonwealth." The formation of a coherent linguistic community serves as the paradigm for the formation of a viable political community. That is, understanding how we come to make common sense out of our myriad, diverse experiences in the world provides the key to how we come to form a commonwealth from our myriad, diverse strivings in life. The emergence from political chaos and the emergence from linguistic confusion are finally one.

Central to the Hobbesian "solution" to political and linguistic anarchy are several principles of central relevance to our discussion here: all speech properly begins with definition; all definitions are arbitrary and thus artificial; and all artificial order and meaning must be held in place by force. The academy, the commonwealth of letters, it would seem, like any polity, originates in a war of all against all until some form of clout, however subtly veiled, establishes itself and begins to speak for all.

Within this all-encompassing theoretical framework, in which political and linguistic coherence converge, and in which all coherence is a matter of control, Hobbes proceeds to define in practice the use and abuse of language. What emerges is a definition of proper speech as univocal speech. One word for one meaning for one thing. In this world of particulars, wherein nothing beyond language is universal, names are essentially numbers assigned to arbitrarily defined entities. Only then can reasoning proceed with mathematical confidence; only if names are numbers, can reasoning be understood as simple addition or subtraction. "In summe," writes Hobbes in his discussion "Of Reason, and Science," "in what matter soever there is place for *addition* and *subtraction*, there is also place for *Reason*; and where these have no place, there *Reason* has nothing at all to do."[3]

Centuries before the computer, Hobbes defined human intelligence as artificial intelligence. Since he perceived no natural correspondence between word and world, between mind and reality, language was of necessity a matter of sheer invention. Words were integers whose assignment required sovereign authority, one original voice speaking for all. Like individual computers, human beings, once programmed in a common language, would be able to process their sensations and share their thoughts without confusion or hostility. They would be fundamentally compatible. Presumably, Hobbes would be not at all surprised and not a little pleased to hear what George Steiner says of the actual age of the computer, an age in which artificial intelligence has come truly into its own:

> Thus it is neither the *Logos* in any transcendent connotation, nor the secular, empirical systems of lexical-grammatical utterance and writing which are now the eminent carriers of speculative energy, of verifiable and applicable discoveries and information or, as French puts it more graphically, *informatique*. It is the algebraic function, the linear and non-linear equation, the binary code. At the heart of futurity lies the "byte" and the number.[4]

Whatever might be said of the future, in any present defined by Hobbes the world of images and the language appropriate to it belong to what he calls "Absurdity," which he says is a privilege, not a right, "to which no living creature is subject, but man only."[5] He goes on to list, in fact, seven causes of absurdity, which nicely describe the character of most everything I do in this book. The first cause he ascribes to

> the want of Method; in that they begin not their Ratiocination from Defini-
> tions; that is, from settled significations of their words: as if they could cast
> account, without knowing the value of the numerall words, *one, two,* and
> *three.*[6]

If there is a single cause at the root of all seven of Hobbes's causes of absurdity, thus at the root of all nonsense, it is metaphor, which for Steiner, Aristotle, and others lies at the root of all human meaning. Of all of the skills of language, writes Aristotle in the *Poetics,* "the greatest by far is metaphor."[7] Metaphor—from *metapherein,* meaning "to convey or to carry across"—allows the mind to pass over what it otherwise might not cross, to go where it otherwise would not or could not go. The activity of metaphor, metaphorical thinking, is, accordingly to Aristotle, "a mark of genius; for it alone cannot be gotten from someone else."[8] The reason for this, Aristotle explains, is that the ability to think metaphorically resides deep within, in the inner eye, the eye of the mind.[9] Apparently, one either has or doesn't have an eye for resemblance, an eye for likeness (*to homoion*). Metaphor is first a matter of theory or sight and only then a matter of rhetoric. Before a metaphor can be expressed, it must be seen.

Not only the poet, of course, requires metaphor. Some would claim that without metaphor there can be no inner world, no life of thought, removed from yet related to the outer world, the life of sense. "It is true," writes Hannah Arendt,

> that all mental activities withdraw from the world of appearances, but this
> withdrawal is not toward an interior of either the self or the soul. Thought,
> with its accompanying conceptual language, since it occurs in and is spoken
> by a being at home in a world of appearances, stands in need of metaphors
> in order bridge the gap between a world given to sense experience and a
> realm where no such immediate apprehension of evidence can ever exist.[10]

The "arc of metaphor," then, to borrow Steiner's phrase, spans always and everywhere the abyss separating the outer world of sense from the inner world of thought, appearance from reality. Indeed, without metaphor "there would have been no bridge whereby to cross from the minor truth of the seen to the major truth of the unseen."[11] Metaphor is no more than a spoken or written image, a word in which one reality is caught in the reflection of another. We need not, however, contrive such an occurrence. Imagination is a matter of insight not invention. Metaphor belongs to reality before it belongs to rhetoric. Images are glimpses not conceits. Such was the profound conviction of Plato, who described, most notably in the *Republic* and in the *Symposium*, the entire movement of the mind in its ascent toward Being as an imaginative progression through a universe of images until the mind at last beholds the reality both concealed and reflected in everything else that is, the One infinitely refracted in the Many. Apart from Being — beheld purely in that time out of time that is contemplation — there is nothing but images.

In book 6 of the *Republic*, Plato provides a diagram of all existence. As a metaphysical geographer, he maps the world as he has come to know it, a world of multiplicity, a world of worlds, the sensible world visible to the eyes and the intelligible world visible to the mind, each world divided from the other and within itself as images are from originals. Yet, with all its layered multiplicity, the world as we first see it is an image of the world as we finally know it. It is one world, in which the least being reflects Being Itself. There are, of course, numerous stages in the mind's full arduous ascent, and each step reflects and repeats the very first step taken. The beginning anticipates the end; so we begin now in the beginning, in the sensory, visible world.

The world as it appears to our eyes contains two kinds of visible things: images and objects. For example, I stand at the edge of a still pond and I see a willow tree spread out across the water. Then I turn around and see a similar willow tree rooted in the solid earth. I see two sights and in a sense two trees. In another sense, I see only one tree; for I realize that the tree in the pond is a reflection of the tree on the bank. Everything in the world of sense, the world of the visible (*to horaton*), is like the one or the other of these two trees.

Plato, in turn, proposes two distinct activities of mind corresponding to these two sights. The first is *eikasia* and the second is *pistis*. *Eikasia* is appropriate to images, such as the tree in the water, while *pistis* is appropriate to originals, such as the tree on the bank. *Eikasia* is not, however, the simple perception of an image; rather it is the discerning recognition of an image *as an image*. Merely seeing the tree in the water is not an act of *eikasia*—not until I look at it with the conscious awareness that it is the reflection of another tree, the one behind me, whose priority is undeniable to whatever common sense I possess.

Without *eikasia*, without the practiced capacity to distinguish appearance from reality in the world of sense, I would be as blind and confused and eventually hungry as Aesop's dog, the one who went after the bone in the "other" dog's mouth and so lost his own to the pond. Without *eikasia*, the simple trust (*pistis*) that what I see is there as I see it would be mere wishful thinking. By virtue of *eikasia,* I know that what I see is not always what is actually there, and I gain practical confidence in my ability to find my way critically through appearances to realities. Optical illusions do exist; and yet all is not illusion. I find utter distrust in the world before my eyes to be both unwarranted and impractical. Critical trust—*pistis* built upon *eikasia*—appears closer to the truth. So it seemed to Plato and so it has seemed, until recently, to most others. "There would be no history as we know it," writes Steiner,

> no religion, metaphysics, politics, or aesthetics as we have lived them, without an initial act of trust, of confiding, more fundamental, more axiomatic by far than any "social contract" or covenant with the postulate of the divine. This instauration of trust . . . is that between word and world. Only in the light of that confiding can there be a history of meaning which is, by exact counterpart, a meaning of history. . . .[12]

What is more, according to Steiner, it is the "break of the covenant between word and world which constitutes one of the very few genuine revolutions of spirit in Western history and which defines modernity itself."[13]

As it happens, these two acts of mind—*eikasia* and *pistis*—provide for Plato the key to every turning, every step of mind in its dialectical ascent towards the pure beholding of Being. Plato proposes, contrary to all common sense and yet not without foundation, that the world revealed to our eyes is, in turn, the image of, not the original for, the world revealed in thought. The world of seen objects, in which we first find and place trust, must be seen through, in a new and higher act of *eikasia,* until we turn from that world as we once turned from the tree in the pond. It is enough for now, however, to recognize that for Plato the mind, until it is released ecstatically from even itself, is confronted incessantly with images and with the challenge of reading them, of discerning what more primary reality is reflected in them. Always this is a movement from multiplicity to unity. For every original, every reality, there are countless possible images or appearances. The movement from images to original, from appearances to reality, however, can never be accomplished by the mere accumulation of images or appearances, as if an object were merely the sum of all the shadows which it casts. Insight is not a matter of simple addition.

It comes down to this: the world we inhabit every day, the world within and the world without, the world we see and the world we think about, are all finally one world, a world of images. Without *eikasia,* without an eye for resemblances or reflections, without trust in what we see and openness to what we do not, we cannot find our way. On this much Plato and the poets concur. But what about the notorious "old quarrel [*diaphora*] between philosophy and poetry,"[14] and the fact that Plato would have banished Homer—"the most poetic of poets and first among tragic playwrights"[15]—from the city of his own design? The truth is that this *diaphora*—this difference or distinction—is, as it were, "in-house." Plato and Homer locate their conflicting affinities on a common map. They manage to quarrel in the same language.

In the world of Homer, the gods are everywhere, mostly unseen, but no less present and active for that. The secular is everywhere transparent to the sacred. In a woman of unspeakable beauty, we learn to glimpse Aphrodite. In a warrior of uncommon might and irresistible fury, we behold Ares. When, during the games in honor of Patroclus, Diomedes drops his whip, it is Apollo that broke his grip and flung the whip from his hand.[16] Moments later in the race, when the yoke of Eumelus's chariot snaps in two and he is hurled to the dust, divine foul play is equally evident. This time Athena's work.[17] In panic we are given to see Panic, in rout Rout, in delusion Delusion. Always, there is more than appears. What we see bears witness to what we do not.[18] Fire—fire blazing in the eyes of warriors, fire lighting up the sky, fire hurled toward the Greek ships, fire consuming the corpse of Patroclus as it will eventually all of Troy—is force and force is divine and what is divine is somehow from Zeus. The arc of his presence and his plan, like a master metaphor, spans and controls the entire poem.

The central movement of the *Iliad*, however, belongs to Achilles; and, indeed, it may be argued, though not here in any detail, that the entire *Iliad* represents his ascent toward vision, toward *eikasia*. He is himself, in the poem's grand vision, the central image or *eikōn*; and his is the central act of imagination or *eikasia*.

Clearly, we learn enough about the love of Achilles for Patroclus to know that he sees himself in him. Patroclus is his other self, his living image, as one beloved friend is to another. This vision is more widely shared once Patroclus dons Achilles' armor and thus becomes the very appearance of Achilles. Not only in the heart of Achilles but to the eyes of all, the death of Patroclus is in that it means the death of Achilles. Hector too, once he appears in the armor stripped from the body of Patroclus, becomes the living and dying *eikōn* of Achilles.

To appreciate the final scene of book 22, we must recall that the past and the future in Greek are conceived in visual, spatial terms. The past, as already suggested, is what lies ahead of us, before our eyes; for we can see the past. The future, always unseen, approaches from behind; so too does the future's darkest face, Fate or Death, which for mortals comes to the same thing. Until now, Achilles, heroically fleet of foot, has outrun his fate. But no longer. Beneath the walls of Troy, Achilles chases himself, whom he cannot hope to outrun. He is his own undoing. Hector, to the eyes of all but himself, is Achilles; and Achilles is sure death. In the poem's vision, death claims them both in the same instant; for when Achilles takes the life of Hector, he loses his own. This much he knows; this much he has already seen. His literal death is, it seems, a slight matter now, a matter of time, no more.

In what lifetime remains, however, Achilles is transformed. His eyes, dilated by death to accommodate realities greater than his own, see well beyond appearances, well beyond the literal. Nowhere is this more clear than in book 24, when Achilles and Priam meet. Their eyes washed with tears and chastened by the sight of their own deaths, they see now further than ever before, across as wide an abyss as any poet has ever opened up. Achilles looks at Priam in his grief and sees his own father mourning him, while the sight of Achilles provokes Priam to weep for his own son Hector. There are tears too for Patroclus, who like Hector died in Achilles' armor and in Achilles' place. In imagination Patroclus and Achilles and Hector are all one, as are Priam and Achilles and Peleus. Theirs is a single grief, a common human grief, whose sound fills the house and, for that matter, the world.

A similar moment of *eikasia* lies at the center of another great ancient epic, the *Gilgamesh*, which like the *Iliad* describes a path of vision, an ascent from appearance to reality. It is the story of a king, Gilgamesh, so powerful and privileged that he appeared divine, and of a stranger, Enkidu, so wild and strong that he appeared bestial; it too is a story of friendship and mortality. At first, Enkidu runs with the animals, and Gilgamesh runs over his subjects. Neither has a true peer, in whom he might see himself and learn his own stature. Only when they first confront each other, lock arms in struggle, and collapse at last in exhaustion, do they stare into each other's eyes and see something each of them has never seen before: himself reflected in another. It is their first glimpse not of themselves, but of humanity. It is a gift, the gift of friendship. In that moment: "They kissed each other and became friends."[19]

After sharing heroes' deeds, the kind that bring fame and a form of immortality, Enkidu is struck down by the gods for offenses that he and Gilgamesh mostly shared. Enkidu dies for them both; and Gilgamesh is left to weep and to wander desolate in a world made strange by the death of his friend, his equal, his companion, the one who went through everything with him. Perhaps more sharply to the point, Gilgamesh, who has learned to see himself in Enkidu, as friends do, sees himself die in Enkidu, not literally, not yet; but, like Achilles bent over Patroclus, Gilgamesh is as good as dead. It is only a matter of time. "I am going to die!" he cries out,

> —am I not like Enkidu?!
> Deep sadness penetrates my core,
> I fear death, and now roam the wilderness—[20]

Enkidu is not Gilgamesh. Enkidu is dead and Gilgamesh is not. No literal truth could be more evident; and yet Gilgamesh no longer lives in a flat, literal world. His own life and death have been caught in the reflection of another. And when that reflection fades into nothingness, so nearly does he.

The truth is that Gilgamesh has become wise, with mortal wisdom, the wisdom shared by his Greek counterpart, Heracles, in Euripides' *Alcestis*.[21] "You there, c'mere," calls out the drunken, braying Heracles to a glum servant of Admetus,

> I'm gonna make you a wiser man.
> Do you know what's what?
> I mean do you know what it means to be human?
> I don't think you do. Anyway, you *lissen* to me.
> We all gotta die.
> There ain't one of us alive today
> That knows whether he'll be around tomorrow . . .
> So there, that's it. You heard what I got to teach . . .
> If you're mortal, you gotta have mortal thoughts.[22]

Human wisdom is mortal wisdom. Halfway between gods and beasts, human beings are hybrids of the two, reflecting both. They enjoy the consciousness of the gods and endure the finitude of the beasts. Human beings are "deathful" (*thnētoi*) not because they die but because they know they are going to die. Not death but the consciousness of death makes them human, distinguishing them from gods and beasts alike, who dwell in deathless oblivion,[23] the gods because they cannot die and the beasts because they cannot conceive of death before it occurs. There is

no death for the gods; and for the beasts death is a fact without significance, a geometric point without extension. For human beings, sighted
with the sense of finitude, death touches everything. It outlines life, giving it definition and depth. Light without limit or shadow is blinding. No
wonder the eyes of the gods are so blind and the eyes of beasts so blank.
From Sîn-leqi-unninnī [24] to Homer to Euripides there is no diminishment
in this conviction: humanity lies in mortality and mortality lies in conscious deathfulness. It did not require Heidegger to discover *Being-
towards-death*.

There can be no mortal wisdom, however, no thinking of mortal
thoughts, without *eikasia*, without imagination. If literal death were
required for the consciousness of death—my death for my consciousness
—then the former would come always too soon and the latter always too
late to be of any use. It is only when death comes *to* me without coming
*for* me that the consciousness of death is ignited without my life's being in
the same moment extinguished. This is what happens when I see my own
death in another's death, when I die imaginatively without dying literally. There is no other way that the reality of my death may be revealed
without my death becoming reality.

Human life is shaped, however, not only by death but by birth. There
are, suggests Steiner, "two defining motions of our existential presence in
the world: that of the coming into being where nothing was . . . and that
of the enormity of death."[25] Mortality is inseparable from natality.[26] It is
because human life is each time new that its passing is so painful and so
significant. In every human life a unique, conscious, willful person comes
and ceases to be. Each human life is only once and each human death is
forever. Someone who never before was will never again be. The radical
beginning marked by my birth is as unseen and inconceivable to me as is
the radical ending marked by my death. I see the former as I see the latter,
reflected in others. The presence of others' births and deaths to me
becomes the presence of my own. This, I learn, is not the fruit of wisdom,
but its mere seed, as even my own beginning and ending become images
whose reality outreaches me. No confusion is greater, Hobbes would say,
than the one I've now proposed. If so, then it is a confusion we must enter
all the same; for the house of images is where we live and die. "Human
beings," writes Erich Fromm, "are half-animal and half-symbolic."[27] And
if they are not, we may at least agree that they once were and that Helen
was among their most splendid creations.

# Notes

## Chapter 1: Helen and History

1. See Gorgias, *Encomium of Helen*, edited with introduction, notes, and translation by D. M. MacDowell (Bristol: Bristol Classical Press, 1982).

2. Ibid., p. 21, section 4.

3. Ibid., p. 30 section 21.

4. Thucydides, *History of the Peloponnesian War*, translated by Rex Warner (New York: Penguin, 1972), p. 151.

5. *Eris*, both the goddess of strife and the name for everyday contention, rivalry, and jealousy, will figure so centrally in this work that I have retained the Greek for the sake of ready recognition.

6. Aeschylus, *Agamemnon* (Loeb), 1455–61, translation mine.

7. Ibid., 1464–67, translation mine.

8. Euripides, *Trojan Women* (Oxford), 498–99, translation mine.

9. T. S. Eliot, *Murder in the Cathedral* (New York: Harcourt, Brace & World, 1935), Part One, p. 25.

10. Aeschylus, *Agamemnon* (Loeb), 973.

11. Martin Heidegger, *Sein und Zeit* (Tübingen: Neomarius Verlag, 1957), see pp. 6, 10, 326, 328, 329, 375, 378, 380, 385.

12. That the seizure of women, however, was a fact of ancient life is not in doubt. Myth, legend, and history—whether or not we can tell the difference in each instance—abound with such stories. More specifically, Herodotus—neither the most, nor the least, reliable source—begins his *History* with an account, based on Persian sources, of the original falling-out between West and East, Greeks and barbarians. It all started, the story goes, with the theft of Io, princess of Argos, by Phoenician traders. The Greeks answered this affront, we are told, by stealing Europa, the daughter of the king of Tyre. The rest, we might say loosely, is his-

tory. Theft followed theft, all the way to Helen and to Troy and, with the redistri-
bution of Troy's women, beyond. Even Herodotus, however, known more for his
love of stories than for anything else, preferred another, less anecdotal, account of
how it was that Greeks and Persians had come to their famous enmity. As for the
series of stolen women culminating in Helen, Herodotus said that he had only
stories, for whose truth or falsity he was in no position to answer; and, as yet, our
position is no better than was his.

13. C. S. Lewis, Preface, *Essays Presented to Charles Williams,* edited by C. S.
Lewis (Grand Rapids: William B. Eerdmans, 1966), p. xiv.

14. Ibid.

15. The understanding of "imagination" informing this entire study will
undoubtedly raise for many readers a range of theoretical questions, to at least
some of which I have endeavored to respond in the appendix to this volume.

16. C. G. Jung, for whom the matrix of myth is the unconscious and for whom
the unconscious is collective, has no difficulty accounting for similar, even identical, myths or mythical images spontaneously generated by diverse individuals or
cultures without any contact between them. According to his theory of myth, the
archetypes, the magisterial myths at work within the human psyche, are primordial, belonging to no specific time or place yet shaping the concrete mythical and
artistic creations of individual persons and cultures. In Jungian terms, then, our
search for Helen represents a search for the Archetypal Feminine, which like any
archetype expresses itself spontaneously in metaphors whose recognizable patterns and similarities are attributable first and foremost to their common psychic
source. See C. G. Jung, *The Archetypes and the Collective Unconscious,* translated by
R. F. C. Hull, *Collected Works* (New York: Pantheon, 1959), 9:i.

17. See John Chadwick, *The Decipherment of Linear B,* 2nd ed. (Cambridge: Cambridge University Press, 1967).

18. According to Chadwick, "we can only begin to speak of Greeks after the
formation of the Greek language," which "was already spoken in Greece in the
Mycenaean age." He argues further that "at least one language was spoken there
before Greek" which was formed by "the grafting of an Indo-European idium on
non-Greek stock" ("Discussion of V.I. Georgiev, 'The Arrival of the Greeks, Linguistic Evidence,' " in *Bronze Age Migrations in the Aegean,* ed. R. A. Crossland and
A. Birchall [London: Duckworth, 1973], p. 255).

19. E. A. Havelock has argued that general literacy emerged in Athens only in
the late fifth century. See his *Preface to Plato* (Cambridge, Mass.: Harvard University Press, 1963), p. 294; and *The Literate Revolution in Greece and Its Cultural Consequences* (Princeton: Princeton University Press, 1982), p. 185. More recently, in a
sweeping study of the character and extent of Greek and Roman literacy, William
V. Harris has suggested that the level of functional literacy in fifth-century Attica
was between 5 percent and 10 percent of the total population (*Ancient Literacy*
[Cambridge, Mass.: Harvard University Press, 1989], pp. 114–15).

20. Tale wandering, which must be only moments less old than the telling of tales, is a curious phenomenon, made rather less startling today by the existence of the mass media, telephones, and the postal service. The range and alacrity of tales in their travels all but defy explanation. For example, a study by Reidar T. Christiansen traces the path of a single story, "The Tale of the Two Travellers," through hundreds of mutations and scores of languages from India to Africa to Korea to Italy to Iceland. The tale's origins are uncertain; but it appears to have had a place in Indian tradition as early as the first half of the first millennium C.E. and to have entered Europe perhaps a thousand years later. See Reidar T. Christiansen, *The Tale of the Two Travellers or The Blinded Men: A Comparative Study* (Hamina: Suomalaisen Tiedeakatemian Kustantama, 1916).

21. Paul Friedrich, *The Meaning of Aphrodite* (Chicago: University of Chicago Press, 1978), p. 21. See Franz Boas, *Race, Language and Culture* (New York: Free Press, 1940), p. 428.

22. See W. R. Halliday, "Notes upon Indo-European Folk-Tales and the Problem of Their Diffusion," *Folk-Lore* 34 (1923): 136–37.

23. Aristophanes, *Peace* (Loeb), 135; *Lysistrata* (Loeb), 695.

24. Herodotus, *The History* (Loeb), 3.121.

25. For a discussion of this story in particular, as well as a general discussion of the transmission of Indian stories and ideas westward, see Jean W. Sedlar, *India and the Greek World* (Totowa, N. J.: Rowman & Littlefield, 1980), particularly chapter 14, "Folk Tales and Fables," pp. 99–106.

26. An excellent summation of the character and extent of Greek travel and commerce, from the Bronze Age to 480 B.C.E., is provided by John Boardman in *The Greeks Overseas: Their Early Colonies and Trade* (London: Thames & Hudson, 1980). See also Lord William Taylour, *The Mycenaeans* (London: Thames & Hudson, 1983), particularly chapter 7, "War and Trade."

27. Colin Renfrew, *Archaeology and Language: The Puzzle of Indo-European Origins* (New York: Cambridge University Press, 1988), p. 168.

28. Ibid. Locating the Indo-European homeland in central and eastern Anatolia prior to 6500 B.C.E., Renfrew associates the dispersion of an early form of Indo-European language with the spread of farming. He suggests that mainland Greece and Crete were among the first points reached by Anatolian immigrants who arrived by sea and established farming settlements in Thessaly, central Greece, the Peloponnese, and Crete.

29. See Boardman, *Greeks Overseas*, 23.

30. The myth of Danaos may well describe the flight of a Hyksos refugee to the Peloponnese at the end of the First Intermediate Period, when the Hyksos were expelled from Egypt, or perhaps the return of a Mycenaean mercenary, who had fought with the Egyptians against the Hyksos. See A. W. Persson, *New Tombs at Dendra near Midea* (Lund: Gleerup, 1942), pp. 176–96; G. Huxley, *Crete and the Luwians* (Oxford: Oxford University Press, 1961), pp. 36–37.

31. N. K. Sandars, *The Sea Peoples: Warriors of the Ancient Mediterranean 1250–1150 BC* (London: Thames & Hudson, 1987), p. 11.

32. See Harriet Crawford, *Sumer and the Sumerians* (New York: Cambridge University Press, 1991), pp. 139–50; Sedlar, *India and the Greek World*, chapter 1, "First Contacts: The Pre-classical Age," pp. 3–7. "The tie between Sumer and Northern India," writes Gertrude Rachel Levy, "may go back to the first settlers among the marshes, for beads probably from the Nilgharry Hills were found in their graves" (*The Gate of Horn: A Study of the Religious Conceptions of the Stone Age, and Their Influence upon European Thought* [London: Faber & Faber, 1948]). Regarding these finds, see C. L. Wooley, *Antiquaries' Journal* 10 (1930): 327–41.

33. Recent excavations at Mehrgarh, Pakistan, have revealed the existence of permanent, sizable agricultural settlements as early as the sixth and fifth millennia, indicating that Baluchistan was a very early center of cereal cultivation. Mehrgarh was already by the mid-fifth millennium a major producer of ceramics and other works of art, including female figurines, importing raw materials, exporting its wares, and so eventually developing "extensive trade networks . . . with eastern Iran and southern Turkmenistan. These lines of communication facilitated the exchange not only of goods but also of ideas" (Jean-François Jarrige and Richard H. Meadow, "The Antecedents of Civilization in the Indus Valley," *Scientific American* 243, No. 2 [1980]: 122–33).

34. See Lucian of Samosata, *Works,* translated by H. W. Fowler and F. G. Fowler (Oxford: Oxford University Press, 1905), 4:97–98; see Crawford, *Sumer and the Sumerians*, p.144. Commenting on the extent of Sargon's influence, Samuel Noah Kramer writes that "it made itself felt in one way or another all over the ancient world from Egypt to India" (*The Sumerians* [Chicago: University of Chicago Press, 1963], p. 59).

35. See Seton Lloyd, *The Archaeology of Mesopotamia* (New York: Thames & Hudson, 1984), pp. 117–18.

36. See C. C. Lamberg-Karlovsky, *Excavations at Tepe Yahya, Iran* (Cambridge, Mass.: Harvard University School of Prehistoric Research, Bulletin #27, 1970); idem, "Excavations at Tepe Yahya," in *Archaeological Researches in Retrospect*, ed. G. R. Willey (Cambridge: Winthrop, 1974).

37. With help from the Hittite royal archives uncovered early in the twentieth century, another Indo-Aryan connection with the Near East may be traced through the Hurrians, whose cultural and political influence on the Hittites was profound. The Hurrians, an apparently indigenous people speaking a language wholly unrelated to any other contemporary Near Eastern language, constituted the greatest part of the population of Mitanni, which became a Hittite dependency in the fourteenth century; but around Mitanni, the Hurrian population "was apparently overlaid with a horse-breeding ruling aristocracy whose language was essentially Old Indic. . . . When about 1380 the weak Mitannian king Sattiwaza . . . sealed by treaty his allegiance to his new leige lord and father-in-

law Suppiluliumas, great king of the Hittites, he listed among the divine guarantors of his loyalty (or punishers of his potential oath breaking) a set of old Indic deities (Mitra, Uruwana/Aruna, Indara, Nasattiya) who are none other than the canonic Vedic Indic grouping of the gods Mitra, Varuna, Indra, and the twin Nāsatyas (or Ásvins). . . . How it (this lost tribe) strayed and briefly flowered in the Near East is a mystery . . ." (Jaan Puhvel, *Comparative Mythology* [Baltimore: Johns Hopkins University Press, 1989], pp. 40–41). We will consider at a later point the assertions of Sir John Marshall and of A. W. Persson regarding the early and extensive connections between the Indus Valley, Mesopotamia, and the East Mediterranean.

38. Greek colonial expansion and/or trade connections, beyond the eastern regions focused on in the body of this text, eventually reached Sicily, North Africa, Italy, Spain, France, Germany, Switzerland, Sweden, Anatolia, the Black Sea area, Soviet Georgia, the Causcasus, Crimea, and the southern Russian steppes. Most significantly, perhaps, for our purposes, they established contact with the Scythians, whose own nomadic connections and conquests were quite extensive, reaching from southern Russia to Palestine, from Asia Minor to unknown points east.

39. Boardman, *Greeks Overseas*, p. 38.

40. See Herodotus, *History* (Loeb), 2.178 concerning the donation and founding of Naucratis.

41. Boardman, *Greeks Overseas*, p. 153.

42. Ibid., pp. 62–63.

43. See Homer, *Iliad* (Loeb), 14.182–83.

44. See A. David Napier, *Masks, Transformation, and Paradox* (Berkeley: University of California Press, 1986), particularly in the section entitled "The Gorgon Reconsidered," pp. 125–34.

45. See P. Walcot, *Hesiod and the Near East* (Cardiff: University of Wales, 1966) for a full discussion of the influence of Near Eastern myth and art, particularly Babylonian and Egyptian material, on Hesiod. He traces the former from North Syria to Euboea to Boetia in the eighth century and the latter from Lower Egypt to Greece in the sixteenth century. Regarding the archaic period, he writes that "while it is foolish to discount the Mycenaean era as a period of time when ideas were freely exchanged throughout the East Mediterranean . . . influence continued to spread westward in the centuries following the Dorian Invasion of Greece"; and "I think we must admit that in the eighth century B.C. the Near East influenced much more than vase decoration, metalwork, and ivories among the Greeks" (pp. 104, 53).

46. "Greece was quite simply in the middle," writes Jaan Puhvel, "at the crossroads of prehistory and history, at the interface of Europe and Asia, at the point were continentality and insularity, land mass and sea vistas met and interacted, where autochthon, northern invader, and eastern trader affected a complex inculturation. Greek culture is a matter not of preserving but of becoming, not so much

130 *Notes to Pages 21–24*

of interrelation but of fusion, in short, a new synthesis. This streak of originality complicates the tracing of antecedents, whether diffusionary or genetic" (*Comparative Mythology*, pp. 126–27).

47. Claude Lévi-Strauss, "The Structural Study of Myth," in *Reader in Comparative Religion: An Anthropological Approach*, ed. William A. Lessa and Evon Z. Vogt (New York: Harper & Row, 1965), pp. 567, 564.

48. Puhvel, *Comparative Mythology*, p. 127.

49. See Friedrich, *Meaning of Aphrodite*, p. 47.

50. Puhvel, *Comparative Mythology*, p. 127.

51. See Friedrich, *Meaning of Aphrodite*, 50–53.


## Chapter 2: The Many Helens

1. The Homeric epithet—*Dios thygatēr*, originally "daughter of the Sky"—is given to Aphrodite and to Athena far more often than to any other Homeric figures. Furthermore, it is the exact cognate of the Vedic epithet *divá(s) duhitár*—exclusively assigned to the dawn-goddess Uṣas, whose Greek counterpart is Eos or Dawn. See Linda Lee Clader, *Helen: The Evolution from Divine to Heroic in Greek Epic Tradition*, MNEMOSYNE, Bibliotheca Classica Batava (Leiden: E. J. Brill, 1976), pp. 53–54; and Gregory Nagy, "Phaethon, Sappho's Phaon, and the White Rock of Leukas," *Harvard Studies in Classical Philology* 77 (1973): 165.

2. With the exception that Persephone is once called *Dios thygatēr* in the Odyssey. As we shall see, however, Helen is closely associated with Persephone.

3. "It is generally agreed that the great daughters of Zeus—Artemis, Athena, Aphrodite—are all powerful goddesses from a place or period when Zeus was not king, and that when the Indo-European sky-god came into conflict with them he made them his daughters, for they were too powerful to become mere consorts" (Clader, *Helen*, p. 54).

4. See Fragment 24, *Hesiodi: Theogonia, Opera et Dies, Scutum*, ed. Friedrich Solmsen, in *Fragmenta Selecta*, ed. R. Merkelbach and M. L. West (Oxford: Clarendon, 1990), p. 122. Okeanos, in the *Iliad*, is said to be "whence the gods have arisen" (14.201) and "whence is risen the seed of all the immortals" (14.246) (*The Iliad of Homer*, translated by Richmond Lattimore [Chicago: University of Chicago Press, 1967]). Aphrodite too, like Helen, is acknowledged by Hesiod to have been spawned from the sea; for he describes her birth from the foam spewing up amidst the waves into which the severed genitals of Ouranos were hurled by Kronos. See Hesiod, *Theogony* (Oxford), 188–200. The only other direct reference in archaic poetry to Aphrodite's birth from the sea is found in the sixth Homeric *Hymn*, though a possible link between Aphrodite and the sea is suggested in the *Iliad* (5.370–71), when Dione is presented as Aphrodite's mother; for, although Dione is described (5.383) as having her home on Olympos, she was among the earliest of the pre-Olympian deities and was herself, by some accounts, a daughter of Okeanos.

5. See Ptolemaeus, in Photius, *Bibliotheca*, ex recensione Immanuelis Bekkeri (Berolini: G. Reimeri, 1824–1825), 149 A f.

6. See *Kypria*, Fragment 6.1-3, in *Epicorum Graecorum Fragmenta*, ed. G. Kinkel (Leipzig: Teubner, 1877), p. 24.

7. See Hesiod, *Theogony* (Oxford), 223–24.

8. See Robert Graves, *The Greek Myths* (Mt. Kisco, N.Y.: Moyer Bell, 1960), 32: a., 2; 62: a., b., 1.

9. *Nemos* means "glade" or "wooded pasture," while the verb *nemein* means "to dispense" or "to bestow." Together these suggest a connection with the earth and vegetation, on the one hand, and with largesse, on the other, which are two similarly central and constitutive elements in that other Hesiodic woman said to be a *pēma* to the race of men, Pandora, whose name means either "the one who bestows all things" or "the one on whom all things are bestowed." See Hesiod, *Works and Days* (Oxford), 79–82, and our later discussion of this figure. A further possible connection between Nemesis and Pandora may be seen in the fact that "the Nemesia, a funeral ceremony at Athens, may associate her with birth and death" (Clader, *Helen*, p. 73). Birth and death, we shall see, are embedded in the symbolism of Pandora and her *pithos*.

10. See Graves, *Greek Myths*, 32: 2; 62: a. An Attic white-ground kylix, found in Rhodes and dated 470–450 B.C.E., reveals Aphrodite astride a bird, which looks more like a goose than anything else, while an earlier, terra-cotta figurine from sixth-century Boeotia presents Aphrodite mounted on a goose or swan. These images provide further reflections of the imaginative coherence of Nemesis, Aphrodite, and Helen.

11. The coincidence in Helen of birth from the sea and birth from an egg makes of her, like Aphrodite in whom the same coincidence is found, an image reflecting the first birth of all things from watery Chaos, when "Eurynome, the Goddess of All Things, rose naked from Chaos . . . divided the sea from the sky, dancing lonely upon its waves. . . . Next, she assumed the form of a dove, brooding on the waves and, in due process of time, laid the Universal Egg. At her bidding (the great serpent) Ophion coiled seven times about this egg, until it hatched and split in two. Out tumbled all things that exist" (Graves, *Greek Myths*, 1: a, b). The central images of this pre-Hellenic account of origins—watery chaos, a creatrix bird, a serpent, and a world egg—are ones to which we will return; for they are as old and as widely dispersed as any images of Helen we will encounter. A similar conception of a world egg, fertilized by the wind, is common to Orphic and Egyptian cosmologies, and is found as well, probably as the result of Egyptian influence, in Phoenicia. The idea of the world egg is also found in India. See Jean W. Sedlar, *India and the Greek World* (Totowa, N. J.: Rowman & Littlefield, 1980), p. 271; and M. L. West, *Early Greek Philosophy and the Orient* (Oxford: Oxford University Press, 1971), pp. 65–66. Interestingly, with respect to the myths of Aphrodite and Helen, in the Orphic cosmology it is Eros that breaks forth from the lunar world egg laid by Night. See E. O. James, *Myth and Ritual in the Ancient Near East* (London: Thames & Hudson, 1958), pp. 174–75.

12. Homer never doubts that Zeus is Helen's father and never mentions Helen's mother by name. Helen herself, however, in the *Iliad*, does speak of "those two, the marshals of the people, Kastor, breaker of horses, and the strong boxer Polydeukes, my own brothers, born with me of a single mother" (3.236–38);

and, in the *Odyssey*, Odysseus himself says how he "saw Leda, who had been the wife of Tyndareos, and she had borne to Tyndareos two sons with strong hearts, Kastor, breaker of horses, and the strong boxer, Polydeukes" (13.298–300), leaving no doubt that Leda too was the mother of Helen. Later in the *Odyssey* (24.199) Tyndareos is clearly said to be the father of Helen's sister, Klytemnestra. See *The Iliad of Homer*, trans. Lattimore; *The Odyssey of Homer*, translated by Richmond Lattimore (New York: Harper & Row, 1965).

13. See E. Bethe in Pauly-Wissowa, *Real-Encyclopädie der Classischen Alterumswissenschaft* (Stuttgart: J. B. Metzler, 1912), s.v. Helene, 2826–27; Graves, *Greek Myths*, 62: a–c.

14. *Sappho*, translated by Mary Barnard (Berkeley: University of California Press, 1958), #13.

15. See Graves, *Greek Myths*, 62: a.

16. See L. R. Farnell, *The Cults of the Greek States* (Oxford: Clarendon, 1896–1909), 2:492.

17. See Graves, *Greek Myths*, 7: 3.

18. See L. R. Farnell, *Greek Hero Cults and Ideas of Immortality* (Oxford: Clarendon, 1921), p. 324.

19. For one indication of the association of Leto and Artemis with swans, see Euripides, *Iphigenia in Tauris*, 1089–1105 (Oxford), translation mine, in which the attendants to the priestess of Artemis sing:

> Halcyon,
> Denizen of sea-carved cliffs,
> Bird of darkest song,
> Keen hearts rend at your mourning
> Laments for a mate long lost.
> Without the grace of winged flight,
> A grave heart within me
> Echoes the saddest of your songs.
> For the noisy fellowship of the market,
> For blessed Artemis worshipped with joy
> By the Kynthian hill,
> I cry out with longing.
> As a bird craves the open sky
> I crave the once familiar palm and laurel,
> The sacred silvered olive boughs,
> Kind to Leto in her labor,
> The glistening pool slowly spun in circles
> By a swan singing service
> To the Muses.

See also Paul Friedrich, *The Meaning of Aphrodite* (Chicago: University of Chicago Press, 1978), pp. 76–77.

20. Friedrich, *Meaning of Aphrodite*, pp. 47, 86.

21. See *Epicorum Graecorum Fragmenta*, ed. Kinkel, pp. 15–31.

22. According to the fifth Homeric *Hymn*, the powers of Aphrodite invariably prevail over anyone's defenses, with three notable divine exceptions: Athena,

Artemis, and Hestia, who traditionally decline sex, from whatever quarter. "But none of the others, neither blessed god nor mortal man, has escaped Aphrodite" (*The Homeric Hymns*, translated by Apostolos N. Athanassakis [Baltimore: Johns Hopkins University Press, 1976], 5.34–35, p. 48).

23. Ibid., 5.45–46, p. 48.

24. Ibid., 5.247–48, 253–55, p. 54.

25. See Deborah Dickmann Boedeker, *Aphrodite's Entry into Greek Epic*, *MNEMOSYNE*, Bibliotheca Classica Batava (Leiden: E. J. Brill, 1974), p. 34.

26. Homer, *The Iliad*, translated by Robert Fagles (New York: Viking Penguin, 1990), 3.470–75 (406–10, Loeb).

27. Ibid., 3.462–65 (400–402, Loeb).

28. Hesiod, *Theogony*, 201, in *Theogony & Works and Days*, translated by M. L. West (New York: Oxford University Press, 1988), p. 9.

29. See *Iliad*, 5.337–38 (Loeb).

30. Aeschylus, *Suppliants*, translated by Janet Lembke (New York: Oxford University Press, 1975), 1376 (1040, Loeb).

31. Walter F. Otto, *The Homeric Gods: The Spiritual Significance of Greek Religion* (Boston: Beacon Press, 1954), p. 102.

32. See Farnell, *Cults of the Greek States*, 5:624.

33. For a thorough presentation and discussion of the images of Helen in the iconographic tradition, in relation to the treatment of Helen in the literary tradition, see Lilly B. Ghali-Kahil, *Les enlèvements et le retour d'Hélène, dans les textes et les documents figurés*, École Française D'Athènes, Travaux et Mémoires (Paris: E. de Boccard, 1955).

34. See Farnell, *Cults of the Greek States*, 5:656.

35. As in Euripides' *Helen*, wherein Helen never went off to Troy or anywhere else with Paris and, throughout the course of the war, heroically resisted, without a single lapse, the ardent advances of the king of Egypt.

36. Euripides, *Iphigenia at Aulis*, 544–51 (Oxford), translation mine.

37. Ibid., 554–55.

38. See *Sappho*, trans. Barnard, #38.

39. Ibid., #53. Kama, god of sexual longing, the Indic counterpart of Eros, carries a quiver containing equally deadly arrows, with names such as "death-bringer." The power of Kama, both that used by him and that used against him, is often described as fire, reducing those whom it afflicts to ashes. See Wendy Doniger O'Flaherty, *Women, Androgynes, and Other Mythical Beasts* (Chicago: University of Chicago Press, 1980), pp. 233–35.

40. Aeschylus, *Agamemnon*, 689 (Loeb), translation mine.

41. Weaving is a polyvalent symbol in Greek culture. It is one of the civilizing crafts bestowed by Athena and assigned especially to women. It is also what the Crones, the Fates, do with the fibers of men's lives. Additionally, in the Indo-European tradition, weaving functions as a symbol of poetic composition. See Marcello Durante, "Ricerche sulla preistoria della lingua poetica greca: La terminologia relativa all creazone poetica," *Atti della Academia Nazionale dei Lincei*, Serie ottava, Rediconti, Classe di Scienze morali, storice e filologiche 15 (1960): 238–44.

42. See *Iliad*, 3.125–28 (Loeb).

43. See C. H. Whitman, *Homer and the Homeric Tradition* (New York: W. W. Norton, 1965), p. 118 and n. 39.

44. See Farnell, *Cults of the Greek States*, 2:652, 665, and n. 110.

45. *Iliad*, 19.325 (Loeb). This is the sole occurrence of *rhigedanēs* in Greek epic. For a discussion of this and of each of Helen's other Homeric epithets, see Clader, *Helen*, pp. 41–62.

46. *Iliad*, 3.404 (Loeb).

47. See Clader, *Helen*, pp. 19–20 and n. 30.

48. See H. Frisk, *Griechisches Etymologisches Wörterbuch* (Heidelberg: Carl Winter, 1960), s.v. *stygeō*; and E. Boisacq, *Dictionnaire étymologique de la langue grecque* (Heidelberg: Carl Winter, 1923), p. 92.

49. *Iliad*, trans. Lattimore, 24.774–75 (773–75 Loeb). See Clader, *Helen*, for a discussion of the other occurrences of *phrissein* in the *Iliad*.

50. Euripides, *Ion* (Oxford), 399–400, translation mine.

51. Euripides, *Medea* (Oxford), 230–31, translation mine.

52. *Iliad* (Loeb), 3.414–17, translation mine.

53. See ibid., 6.342–68.

54. *Iliad*, trans. Lattimore, 6.344.

55. See *Iliad* (Loeb), 3.180; 6.244, 356. For a catalogue of all of the occurrences of *kyōn* in the *Iliad* and the *Odyssey*, see Manfred Faust, "Die künstlerische Verwendung von *kuōn* 'Hund' in den homerischen Epen," *Glotta* 48 (1970): 8–31. See also Paul Friedrich, "Sanity and the Myth of Honor," *Ethos* 5:3 (1977): 289–90.

56. See Pindar, *Pythian*, 487.

57. See Hesiod, *Theogony* (Oxford), 934.

58. Jean-Pierre Vernant, "Feminine Figures of Death in Greece," in *Mortals and Immortals, Collected Essays,* ed. Froma I. Zeitlin (Princeton: Princeton University Press, 1991), p. 97.

59. Hesiod, *Theogony*, 205–6, in *Theogony & Works and Days*, trans. West, p. 9.

60. Emily Vermeule, *Aspects of Death in Early Greek Art and Poetry* (Berkeley: University of California Press, 1979), p. 148.

61. Vernant, "Feminine Figures of Death in Greece," pp. 95–96.

62. Vermeule, *Aspects of Death*, p. 40. Vermeule goes on to add that "the *ker*'s nature is mixed of life and death. She is analogous to kind black earth opening to swallow men, like an animal swallowing her young"(pp. 40–41). This fuller, more ambiguous conception of the *Ker* will coincide with the fuller, more ambiguous conception of Helen to be developed here.

63. See *Iliad* (Loeb), 13.291. See also Vermeule's discussion of *polemou oaristun*, which she translates as the "enchanting love-talk of war," in *Aspects of Death*, p. 103.

64. Vermeule, *Aspects of Death*, pp. 157, 159. That Demeter and her mysteries, celebrated at Eleusis, instilled both fear and bliss in mortals, is discussed at length in Helene Foley's excellent study entitled *The Homeric Hymn to Demeter* (Princeton: Princeton University Press, 1994).

65. Helen's beauty was of no use to her, however, against the women of Rhodes, widows of the war against Troy. In Pausanias's account (3.19.9), these women, led by Polyxo, hung Helen from a tree in revenge for what they had suf-

fered because of her. West and others explain this story as an invention "to explain a cult practice of hanging her image [the image of Helena Dendritis, "Helen of the Tree"] on a tree" (M. L. West, "Immortal Helen," Inaugural Lecture, Bedford College, University of London, 30 April 1975). The deaths by hanging of both Ariadne and Phaedra, her sister, may likewise be traced to a shared tree cult. See Pausanias 1.22.2; 2.32.3; and S. Wide, *Lakonische Kulte* (Leipzig: Teubner, 1893), p. 343.

66. The Scholiast on Euripides' *Andromache* (628) tells how Menelaos dropped his sword out of love when he came upon Helen, who had taken refuge in the temple of Aphrodite. See J. M. Edmonds, ed., *Lyra Graeca*, Loeb Classical Library (London: William Heinemann, 1928), 2:104.

67. According to Lesches, a poet of the seventh century, it was the sight of Helen's breasts that made Menelaos drop his sword. See Hugh Evelyn-White, trans. and ed., *Hesiod, The Homeric Hymns, and Homerica*, Loeb Classical Library (Cambridge, Mass.: Harvard University Press, 1967), p. 519. See also Stesichorus, frag. 201 (*Poetae Melici Graeci*, ed. D. L. Page [Oxford: Oxford University Press, 1962]).

68. I owe this proposal to Professor Lou Goble of the Department of Philosophy at Willamette University, though the oral tradition that conveyed it to me may have a written source, as suggested by M. L. West, who attributes it to a correspondence carried some years ago by the *New Scientist*.

69. See Homeric *Hymn to Apollo*, 194–95 (Loeb) and *Hymn to Aphrodite*, (#5) 117–18 (Loeb); *Odyssey*, 18.194 (Loeb); Lucian, *On the Dance*, II (Loeb, vol. 5). See also Boedeker, *Aphrodite's Entry into Greek Epic*, chapter 2, "Aphrodite and the Choros," pp. 43–63.

70. See Farnell, *Cults of the Greek States*, 2:750–51 (n. 107), where he lists and traces the ancient cults of Aphrodite in her function as a fertility goddess, and 2:642–43, where he discusses this function.

71. See Plutarch, *Parallel Lives*, "Theseus" 31.2 (Loeb, vol. 1).

72. See Homeric *Hymn to Aphrodite*, (#5) 117–20 (Loeb).

73. *Iliad*, trans. Lattimore, 3.390–94.

74. See *Iliad* (Loeb), 3.35–37.

75. *Iliad*, trans. Lattimore, 3.39.

76. Ibid., 3.54–55.

77. Ibid., 24.259–61.

78. *Odyssey*, trans. Lattimore, 8.249–53.

79. See *The Epic of Gilgamesh*, translated by Maureen Gallery Kovacs (Stanford: Stanford University Press, 1985), Tablet I, pp. 5–11, lines 75–225.

80. See Jeffrey H. Tigay, *The Evolution of the Gilgamesh Epic* (Philadelphia: University of Pennsylvania Press, 1982), chapter 10, "The Creation of Enkidu," pp. 192–97, and chapter 11, "The Early Life of Enkidu," pp. 198–213; also Morris Jastrow, "Adam and Eve in Babylonian Literature," *American Journal of Semitic Languages and Literatures* 15 (1899): 193–214.

81. For a discussion of prostitution in Mesopotamia and its connection with the cult of Inanna/Ishtar, as well as a specific discussion of Enkidu's encounter with her love-priestess, see Gerda Lerner, *The Creation of Patriarchy* (New York: Oxford University Press, 1986), chapter 6, "Veiling the Woman," pp. 123–40.

82. So close was Ishtar's association with not only temple but also commercial prostitution that an early text reads: "When I sit in the entrance of the tavern, I, Ishtar, am a loving *harimtu.*" See *Assyrian Dictionary of the Oriental Institute of the University of Chicago* (Chicago: University of Chicago Press, 1968), 6:101–2.

83. See "Inanna and the God of Wisdom" in Diane Wolkstein and Samuel Noah Kramer, *Inanna: Queen of Heaven and Earth, Her Stories and Hymns from Sumer* (New York: Harper & Row, 1983), pp. 11–27, 16–18.

84. See Tigay, *Evolution of the Gilgamesh Epic,* pp. 212–13.

85. *Iliad,* trans. Lattimore, 5.330, 425, 428–29.

86. See Aristotle, *Poetics,* 4.1448b–1449a (Loeb).

87. See Donald Ward, "On the Poets and Poetry of the Indo-Europeans," *Journal of Indo-European Studies* 1 (1973): 128–44; see also A. W. H. Adkins, "Threatening, Abusing and Feeling Angry in the Homeric Poems," *Journal of Hellenic Studies* 92 (1972): 7–21.

88. Ward, "On the Poets and Poetry of the Indo-Europeans," p. 142.

89. *Poems of Love and War,* translated by A. K. Ramanujan (New York: Columbia University Press, 1985), p. 290.

90. Ibid., 291.

91. Ibid., p. 309, note to page 186.

92. Ibid., p. 186.

93. Sigmund Freud, "The Antithetical Sense of Primal Words, A review of a Pamphlet by Karl Abel, *Über den Gegensinn der Urworte,* 1884," in Sigmund Freud, *Collected Papers* (New York: Basic Books, 1959), 4:184.

94. Ibid., p. 185.

95. Ibid., p. 186.

96. Ibid., p. 191.

97. Ibid., p. 186.

98. Rene Girard, *Violence and the Sacred* (Baltimore: Johns Hopkins University Press, 1977), p. 145.

99. See ibid., p. 145.

100. Ibid., p. 146.

101. In case this analysis seems both too technical and too farfetched, I will recount briefly a story I know to be true. A woman in the west of Ireland, who collects and sells from her own cottage antique copper kettles, told me of a remarkable encounter several years ago. A man and a woman, the latter wrapped in furs, tourists from America, came to her cottage to look at kettles. When the American woman's eyes fell on one particular kettle, they lit up and she was greatly excited. Examining the kettle, she declared that it was perfect. The kettle she had already dreamt of but never yet set eyes on! The only question was whether so perfect a kettle could be afforded. To the Irish woman it seemed a rather ordinary kettle, which she said had a rather ordinary price. It could be had for forty pounds, or sixty-five dollars. On hearing this, the American woman's face fell and she put the kettle down. Her interest in the kettle had changed like the Irish weather, without warning. It was, she said, not the kettle she had thought it was. She had wanted something more "in the five-hundred dollar range," a real treasure to bring home—which, in fact, this kettle was. But this fact

could not be seen by someone who measured an object's value not by how much she desired it but by how much others desired it. If the kettle could be relinquished for so little, it wasn't worth having; so they left without it.

102. See Girard, *Violence and the Sacred*, p. 152; see also Emile Beneviste, *Le Vocabulaire des institutions indo-européennes* (Paris: Editions de Minuit, 1969), vol. 2, book 1, chap. 6.

103. *Iliad*, trans. Lattimore, 19.282. See also the discussion "Briseis: The Second Helen," in Mihoko Suzuki, *Metamorphoses of Helen* (Ithaca: Cornell University Press, 1989), pp. 21–29.

104. Friedrich, "Sanity and the Myth of Honor," 285.

105. *Iliad*, trans. Lattimore, 2.354–56.

106. Ibid., 22.410–11.

107. See Friedrich's discussion entitled "The Symbolism of the Veil" in "Sanity and the Myth of Honor," pp. 295–96; see also M. N. Nagler's discussion of this same theme in "Towards a Generative View of the Oral Formula," *Transactions of the American Philological Association* 98 (1967): 269–311.

108. See Cyrus H. Gordon, *The Common Background of Greek and Hebrew Civilizations* (New York: W. W. Norton, 1965), pp. 270–71. Concerning the many parallels and mutual influences uniting the early literatures of the ancient East Mediterranean, see also Cyrus Gordon, *The Ancient Near East* (New York: W. W. Norton, 1965); idem, "Homer and the Bible," *Hebrew Union College Annual* 26 (1955): 43–108.

109. Central to both the *Ramayana* and the *Mahabharata* is a great war, involving both human and divine figures and forces, and at the center of each war is a woman of surpassing beauty. In fact, the parallels between these two vast Sanskrit epics and the *Iliad* are so numerous and so intriguing that to explore them with any adequacy would require a volume in itself. All that can be offered here are several brief glances out over what is admittedly an ocean.

In the *Ramayana*, Rama's captivatingly beautiful wife Sita is abducted and eventually, in a universal war, retrieved. Sita, whose name means "furrow," was found as an infant by Janaka, her earthly father, in a freshly plowed field. Sita, the gift of Mother Earth, was found lying there, newborn, in the turned soil. When she grew into her full beauty, a cloud of rival suitors descended on her father's house and a war over her was narrowly averted. Only he who could lift, bend, and string the bow of Shiva, a holy heirloom in the house of Janaka, would be given the hand of Sita, whom Ravana, her abductor, later likened to a swan. Rama, her godlike spouse, was forced to win her twice, once from her father and once from her abductor. Finally, after a war which Rama admitted he had fought not for love of Sita but to avenge his own honor, he rejected her as a woman shamed. Not until Sita leaped into the sacred flames and emerged pure in the arms of Agni, god of fire, did Rama take her back. In the final, seventh book of the *Ramayana*, at the close of Sita's life, the earth from which she had come opened up again and a throne appeared for her. Enthroned by her mother, Earth, amidst a rain of celestial flowers, Sita, or "Furrow," returned whence she came.

The *Mahabharata*, approximately seven times the length of the *Iliad*, is not so easily distilled. At its core, however, is a war encompassing heaven and earth; a

godlike warrior armed with divine weapons, Arjuna, "the terrifier," who with-
holds himself from the great battle until he is persuaded to fight by his charioteer;
and a spell-bindingly beautiful woman, Draupadi, as lethal as she is alluring.
"Created by the Creator himself," Draupadi "surpassed all other women and
beguiled all creatures" (J. A. B. van Buitenen, trans. and ed., *The Mahabharata*
[Chicago: University of Chicago Press, 1973), Book One, p. 358). Unlike Helen,
whose five marriages were sequential, Draupadi was married to five men at once,
consummating her unions on five consecutive nights, each time miraculously
recovering her virginity in the morning. One of these husbands was Arjuna,
whose likeness to Achilles is most striking.

   One point at which the stories of Arjuna and Achilles cross unmistakably is in
the legend of Achilles' withdrawal to the island of Skyros (see *ΣIl*. XVI 326 and
Pausanias 1.22.6; also Dale S. Sinos, *Achilles, Patroklos and the Meaning of Philos*
[Innsbruck: Innsbrucker Beiträge zur Sprachwissenschaft, 1980], pp. 55–56),
where he hid among girls to avoid being induced to fight at Troy. He was found
out, however, by Odysseus, who tricked Achilles by setting before him a shield
and spear, which Achilles seized at the blast of a trumpet. In the *Mahabharata*, a
remarkably similar story is told of Arjuna, who disguised himself among the
daughters of the court as a eunuch dance teacher with a feminine name, meaning
"large reed" or "having a large reed," echoing both the double meaning of *kouros*
as "lad" or "sprout" and Thetis's likening of her son Achilles to a young tree
sprout (see *Iliad*, 18.437–38 [Loeb]). Finally, after comically playing with weapons,
Arjuna took them up, revealed himself for who he truly was, went into battle, and
in the end signaled victory with a blast of his trumpet. (See *The Mahabharata*,
trans. and ed. van Buitenen, Introduction to Book Four, pp. 7, 9, 15–17.)

   A more elusive yet more embracing correspondence between the *Iliad* and the
*Mahabharata* may lie in the centrality of fire to each. The entire *Mahabharata* may
be read as an extended fire sacrifice, just as the inhuman, unwearying blaze of
divine fire may be said to be the master image of the *Iliad*. Finally, just as the
*Mahabharata* ends with a horse sacrifice, so the *Iliad* ends with the flames of
Patroklos's pyre, on which men and horses burn together, the pyre of Hector,
breaker of horses, and the anticipation of the flames of Troy, in which will burn
the enigmatic wooden horse.

   110. Genesis 12:10–20; 20:1–18; 26:6–11. See E. A. Speiser's discussion of these
three accounts and their likely Hurrian source in *Genesis*, Anchor Bible (Garden
City, N.Y.: Doubleday, 1987), pp. XL–XLI and 91–94.

   111. Apart from Eve, Sarai/Sarah is perhaps Helen's nearest counterpart in the
*Pentateuch*. The legendary beauty of Sarai/Sarah in the Jewish tradition is
reflected quite interestingly in one of the Qumran scrolls, a text entitled "Memoirs
of the Patriarchs," in which Sarah's charms, after having been detailed, are
summed up in the following claim: "Her beauty is greater than all other women's,
and she excels them all" (see Theodor H. Gaster, *The Dead Sea Scriptures* [New
York: Anchor/Doubleday, 1976], p. 365).

   112. Michael David Coogan, trans. and ed., *Stories from Ancient Canaan*
(Philadelphia: Westminster, 1978), p. 59.

   113. Ibid., p. 65.

114. The same may not be said for the house of Pabil. Indeed, beauty often leaves destruction in its wake. Nowhere is this theme more poignantly concentrated than in the following ancient Tamil poem, from *Poems of Love and War*, p. 188, entitled "When a King Asks for a Chieftain's Daughter":

> The king scrapes the sweat
> off his brow
> with the blade of his spear
> and says terrible things.
> The girl's father
> rants as well
> and will not speak softly.
>
> This is their natural way of speaking.
>
> And come to think of it,
> this lovely girl,
>
> > sharp teeth, cool eyes
> > streaked with red,
> > skin the color
> > of young mango leaf,
>
> this goddess,
>
> > like a fire
> > sparked by the wood itself,
>
> will devastate
> the very place of her birth.

Ramanujan's commentary on this poem runs as follows: "A king would often ask a chieftain for his daughter's hand. If the chieftain refused, enmity and war would follow. This poem speaks of the destructive power in beautiful women (and in warriors, war drums, etc.). Such magical power is *aṉaṅku*, also a goddess" (p. 309, note to p. 188)

115. See P. Walcot, *Hesiod and the Near East* (Cardiff: University of Wales, 1966), p. 23.

116. See Farnell, *Cults of the Greek States*, 2:635–36 and nn. 99c, 99g regarding sacred prostitution among the Corinthians and Locrians, as well as on Cyprus.

117. That Aphrodite's origins are to be found in the ancient Near East and that she is a relatively late import to Greece is a theory widely held by classical scholars. To claim the Oriental and likely Semitic origin of the myths, iconic images, and cults of Aphrodite, however, is a more complex and questionable matter. See Farnell, *Cults of the Greek States*, vol. 2, chaps. 21 and 22, especially pp. 618–29; Ulrich von Wilamowitz-Moellendorff, *Der Glaube der Hellenen* (Berlin: Weidmann, 1931), 1:95–98; Otto, *Homeric Gods*, pp. 91–92; and Martin P. Nilsson, *Geschichte der griechischen Religion*, 2nd ed. (Munich: Beck, 1955), 1:519–20. For a concise assessment and reexamination of the "Aphrodite question," see Boedeker, *Aphrodite's Entry into Greek Epic*, pp. 1-17, wherein she argues that "Aphrodite originated as a hypostasis of the Indo-European Dawn-goddess" (p. 15). The fact that Aphrodite's name is not found among those divinities attested on extant Linear B fragments may reveal, in the assessment of John Chadwick, no more than the operation of

"mere chance" (see John Chadwick, *The Decipherment of Linear B*, 2nd ed. [Cambridge: Cambridge University Press, 1970], p. 124). Furthermore, the common claim that Aphrodite first surfaced in the Greek world at Cyprus, whence her name *Kypris*, and that the Phoenicians were responsible for her presence there, is made all the more questionable by excavations on Cyprus, indicating that the Mycenaeans had settled there long before the arrival of the Phoenicians (see Vassos Karageorgis, *The Ancient Civilization of Cyprus* [Geneva: Nagel, 1969], pp. 62–67, 135–50), whose contact with the Greeks in the early Iron Age seems too minimal and too late to be the main font for the myths and cult of Aphrodite. "If Cyprus is really her homeland, as the ancient tradition maintains," suggests Boedeker, "Aphrodite was probably introduced there by Mycenaean Greeks. After a period of relatively isolated evolution, which would have included a certain amount of assimilation to the Eastern goddesses, Aphrodite may have been reintroduced from Cyprus to the rest of the Greek world" (*Aphrodite's Entry into Greek Epic*, p. 3).

Aphrodite and, for that matter, Helen, however, are never singular, completed objects whose manufacture and transmission can be traced with confidence. Their living roots reach, for the most part invisibly, in myriad directions. Cultic parallels, iconic resemblances, common mythic and narrative patterns, ancient claims and enduring evidence of contacts and influences all together may allow us to imagine Aphrodite and Helen's vast relations but never to draw in any detail the family tree.

118. Aeschylus, fr. 525, translated by John Herington, in his *Aeschylus* (New Haven: Yale University Press, 1986), p. 102.

119. *The Homeric Hymns*, translated by Charles Boer (Chicago: Swallow, 1970), pp. 74–75.

120. For a longer list, see Clader, *Helen*, p. 71.

121. See Graves, *Greek Myths*, p. 164n.

122. See R. M. Dawkins, *Annual of the British School at Athens* 16 (1909/1910): 5; see also Martin P. Nilsson, *The Minoan-Mycenaean Religion and its Survival in Greek Religion* (Lund: Gleerup, 1950), pp. 471, 529.

123. Herodotus (6.61) speaks of a shrine to Helen at Therapnai, while Pausanias (3.19.9) locates this site and its temple as the burial place of Helen and Menelaos, where Isocrates (*Helen* 63) tells of sacrifices made to Helen and Menelaos, not as heroes but as gods. Nilsson points out that Helen had two temples at Sparta, the one not far from the Platanistas and the other at Therapnai (*Minoan-Mycenaean Religion*, p. 529).

124. See A. J. B. Wace, M. S. Thompson, J. P. Droop, "Excavations at Sparta, 1909: §6. The Menelaion," *Annual of the British School at Athens* 15 (1908/1909): 108–9, 124.

125. Aphrodite may be considered "cognate" with Artemis, Hekate, Demeter, and Persephone, as they are also with each other. See Farnell, *Cults of the Greek States*, 2:425.

126. See Clader, *Helen*, pp. 64–80; also Nilsson, *Minoan-Mycenaean Religion*, p. 530. Baskets were frequently carried, sometimes on the head, in cult rituals belonging to Dionysos, Artemis, Demeter, Athene, and Aphrodite. See Lillian B.

Lawler, *The Dance of the Ancient Greek Theatre* (Iowa City: University of Iowa Press, 1964), pp. 39-41. Further, Ariadne is said to have given to Theseus a wooden image of Aphrodite, carved by Daedalus, which after the death of Ariadne Theseus dedicated to Apollo at Delos, where he danced the *geranos* or crane dance of Crete (Lawler, *Dance in Ancient Greece*, pp. 46–47).

127. Concerning Helen's cultic association with trees, particularly the plane tree, see Wide, *Lakonische Kulte*, pp. 340ff.; and Nilsson, *Geschichte der griechischen Religion*, 1:315.

128. Not surprisingly, both Helen's and Aphrodite's connection with Ariadne, which we will discuss further at a later point, is very close indeed. For a discussion of the theory that the cult of Aphrodite replaced that of the once-divine Ariadne, thus reducing her to mortal status, see Farnell, *Cults of the Greek States*, 2:631–34. Both Aphrodite and Ariadne were closely associated with ritual dance. Aphrodite's roots in Crete and her involvement in Cretan cultic dance are suggested by Sappho when she calls out to Aphrodite to "leave Crete and come to us" (*Sappho*, trans. Barnard, #37) and in another of her poems, written, quite likely, with Aphrodite and Eros in mind:

And their feet move
Rhythmically, as tender
feet of Cretan girls
danced once around an
altar of love, crushing
a circle in the soft
smooth flowering grass. (Ibid., #23)

129. For a discussion of abduction or rape as designating a fertility goddess, see Nilsson, *Geschichte der griechischen Religion*, pp. 475ff. Nilsson has suggested that the story of Helen's abduction has its origin in some element in the Spartan religious calendar, such as the temporary absence of the goddess (*Mycenaean Origin of Greek Mythology*, pp. 73–75). For a discussion of this theme as embodied in the Hymn to Demeter and variant myths, see Foley, *Homeric Hymn to Demeter*, pp. 84–103.

130. The divine "mountain mother" is an image of untraceable age. The mountain or cone on which she stands appears to represent the earth's navel, the first mound of earth to emerge from chaos, the earth-womb from which comes all life. At Byblos, this cone was a symbol of Astarte. See B. Johnson, *Lady of the Beasts: Ancient Images of the Goddess and Her Sacred Animals* (New York: Harper & Row, 1988), p. 29. A colossal thirty-foot statue of the mountain mother, which Pausanias (3.22.4) said was the most ancient image of the Great Goddess in the East, was cut from the rock face of Mount Siplylus near Ismir. See Leonard Wooley, *History Unearthed* (New York: Frederick A. Praeger, 1963), p. 139. Countless equivalent images have been found throughout the East Mediterranean, of which one of the most frequently represented is that of the mountain mother flanked by lions on a seal found at Knossos and dated ca. 1600 B.C.E.

131. For all of the following passages from the penultimate stasimon of Euripides' *Helen*, see my translation of that play (Amherst: University of Massachusetts Press, 1986), pp. 92–94.

132. See Hesiod, *Theogony* (Oxford), 984–91.

133. See Gregory Nagy, "Phaethon, Sappho's Phaon, and the White Rock of Leukas," *Harvard Studies in Classical Philology* 77 (1973): 157.

134. Gregory Nagy in the essay cited above offers a brilliant excursion through the mythic world shared by Aphrodite and Eos.

135. See Ernest Maass, "Aphrodite und die hl. Pelagia," *Neue Jahrbücher fur das klassische Alterum* 27 (1911): 457–68; Vittore Pisani, "Akmon e Dieus," *Archivo glottologico italiano* 24 (1930): 65–73.

136. See *Iliad*, 18.403 (Loeb). Although nowhere in extant Greek texts does *aphros* mean "mist" or "cloud," this use of *aphros* to refer to celestial waters may serve to support an argument, based on phonetic correspondences, for its being related to the Indic *abhrá-*, meaning "cloud," derived from a tentatively reconstructed proto-Indo-European *\*abhrós*. See Friedrich, *Meaning of Aphrodite*, p. 202.

137. Aphrodite's celestial roots may well be preserved, not only in her name, but in the cult title of Ourania, and in the fact that at Athens, offerings called *nephalia*, "wineless" offerings, were made to Aphrodite Ourania, along with the celestials Helios, Eos, and Selene. Summing up the evidence, epic, cultic, and iconic, Boedeker suggests that "Aphrodite originated as a hypostasis of the Indo-European Dawn-Goddess," whose Greek form is Eos (*Aphrodite's Entry into Greek Epic*, pp. 14–15).

138. For a further discussion of this epithet, its possible derivations and meanings, see Clader, *Helen*, pp. 55–58. See also Frisk, *Griechisches Etymologisches Wörterbuch*, s.v. *argos* and *Argos*; and P. Chantraine, *Dictionnaire étymologique de la langue grecque* (Paris: Klincksieck, 1968), s.v. *argos* and *Argos*. Additionally, it is perhaps interesting to note that *Argos* is the name of another famous *kyōn* or "dog," that of Odysseus (*Odyssey*, 17.292).

139. See Douglas Frame, "The Origins of Greek NOUS" (dissertation, Harvard University, 1971), *passim*. Frame derives *nostos* from the Greek root *\*nes-*, connoting not only the return to light (sunrise) but also the return to consciousness (rebirth).

140. Vedic Uṣas and Greek Eos have a common Indo-European root reconstructed as *\*áwsōs*. See Friedrich, *Meaning of Aphrodite*, Appendix 5, pp. 199–201.

141. Ibid., p. 48.

142. Helen's and Aphrodite's Homeric epithet *Dios Thugatēr* is the exact cognate of the Vedic *divá(s) duhitár-*, which is given to Uṣas and to no one else. See Nagy, "Phaethon, Sappho's Phaon, and the White Rock of Leukas," pp. 165–66; R. Schmitt, *Dichtung und Dichtersprache in indogermanischer Zeit* (Wiesbaden: Harrassowitz, 1967), pp. 169–73.

143. See Boedeker's discussion of "Aphrodite and the *Choros*," in *Aphrodite's Entry into Greek Epic*, pp. 43–63; and the Appendix, "Chôros and Choros," pp. 85–91.

144. See *Iliad*, 19.1–2; 8.485; Homeric *Hymn to Aphrodite*, 227. While Uṣas is said to be conveyed in a shining chariot (*Rigveda*, 7.78,I; I.23.7), drawn by horses (7.75.6) or cows (1.92.2), only the names of Eos's horses (*Odyssey*, 22.246) and nothing of her chariot finds mention in Greek epic. The Dioskouroi, on the other hand, while usually portrayed as horsemen, are likewise depicted in a sky-borne

chariot. See Euripides' *Helen*, 1495. There appears to be a further close connection, however, between the *Harits* of the *Rigveda*, the winged horses of the sun, who bring prosperity and well-being, and the *Charites*, or Graces, who accompany Aphrodite and Helen. See Friedrich, *Meaning of Aphrodite*, Appendix 2, "Proto-Indo-European *ghár-i-s,"* pp. 196–98.

145. In Vedic poetry, dawn, not sunset, marks the division between past and future. See Henry De Witt Griswold, *The Religion of the Rigveda* (Delhi: Motilal, 1971), p. 252. With each new dawn, Usas, Eos, and Aphrodite are reborn, virginal and forever in the blush of beauty. Not so their mortal lovers, for whom they cause time to pass, and to whom they thus bring age and death. See *Rigveda*, 1.124.2a; Hesiod, *Works and Days*, 578; and *Hymn to Aphrodite*, 225–45.

146. The Morning Star (*Hesperos*) and the Evening Star (*Heōsphoros*) are, of course, a single star, the planet Venus, the astral emblem of Aphrodite, Astarte, and Ishtar/Inanna.

147. See *Rigveda*, 10.85.9

148. See *The Rig Veda*, translated by Wendy Doniger O'Flaherty (New York: Penguin, 1981), p. 267.

149. See *Rigveda*, 10.85.40.

150. See *Rigveda*, 4.43.6; 1.119.5. Among Sūryā's other marriages, perhaps reflected in Aphrodite's cult association with Hermes, is her marriage to Pūsan, the solar charioteer, god of road and journeys. In fact, Usas too, like Sūryā, was said to be both the sister of the Ásvins and their lover. See *Rigveda*, 7.71.1; 4.52.1–3.

151. See Puhvel, *Comparative Mythology*, p. 84.

152. See Donald Ward, *The Divine Twins*, Folklore Studies 19 (Berkeley, University of California Press, 1968).

153. See ibid., p. 21; and *Rigveda*, 5.78.2.

154. See *Rigveda*, 4.43.3.

155. See *Rigveda*, 4.45.4.

156. See Adolf Furtwangler, "Dioskuren," in *Ausführliches Lexicon der griechischen und römischen Mythologie*, ed. W. H. Roscher, 10 vols. (Leipzig: Teubner, 1884–1937), vol. 1, no. 1, col. 1159.

157. See James Rendel Harris, *Boanerges* (Cambridge: Cambridge University Press, 1913), p. 310.

## Chapter 3: The Duality of Helen

1. Robert Lamberton, in his work on Hesiod, finds the "echoes" of Hesiod's virulent sexism to be "omnipresent in Greek literature and in the sphere of its influence. The exclusion of the female from the world of discourse in Hesiod, constitutes, along with the degradation of the female into a series of bestial grotesques in the poetry of Semonides of Amorgos, the principal archaic manifestation of a hostility that is one of the most problematic aspects of the subsequent tradition" (*Hesiod* [New Haven: Yale University Press, 1988], p. 103).

2. P. Walcot argues that the *floruit* of Hesiod was approximately 730 B.C.E. and

that the *Theogony* preceded *Works and Days* (*Hesiod and the Near East* [Cardiff: University of Wales, 1966], pp. 109, 81). Chester G. Starr, however, who argues for different authors for the above works, places the *Theogony* in the early or mid-seventh century, which is in general agreement with G. S. Kirk's linguistic comparisons of the *Theogony* with the *Iliad* and the *Homeric Hymns*. See Chester G. Starr, *The Origins of Greek Civilization* (New York: Knopf, 1961), pp. 268, 270–71; G. S. Kirk, *Hesiode et son Influence*, Entretiens sur l'antiquité classique 7 (Geneva, 1962), pp. 63–64.

3. Many of the arguable "sources" of Homeric and Hesiodic poetry are not altogether invisible, of course; for the emergence of written from oral traditions occurred much earlier in Egypt and the Near East than on the Greek mainland.

4. See Hans G. Güterbock, *Kumarbi*, in *The American Journal of Archaeology* 52 (1948): 123–34. H. W. F. Saggs suggests that the ultimate source for both the Greek and the Hurrian/Hittite succession myths may be the Babylonian Myth of Harab (*Civilization Before Greece and Rome* [New Haven: Yale University Press, 1989], p. 294). See also Thorkild Jacobsen, "The Harab Myth," in *Sources from the Ancient Near East* (Malibu, Calif.: Undena, 1984), vol. 2, fasc. 3, pp. 6–26.

5. See Hans G. Güterbock, *The Song of Ullikummi* (New Haven: Yale University Press, 1952).

6. See *The Epic of Creation*, in *Myths from Mesopotamia*, translated by Stephanie Dalley (New York: Oxford University Press, 1989), pp. 228–77.

7. See Hesiod, *Theogony & Works and Days*, translated by M. L. West (New York: Oxford University Press, 1988), Introduction, p. xii; Walcot, *Hesiod and the Near East*, pp. 121–23. Walcot suggests, as well, that the same route may have been taken by the Phoenician alphabet, brought home by Greeks who had been resident in northern Syria.

See also Roland Hampe, *Frühe griechische Sagenbilder in Böotien* (Athens: Athen. Dt. Arch. Inst., 1936), p. 55; Pierre Guillon, *La Béotie antique* (Paris: Belles Lettres, 1948), p. 27.

8. Walcot, *Hesiod and the Near East*, pp. 30, 32, 129.

9. For a discussion of the influence of Babylonian materials, most specifically the *Enuma Elish*, on Hesiod, see Walcot, *Hesiod and the Near East*, pp. 27–54. Concerning the origins and development of the cult of Yahweh in ancient Israel, see Mark S. Smith, *The Early History of God* (New York: Harper & Row, 1987). And for a comparison of the Hebrew and Babylonian materials regarding the origins of the cosmos and of humanity, as well as the ascendancies of Marduk and of Yahweh, see Alexander Heidel, *The Babylonian Genesis* (Chicago: University of Chicago Press, 1951). Gerda Lerner considers all three traditions, though most substantially those of Mesopotamia and Israel, in *The Creation of Patriarchy* (New York: Oxford University Press, 1986).

10. Lamberton, *Hesiod*, p. 77.

11. Hesiod, *Theogony* (Oxford), 585, translation mine.

12. Ibid., 600–601.

13. Ibid., 570. A further, admittedly remote, though possible, connection between Pandora and stolen fire may be glimpsed in legends recounting how woman once kept fire in her vagina. See Mircea Eliade, *The Forge and the Crucible* (New York: Harper & Brothers, 1962), p. 80.

14. Ibid., 560.

15. See ibid., 540, 547, 550, 555, 560, 562.

16. Ibid., 160; see 175.

17. Hesiod, *Theogony & Works and Days,* trans. West, p. 8.

18. Hesiod, *Theogony* (Oxford), 496.

19. Ibid., 589.

20. I use the categories "appearance" and "reality" advisedly here, where one might be tempted to use, instead, "form" and "matter" (particularly as Hesiod refers to woman as a likeness or form); for the latter more technical categories are quite volatile and prone to change. In the metaphysics of Plato and Aristotle, form—not matter—is the more real of the two; and Aristotle explicitly contrasts the sexes by likening man to form and woman to matter.

21. Hesiod, *Theogony* (Oxford), 581.

22. Ibid., 589.

23. Ibid., 592.

24. Ibid., 535–37.

25. Ibid., 613.

26. For a fuller discussion of what the figure of Prometheus represents, see Jean-Pierre Vernant, "The Myth of Prometheus in Hesiod," in *Myth and Society in Ancient Greece* (New York: Zone, 1980), pp. 183–201; and Robert Emmet Meagher, "*Technē,*" in *Perspecta 24, The Yale Architectural Journal* (New York: Rizzoli, 1988), pp. 159–64. If, indeed, the threat posed by Prometheus, in concert with human-kind, is that men might become like gods, it may be of interest to note that a similar promise is presented to Adam and Eve by the serpent who tells Eve that if she and her mate will eat of the forbidden tree they "will be like divine beings" (*Tanakh* [Philadelphia: Jewish Publication Society, 1988], Genesis 3:5). At the outset of this encounter, the serpent is described as "the shrewdest of all the wild beasts" (2:25), while Adam and Eve are depicted as naked but as yet feeling no shame (3:1). What is obvious only in the original Hebrew is that the author of this account has created a pun here. The serpent is "shrewd" (ʿarum) and the first humans are "naked" (ʿarom), words written alike but vocalized differently. Soon Adam and Eve, in seeking to be shrewd like the serpent realize their nakedness, knowing desire and shame in the same instant. This same convergence of naked-ness, desire, and would-be resemblance to the gods is suggested in the *Gilgamesh,* wherein the temple prostitute "exposes her sex" to the primordial man Enkidu, and six days later, we are told, "he drew himself up,"

for his understanding had broadened.

Turning around, he sat down at the harlot's feet,

> gazing into her face,
>
> his ears attentive as the harlot spoke.
>
> The harlot said to Enkidu:
>
> > "You are beautiful, Enkidu,
> >
> > you are become like a god."

(*The Epic of Gilgamesh*, translated by Maureen Gallery Kovacs [Stanford: Stanford University Press, 1985], p. 9, lines 183–88).

The correspondence of these earlier Near Eastern stories with that of Prometheus and Pandora is evident. Aided and abetted by Prometheus, men will soon be as shrewd as Zeus, and possibly more so. God-like cleverness combined with divine force is all the provocation Zeus needs to act. He will give to man, in the person of Epimetheus, a woman to consume him and his desires. Man will know nakedness, the secrets of woman, not the secrets of god. Intimacy with woman will spell estrangement from god, as it does in Genesis and *Gilgamesh*. See David Damrosch, *The Narrative Covenant: Transformations of Genre in the Growth of Biblical Literature* (New York: Harper & Row, 1987), chapter 3, "Gilgamesh and Genesis," pp. 88–143, esp. pp. 138–43.

27. Particularly when this account is conflated with its synopsis in *Works and Days* (47–58), Prometheus emerges as the First Man, or precisely as the most threatening of the several aspects of original man reflected in the sons of Iapetos and Klymene. This is made clear when Zeus tells him that the First Woman, whose creation he is about to commission, will be a *pēma mega* for Prometheus himself and "for future men" (*andrasin essomenoisin*, 56).

28. In the slaughtering of a willing beast, both the fellowship and the divide between men and animals is made evident; and in the meat feast that follows, wherein the choice portions are raised to the gods and the lesser portions are shared among men, both the fellowship and the divide between men and gods is made evident. In the sacrificial ritual, duly performed, the hierarchical ordering of god, man, and beast is articulated and enacted. For a further and fuller consideration of animal sacrifice, see Walter Burkert, *Homo Necans, The Anthropology of Ancient Greek Sacrificial Ritual and Myth* (Berkeley: University of California Press, 1983), *passim*, and *Greek Religion* (Cambridge, Mass.: Harvard University Press, 1985), pp. 55–68. See also Jean-Pierre Vernant, *Mortals and Immortals: Collected Essays*, edited by Froma I. Zeitlin (Princeton: Princeton University Press, 1991), chapter 17, "A General Theory of Sacrifice and the Slaying of the Victims in the Greek *Thusia*," pp. 290–302; and Robert Emmet Meagher, *Mortal Vision, the Wisdom of Euripides* (New York: St. Martin's, 1989), pp. 64–65. For a more specific discussion of the Athenian Buphonia, the slaying of an ox for "Zeus of the City," see Burkert, *Homo Necans*, pp. 136–43.

29. Actually, this simplified schema is complicated and contradicted by Hesiod's insertion of a fifth race of heroes between the brazen and the iron races. The delineation of world ages in steady decline and their association with specific

metals of diminishing value may be traced to Babylonian materials. See A. Jeremias, "Ages of the World (Babylonian)," *Encyclopedia of Religion and Ethics* ( New York: Charles Scribner's Sons, 1908), 1:183–87. The same idea is found in other traditions as well, such as the Persian *Avesta* and the Hebrew *Book of Daniel*, wherein Daniel interprets for the Babylonian king Nebuchadnezzar his dream of a brilliant and dreadful statue with a gold head, silver chest and arms, bronze belly and thighs, iron legs, and feet of both iron and clay, a statue that fell apart into tiny pieces before the king's eyes. Daniel takes it all to mean the rise and fall of five kingdoms to be succeeded by the never-ending kingdom of the God of heaven (2:31–45).

30. Pietro Pucci provides an illuminating schematization of the differences between life before woman and life with woman. In the oppositions listed below, which Pucci calls "the *edifying* intentions of the text," Hesiod's original man and original woman are neatly distilled for us:

| | |
|---|---|
| Godlike man | Woman resembling the goddesses |
| Identity | Imitation, copy |
| Symmetry | Addition, excess, loss |
| Natural birth from earth | Manufacture with earth and water |
| No reproduction, unicity | Sexuality, reproduction |
| Spontaneity | Artifice, art, toil |
| Truth | Falsity |
| Natural sleep | Diseases, death |

See Pietro Pucci, *Hesiod and the Language of Poetry* (Baltimore: Johns Hopkins University Press, 1977), p. 106.

31. The dressing and adorning of Pandora in *Works and Days* (72–76), together with the corresponding account in the *Theogony* (573–89), find a close parallel in the second Homeric *Hymn to Aphrodite*, wherein Aphrodite, when she emerges newborn from the sea at Cyprus, is enrobed and crowned by the Horai, the daughters of Zeus and Themis, whereupon she is brought before the immortals, who wonder at her. Although the first woman, fashioned from moistened clay, may be said to emerge from the earth, she is crowned at once with a golden diadem, wrought by Hephaestos, on which were worked images of "all the myriad creatures spawned by the solid land and the sea" (*Theogony*, 582). Like Aphrodite, who steps from the sea onto dry land to be welcomed, adorned, and gazed upon, so the first woman is at once associated with both earth and sea.

Walcot, on the other hand, emphasizes the likeness between the Hesiodic scenes of the First Woman's being robed, adorned, crowned, admired, and named and similar scenes of the Egyptian queen Hatshepsut's birth and coronation presented in a series of reliefs and inscriptions on a colonnade of her memorial temple at Deir el-Bahari in West Thebes. In order to explain the possible influence of these scenes from fifteenth-century Egypt on eighth-century Greek poetry, Walcot cites evidence of direct Mycenaean contact with Egypt in the period after approximately 1570 B.C.E. and the resulting Egyptian influences discernible in Mycenaean ideas and images of sacred kingship. Finally, he endeavors to trace those same influences still further into archaic Greek poetry and concludes that "there is nothing improbable after all in the theory that Hesiod's description of the preparation of Pandora may be traced back to the Mycenaean period, and that, when we start to look for its origins, we must go beyond the confines of the Greek world" (Walcot, *Hesiod,* pp. 65–74). See also Edouard Henri Naville, *The Temple of Deir el Bahari* (London: Egypt Exploration Fund), Part II (1897), pp. 12–18 and plates 46–55; Part III (1898), pp. 1–9 and plates 56–64; James H. Breasted, *Ancient Records of Egypt II* (Chicago: University of Chicago Press, 1906), pp. 75–100; H. Brunner, *Die Geburt des Göttkonigs,* Ägyptologische Abhandlungen 10 (Wiesbaden: O. Harrassowitz, 1964).

32. See Hesiod, *Works and Days* (Oxford), 60-68.

33. See ibid., 68, 77.

34. Ibid., 81–82, translation mine. M. L. West (*Theogony & Works and Days* [New York: Oxford University Press, 1988], p. 39) translates this line as follows: "and he named this woman Pandora, Allgift, because all the dwellers on Olympus made her their gift—a calamity for men who live by bread." Presumably, "Allgift" is intended to mean both "recipient" and "source," both "all-gifted" and "all-giving," while emphasizing that Pandora is from the outset intended and "gifted" by the gods as a deadly "gift" to men. In short, the gift (*dōron*) of woman comes down to grief (*pēma*).

35. See Hesiod, *Works and Days* (Oxford), 100.

36. See Dora and Erwin Panofsky, *Pandora's Box: The Changing Aspects of a Mythical Symbol,* Bollingen Series 52 (Princeton: Princeton University Press, 1962), pp. 17–20, for a discussion of Erasmus's possible reasons for what must have been a conscious substitution of *pyxis* for *dolium,* which surely the learned Erasmus knew to be the Latin equivalent for the Greek *pithos.* The Latin word *pyxis,* on the other hand, properly translates its exact phonetic equivalent in Greek.

37. Walcot has argued that Pandora's *pithos* or jar referred to in *Works and Days* is a magic cauldron or pot, made of metal, most probably bronze ("Pandora's Jar, Erga 83–105," *Hermes,* 89 [1961]: 250). Concerning the magical properties of bronze, see G. Germain, *Essai sur les origines de certains thèmes odysséens et sur la genèse de l'Odyssée* (Paris: Thèse Fac. des Lettres Paris Presses Universitaires, 1954), pp. 153 ff. Walcot suggests elsewhere that the Homeric counterpart to Hesiod's jar, a place of imprisonment and not merely storage, is the bronze cauldron in which Ares was chained for thirteen months by the sons of Aloeus, until, nearly dead from his long ordeal, he was rescued at last by Hermes, presumably in his capacity as *psychopompos,* guide of souls lost to the light (*Hesiod and the Near East,* p. 61). See also Homer, *Iliad* (Loeb), 5.385–91. The idea that bronze might be an appropriate material for Pandora's jar finds support in the Old Anatolian myth entitled "The Disappearance of Telipinu," the son of the great storm god, in which we read:

Down in the Dark Earth stand great *pahli*-vessels.
Their lids are of lead. Their latches are of iron.
That which goes into them doesn't come up again;
it perishes therein. So may they seize Telipinu's
anger, wrath, sin, and sullenness, and may they not
come back (here).

Bronze *pahli*-vessels, were wide-mouthed storage pots with lids, essentially bronze *pithoi*. An identical account of these vessels and their function appears in the corresponding myth of "The Disappearance of Hannahanna," the Hurrian-Hittite Mother Goddess frequently associated with myths of vanishing gods. See Harry A. Hoffner, Jr., trans., and Gary M. Beckman, ed., *Hittite Myths* (Atlanta: Scholars Press, 1990), pp. 17, 28.

38. Long before this, as early as 3500 B.C.E., burial in large earthenware jars may be traced to Asia Minor. Also very early and quite widespread was the use of honey in the cult of the dead. See Erich Neumann, *The Great Mother*, Bollingen Series 47 (Princeton: Princeton University Press, 1963), pp. 264–67; and A. W. Persson, *The Religion of Greece in Prehistoric Times*, Sather Classical Lectures 17 (Berkeley: University of California Press, 1942), pp. 13–18. In fact, burial in fetal position within egg-shaped earthenware pots is documented throughout southern and southeastern Europe from the Neolithic period onward, which practice clearly expresses "the idea of burial in the mother's womb. Burial in the womb is analogous to a seed being planted in the earth, and it was therefore natural to expect new life to emerge from the old" (Marija Gimbutas, *The Language of the Goddess* [New York: Harper & Row, 1989], p. 151).

39. The *choe*, drink offerings poured out from large vessels over the earth to the dead and to chthonic deities, may include honey, milk, water, oil, and wine. See Burkert, *Greek Religion*, pp. 70–72. Thus Odysseus, in preparation for his visit to the land of the dead, digs a pit and pours into it three cups for the dead and the gods below to drink: the first of honey mixed with milk, the second of sweet wine, and the third of water. See Homer, *Odyssey* (Loeb), 10.517–20. See also Aeschylus, *Persians* (Oxford), 607–22 and *Libation Bearers* (Oxford), 84–164; Sophocles, *Oedipus at Colonus* (Oxford), 466–92; Euripides, *Iphigenia in Tauris* (Oxford), 157–66.

40. From the Geometric period onwards, simple pot burials were regularly given to infants and children, a practice that persisted in the classical period. See Robert Garland, *The Greek Way of Death* (Ithaca: Cornell University Press, 1985), p. 78. For a full discussion of the myth of Glaukos, see Persson, *Religion of Greece in Prehistoric Times*, pp. 9–24.

The expression "to fall into a jar of honey" means simply and euphemistically "to die." See Persson, *Religion of Greece in Prehistoric Times*, p. 12. Curiously, there is one preserved instance of a child's having "fallen" not only into honey but into the honeycomb itself. In the museum at Vrana near Marathon, there are kept the local remains of a child buried in two beehives, placed end to end to make his coffin. It is perhaps mistaken to suggest, however, as Garland does, that these two hives provided merely a "cheap" form of makeshift burial. "In the light of this evidence"—namely, the evidence for burying children in simple pots and even beehives—Garland concludes, "it is difficult to resist the impression that any serviceable container was acceptable for the body of a child" (*Greek Way of Death*, pp. 78, 81). Yet it may be that we would do well to resist just this impression in the additional light shed by the central significance of honey and of bees in the cult of the dead. See Gimbutas, *Language of the Goddess*, pp. 270–75, and *The Gods and Goddesses of Old Europe* (Berkeley: University of California Press, 1989), pp. 181–85. See also E. Richards-Mantzoulinou, "Melissa Potnia," *Athens Annals of Archaeology* 12 (1980): 1.72–92; and Anne Baring and Jules Cashford, *The Myth of the Goddess* (London: Arcana/Penguin, 1993), pp. 118–20.

In this context, it is interesting to recall that the infant Zeus, born in a Cretan cave inhabited by bees, was said to have been nourished by them. The fact that this Zeus was a year-child, dying and being reborn annually, would suggest that the bees and their nourishment may have played a role in his rebirth. See Martin P. Nilsson, *The Minoan-Mycenaean Religion and its Survival in Greek Religion* (Lund: Gleerup, 1950), pp. 542–43.

Also, Gorgons, who can draw out one's very life-breath and turn living flesh to stone, sometimes have the heads of bees, as depicted on a proto-Attic vase found at Eleusis and dated ca. 675–650. See G. M. A. Richter, *A Handbook of Greek Art* (London: Phaidon Press, 1959), p. 286, fig. 405.

Finally, we may note that in the Old Anatolian myths of vanishing gods, it is the bee, "holding honey in its heart," that is sent repeatedly to search for the lost god, perished in the land of no return. It is the bee that stings him back to consciousness, soothes him with the sweet balm of its wax, and brings him home. See Hoffner and Beckman, *Hittite Myths*, pp. 13–16, 18, 21, 29, 30, 32–33, 36.

41. The owl, an early symbol for the uterus, commonly presides over the cult of the dead. The figure of the owl served for the Egyptians as the hieroglyph for death. The Burney plaque, from the late Sumerian period (2300 B.C.E.), depicts a winged demon, flanked by owls. She is commonly identified with the Hebrew Lilith, hag of the night and of the dark realms, whose name means "screech owl." See B. Johnson, *Lady of the Beasts* (New York: Harper & Row, 1988), p. 82; and Isaiah 34:14. Lilith appears in Sumerian myth as *Lillake*, a demon inhabiting, along with the *Anzu*-bird and the serpent, the *huluppu*-tree (possibly a willow), planted and tended by the goddess Inanna. See Samuel Noah Kramer, *Sumerian Mythology* (Philadelphia: University of Pennsylvania Press, 1961), p. 33. Eventually, according to a Sumerian tablet from Ur, the hero Gilgamesh strikes the serpent, smashes the home of Lillake, sending her off like the *Anzu*-bird to live in the wild, and carves from Inanna's holy tree a throne and a bed. See Diane Wolkstein and Samuel Noah Kramer, *Inanna: Queen of Heaven and Earth, Her Stories and Hymns from Sumer* (New York: Harper & Row, 1983), pp. 3-9, 178-80. Lilith was later said to have been the first wife of Adam, rejected for her refusal to lie beneath him in a

posture of submission, and sent off to the wilderness, like her Sumerian counterpart, to live in the company of animals. See Robert Graves and Raphael Patai, *Hebrew Myths: The Book of Genesis* (New York: Doubleday, 1964), pp. 12, 65–69, 101. Interestingly, in a story dating from sixteenth-century Palestine, Helen of Troy is closely associated with Lilith. See H. Schwartz, *Lilith's Cave* (New York: Oxford University Press, 1988), pp. 40–51. For a full discussion of the archaeological evidence linking the owl with death both in Greece and beyond, see Gimbutas, *Language of the Goddess,* pp. 185, 187, 189, 190–95, 207, 319, 321.

42. Mysteriously emerging from and returning to earth and water, and residing in the tree of life, the serpent is commonly associated both with death and with life, with the world above and the world below. See Gimbutas, *Language of the Goddess,* pp. 121, 133, 135, 207. The observed fact that the serpent sloughs its dry, dead skin and thereby rejuvenates itself makes it a powerful symbol of rebirth. So embedded was this phenomenon in the Greek imagination that the same word, *gēras,* means both old age and the slough of the serpent. Frequently, in the mythologies of the ancient Near East, the serpent is associated not only with death but also with regeneration. Thus, in the epic of *Gilgamesh,* when the wife of Utanapishtim, the Sumerian Noah, persuades her husband to share with Gilgamesh the gift of immortality granted them by the gods, this gift comes in the form of a plant. This plant, pulled up from the *Apsu,* the fresh, sweet waters below the earth, restores youth each time it is eaten. (The *Apzu,* the waters of Enki, god of the abyss, like semen and amniotic fluid, are alive with engendering power. Enki presides over all three: the sweet waters that impregnate the earth, the semen that impregnates the mother, and the "birth water" that issues forth from the womb. The Sumerian language makes no distinctions here. So, when Gilgamesh plunges into the Apzu in search of rejuvenation, he is returning to the fecund earth and its fertile waters, to the womb of all life. See Thorkild Jacobsen, *The Treasures of Darkness: A History of Mesopotamian Religion* [New Haven: Yale University Press, 1976], p. 111; and Sylvia Brinton Perera, *Descent to the Goddess* [Toronto: Inner City, 1981], p. 67).

Gilgamesh, however, does not eat the magical plant at once. Instead, exhausted by his efforts to secure the plant, he decides to rest; and, while he is sleeping, a serpent slithers up, eats the plant, and sloughs its skin as it slithers off again. When he awakes, Gilgamesh weeps not only for himself but for all of humankind; for this was the last chance not to die, one by one, forever. See *The Epic of Gilgamesh,* trans. Kovacs, pp. 106–7, lines 266–309.

The serpent in Genesis, of course, requires no introduction. There too, through the intervention of the serpent, the tree of life is lost and, with it, immortal youth.

Finally, a possible and intriguing link between Helen and the cultic elements preserved in the Glaukos myth is suggested by Nilsson when he states: "From the archaic age onwards the symbols of the Dioscuri are two amphoras, and reliefs and coins show one or both of the amphoras entwined with snakes, or snakes approaching the amphoras" (*The Minoan-Mycenaean Religion and its Survival in*

*Greek Religion*, p. 320). Like the snake in the Glaukos myth, the Dioskouroi are here understood as house gods, who appear as snakes and receive offerings left for them in earthenware vessels.

43. See Robert Graves, *The Greek Myths* (Mt. Kisco: Moyer Bell, 1960), 90: d, e.

44. Hope, which remains in the pithos to greet those who reenter it in death, is accorded little if any significance in Hesiod. The *Works and Days* presents what no one I know would call a hopeful picture. The timeless hope that the earth, the womb of all life, is a place from which anyone is born a second time seems to have left the kind of impression in Hesiod that plants leave in stones: the silent trace of life in the lifeless. *Elpis* or hope is nothing but a fossil from a forgotten time when the womb of woman and of the Mother Earth was the source not only of life but of its endless renewal.

45. Erich Neumann holds the central archetypal symbol of woman as vessel to be "the essence of the feminine." "The basic symbolic equation woman = body = vessel corresponds," by his account, "to what is perhaps mankind's—man's as well as woman's—most elementary experience of the Feminine" (*Great Mother*, p. 39). Interestingly, the Old Egyptian hieroglyph for woman is a pot. See Robert Briffault, *The Mothers* (New York: Johnson Reprint, 1969), 3:473–74.

46. See Gimbutas, *Language of the Goddess, passim*, particularly pp. 7, 21, 22, 37. Frequently, these vessels took the form of a bird-woman, surrounded by symbols indicating the presence of water and/or trees, the primeval waters and the tree of life. Clearly, both Aphrodite's and Helen's close association with fertility, death, trees, birds, and water suggest that we may find in these oldest pots their faint reflection. Indeed, the claim was made in ancient times that the very first bowl was shaped by using Helen's breast as a mold. See Briffault, *The Mothers*, 1:473.

Commenting on the identification of woman and pot, Erich Neumann points out: "The vessel character of the Feminine is often emphasized by a duplication of the jar: the woman represented as a jar carries a second jar" (*Great Mother*, p.121). In this same context, B. Johnson writes: "A figure from the Hisarlik site of Troy furnishes a curious duplication: The Pot Mother holds a jar on her head; at the same time she carries in her hands a small vessel connected to her larger pot body. The pot, in turn, represents the inexhaustible womb of the Bird Goddess, the primeval deep" (*Lady of the Beasts*, p. 49; see also pp. 38–50).

47. See Hesiod, *Theogony* (Oxford), 571; *Works and Days* (Oxford), 60–62. P. Walcot finds a possible model for this episode in a scene depicted in the already mentioned reliefs on the funerary temple of Hatshepsut at Deir el-Bahari. In a series of these reliefs, the ram-god Khnum is ordered by the high god Amon to fashion Hatshepsut and her *ka*, her life-force, which he proceeds to do on what appears to be a potter's wheel (*Hesiod and the Near East*, p. 67). See also Brunner, *Die Geburt des Göttkonigs*, p. 68.

48. In referring here and in the following discussion to Hephaestos as a "man," I am underlining his anthropomorphic masculinity. If it were not unduly awk-

ward, I might refer to him as a "man-god" or "he-god" in the same way that we speak of a "she-witch" or a "she-goat."

49. See John J. Winkler, *The Constraints of Desire: The Anthropology of Sex and Gender in Ancient Greece* (New York: Routledge, 1990), Appendix 2, "*Phusis* and *Natura* Meaning 'Genitals,'" pp. 217–20.

50. According to Robert Lamberton, the unspoken claim of Hesiod is that "the female genitals are the source of all evil" (*Hesiod*, p. 102).

51. The name given to the first woman by Adam, after the Fall, is Eve or *hāwwa*, the "mother of all the living" (Genesis 3:20). Quite another interpretation of Eve's name, however, is suggested by the fact that in Aramaic it means "serpent." See Stephen Langdon, *The Sumerian Epic of Paradise, the Flood and the Fall of Man,* University Museum Publications of the Babylonian Section, vol. 10, no. 1 (Philadelphia: University of Pennsylvania Press, 1915), pp. 36–37.

The prior and more essentially definitive name given to the first woman by God Yahweh at her creation is *ʾissā*, the one "taken from man" (*ʾīs*, Genesis 2:23). Here, she appears to be the source neither of all living things as they were meant to be, nor of Adam, original "man." Her only brood is fallen human beings, who were never meant to be and must wrest their livelihood from nature. They must take everything they get from the earth's withholding grasp until it holds them in its grasp forever.

Eve's organic derivation from Adam in the J text is indeed curious. There are myriad interpretations of Eve's origination from Adam's rib, which mostly come down to her inferiority, dependence, and consequent subservience. An interesting alternative is suggested by a Sumerian poem, which Kramer entitles "Enki and Ninhursag: The Affairs of the Water-God." Its two central characters are Enki and Ninhursag, who, under the name of Nintu, may have once been identical with Earth. In this poem, Enki is cursed by Ninhursag for having eaten eight plants, sprouts from Uttu herself, great-granddaughter of Ninhursag and goddess of plants. Eventually, Ninhursag withdraws her curses from the ailing Enki, who hurts all over. For each of his many pains, Ninhursag gives birth to a healing deity. The most relevant section reads as follows:

*Ninhursag:* "My brother, what hurts thee?"

*Enki:* "My rib hurts me."

*Ninhursag:* "To the goddess Ninti I gave birth for thee."

(Kramer, *Sumerian Mythology*, pp. 54–59).

Gerda Lerner, in commenting on this same passage, adds the salient fact that "in Sumerian, the word 'Ninti' has a double meaning, namely 'female ruler of the rib' and 'female ruler of life,' a meaning so close to the meaning of Hebrew *hāwwa*, that "there may be a fusion of the Sumerian Ninti with the Biblical Eve" (*Creation of Patriarchy*, p. 185).

52. Briffault, *The Mothers*, 1:466.

53. See Kramer's discussion of the myth of *Enki and Ninmah*, the Sumerian forerunner to *Atrahasis* (*Sumerian Mythology*, pp. 68–72). In the Old Babylonian ver-

sion of *Atrahasis*, Nintu, "birth-lady"—also called Mami, identical with Ninhursag, whose epithets include "womb-goddess," "mother of the gods," and "mother of all children"—entered the "room of fate" where "the womb-goddesses were assembled." There she pinched off fourteen pieces of clay, which she gave to the womb-goddesses, who created seven males and seven females. See *Atrahasis I*, in *Myths from Mesopotamia*, trans. Dalley, p. 14. In the *Gilgamesh*, it is this same goddess, under the name of Aruru, who pinches off a piece of clay and fashions Enkidu. See *Gilgamesh*, in *Myths from Mesopotamia*, trans. Dalley, pp. 52–53; and Jeffrey H. Tigay, *The Evolution of the Gilgamesh Epic* (Philadelphia: University of Pennsylvania Press, 1982), chapter 10, "The Creation of Enkidu," pp. 192–97. For a discussion of similarities between the creation of Enkidu and the creation of Adam and Eve, see Morris Jastrow, "Adam and Eve in Babylonian Literature," *American Journal of Semitic Languages and Literatures* 15 (1899): 193–214; and *The Religion of Babylonia and Assyria* (Boston: Ginn, 1898), chapter 23. See also Alexander Heidel, *The Babylonian Genesis* (Chicago: University of Chicago Press, 1942).

54. See Marilyn B. Arthur, "Cultural Strategies in Hesiod's *Theogony*: Law, Family, Society," *Arethusa* 15 (1982): 74–79, and "The Dream of a World without Women: Poetics and Circles of Order in the Theogony Prooemium," *Arethusa* 16 (1983): 102–4, for a consideration of the meaning of *gastēr* in Hesiod and Homer.

55. Hesiod, *Theogony* (Oxford), 158.

56. Ibid., 487.

57. Ibid., 483.

58. See ibid., 596–99.

59. M. B. Arthur lists a number of epithets attached to the *gastēr* in the *Odyssey*: "hateful" (*stygerē*), "deadly" (*oulomenēs*), "greedy" (*analton*), "insistent" (*memauian*), "dismal" (*lygrēs*), "unappeasable" (*margēi*), "evildoing" (*kakoergos*), and a cause for reproach (*oneidizōn*) ("The Dream of a World without Women," p. 102). See Homer, *Odyssey*, 7.216, 15.344, 17.228 = 18.364, 17.286, 17.473, 18.2, 18.53, 18.380.

60. Hesiod, *Theogony & Works and Days*, trans. West, p. 25, line 731.

61. See *Theogony* (Oxford), 721–33.

62. See Hesiod, *Theogony & Works and Days*, trans. West, p. 70, note to line 727; and Walcot, *Hesiod and the Near East*, p. 61. The *pithos* imagined by Hesiod in his description of Tartaros is made not of clay but of bronze, like the jar in which Ares was confined and from which he was delivered by Hermes. See Homer, *Iliad* (Loeb), 385–91. Whether made of bronze or of clay, however, the pithos was widely understood as a symbol of the underworld. "It is of interest to note," comments Persson, "that one of the meanings of the word pithos during the classical period was 'the kingdom of the dead,' Hades. The frequent, often humorous stories which are connected with the the pithos or storage vessel in later mythology show how widespread this idea must have been at one time (cf. Gruppe, *Griechische Mythologie*, p. 816)" (*Religion of Greece in Prehistoric Times*, p. 17).

That the Romans too envisioned the underworld as a kind of pot is argued by H. Wagenvoort, *Studies in Roman Literature, Culture and Religion* (Leiden: E. J. Brill, 1956), pp. 102–31.

63. See Garland, *Greek Way of Death,* p. 54, on whose description of this vase I rely in my account. The scene on this vase would appear to confirm the identification of Ares' "*pithos*-prison," discussed above, as indeed Tartaros.

64. See Hesiod, *Theogony & Works and Days,* trans. West, p. 64, note to line 116 of the *Theogony.*

65. Hesiod, *Works and Days* (Oxford), 563.

66. See Hesiod, *Theogony* (Oxford), 116–17.

67. Among the several prominent Egyptian myths of creation, the Heliopolitan, which may be traced to the second and third dynasties in the Old Kingdom, came to be the most widely accepted. This myth was centered in On, or Heliopolis (its Greek name), the eminent center of the Egyptian cult of the sun. It was here (six miles northeast of modern Cairo), at the apex of the Nile delta, that the annual floodwaters of the Nile would first begin to recede, revealing the rich earth buried below. This yearly sight was, for the Egyptians, an image of the first emergence of earth, on which the creation of the world took place. The sun-temple of On was itself said to have been built over that primeval hill on which creation began.

In the Hermapolitan myth, referred to in Pyramid texts, that same primeval hill was envisioned as an island—the Isle of Flames—circled by the waters of chaos and death. This island, before the drama of creation began, rose from the dark chaotic waters and provided a place of appearance for the Ogdoad, the eight deities—four male and four female—who created an egg from which broke forth the sun who fashioned humankind and ordered the world. In a variant version, the sun was born on this same hill from a lotus flower, while from the primordial egg there came the first sacred goose. For texts and commentary, see James B. Pritchard, *The Ancient Near East* (Princeton: Princeton University Press, 1958), 1:1–3; H. Frankfort, H. A. Frankfort, J. A. Wilson, Thorkild Jacobsen, and W. A. Irwin, *The Intellectual Adventure of Ancient Man* (Chicago: University of Chicago Press, 1946), pp. 50–61; Henri Frankfort, *Ancient Egyptian Religion* (New York: Harper & Row, 1948), pp. 20–22, 154.

68. Hesiod, *Theogony & Works and Days,* trans. West, p. 40, lines 106–8. See also fragment 1.6 in Merkelbach-West, *Fragmenta Hesiodea* (Oxford: Oxford University Press, 1967), pp. 3ff. For a discussion of this passage and of counterinterpretations to that one suggested here, see Pucci, *Hesiod and the Language of Poetry,* pp. 88–89, and n. 14, p. 117–18.

69. Hesiod, *Theogony* (Oxford), 582, translation mine. The word for earth here is *ēpeiros,* "solid land," as opposed to sea. Specifically in Egypt, this word was used to name that land rising above the floodwaters, suggesting a clear link to the primeval hillock of creation. See Liddell and Scott, revised by Jones with McKenzie, *A Greek-English Lexicon* (Oxford: Clarendon, 1968), p. 7776, s.v. *ēpeiros.*

70. See Hesiod, *Theogony* (Oxford), 211–25.

71. See ibid., 226–33.

72. Ibid., 126.

73. Ibid., 120.

74. Ibid., 881–85.

75. Marduk of Babylon, Assur of Assyria, Yahweh of Israel, and Zeus of Greece represent a new breed, as it were, of Iron Age "strongmen," who are marked by militarism and absolute power. See Mark S. Smith, *Early History of God*, p. 56. Two other Near Eastern storm-gods, Baal and Teshub, in their respective myth cycles, know defeat as well as victory, and even when victorious are not always single-handedly so. See Walcot, *Hesiod and the Near East*, p. 25. Many of Baal's enemies, for example, are defeated not by him but by Anat. A mythic cycle with perhaps even closer links to the *Theogony* is the Hurrian Kumarbi Cycle, in which the central contest for kingship among the gods is between Teshub and Kumarbi. Ea, the Mesopotamian god of wisdom, who in the *Song of Kumarbi* is the foe of Teshub and the ally of Kumarbi, eventually changes sides and, in the *Song of Ullikummi*, becomes altogether crucial to Teshub's final success. See Hoffner and Beckman, *Hittite Myths*, II. "Hurrian Myths," pp. 38–61, especially Nos. 14 and 18. Then too, there is the cosmic and dynastic combat of Seth and Horus (see E. A. Wallis Budge, *The Gods of the Egyptians* [New York: Dover, 1969], 2:241–60) in which the victory of Horus is neither unassisted nor total, as indicated by the fact that in the reliefs depicting Queen Hatshepsut's coronation, the twin crowns of upper and lower Egypt are placed on her head not by Horus alone but by both Horus and Seth together (see Henri Frankfort, *Kingship and the Gods* [Chicago: University of Chicago Press, 1972], pp. 106–7).

76. Hesiod, *Theogony* (Oxford), 884.

77. In books 1 and 2 of the *Iliad*, this issue informs and even defines the contest between Agamemnon and Achilles over who is the "Best of the Achaeans." It is at root a contest between the scepter, which Agamemnon carries and claims to be traceable to Zeus, and the spear, in the use of which Achilles is peerless. These two symbols, the scepter and the spear, represent the two essential elements of divine kingship: authority and force. Both are ultimately divine. Clearly, Zeus possesses both and rules accordingly. When his word is questioned, his fire decides the matter (see Homer, *Iliad* [Loeb], 1..580–81; 8.5–27). On earth, in cities, among men, there is rarely if ever the convergence of wisdom and power. Homer knew this as well as did Plato. The question this raises is whether the Olympian paradigm—the perfect coincidence of authority and power—can ever be replicated in the human realm. Then, if the answer is no, if we must choose between brute force and right counsel, the question becomes whether we choose to be governed by only one element of the divine paradigm or find, instead, another paradigm altogether for the formation and governance of human community. Homer, I believe, sought the latter path and with it a new definition of "the Best of the Achaeans."

78. See *Myths from Mesopotamia*, trans. Dalley, *The Epic of Creation*, tablet VII, pp. 267–74.

79. Ibid., p. 272.

80. Ibid., p. 273: "With fifty epithets the great gods called his fifty names, making his way supreme."

81. Hesiod, *Theogony* (Oxford ), 886.

82. Marcel Detienne and Jean-Pierre Vernant, *Cunning Intelligence in Greek Culture and Society* (Chicago: University of Chicago Press, 1991), p. 109. From this they go on to explain: "Because all the *mētis* in the world, all the unexpected possibilities which cunning time conceals are now within Zeus, sovereignty ceases to be the stake played for in a series of indefinitely repeated conflicts and becomes, instead, a stable and permanent state. At this point the king of the gods can celebrate his marriage to Themis and beget fine children for her: the Seasons and the Fates. His irrevocable decisions have fixed the succession of future events as it has [*sic*] the hierarchy of the different functions, ranks and honours. He has settled them by ordinance once and for all. Whatever comes to pass in the future has, for all time, already been foreseen and determined in the head of Zeus."

83. Hesiod, *Theogony* (Oxford ), 899.

84. Ibid., 891. The reaction of Gaia to the birth of Athena, as recorded in the first Homeric *Hymn to Athena*, seems a bit more authentic. When she, we are told, together with the rest of the immortals, saw Athena "jump suddenly out of his [Zeus's] sacred head shaking her sharp spear . . . the earth groaned awfully" (*The Homeric Hymns*, translated by Charles Boer [Chicago: Swallow, 1970], p. 137).

85. See Jane Ellen Harrison, *Prolegomena to the Study of Greek Religion* (Princeton: Princeton University Press, 1991), pp. 300–307.

86. Walcot, *Hesiod and the Near East*, pp. 113–14.

87. See F. Brommer, "Die Geburt der Athena," *Jahrbuch Römisch-Germanisches Zentralmuseum* 8 (1961): 72–73.

88. Jean-Pierre Vernant, "Hestia Hermès: Sur l'expression religieuse de l'espace et du mouvement chez les Grecs," in *Mythe et pensée chez les Grecs* (Paris: F. Maspero, 1965), p. 124; see Arthur, "The Dream of a World without Women," p. 97.

89. Christine Downing, *The Goddess* (New York: Crossroad, 1987), p. 154.

90. Arthur, "Cultural Strategies in Hesiod's *Theogony*," p. 75.

91. See L. R. Farnell, *The Cults of the Greek States* (Oxford: Clarendon, 1896–1909), 3:25.

92. Hesiod, *Theogony* (Oxford), 591.

93. Walter F. Otto, *The Homeric Gods: The Spiritual Significance of Greek Religion* (Boston: Beacon Press, 1954), p. 102. Pucci points out that "Aphrodite does not appear, but sends in her place some of her occasional helpers to beautify Pandora. The goddess is, then," he concludes, "*vicariously* represented by the Charities, Peitho, and the Horai, all of whom may bespeak her, but none of whom is a univocal 'sign' of Aphrodite" (*Hesiod and the Language of Poetry*, p. 96).

94. See Farnell, *Cults of the Greek States,* 5:624.

95. *Sappho,* translated by Mary Barnard (Berkeley: University of California Press, 1958), #65.

96. Again, for a thorough presentation and discussion of the ancient iconographic tradition depicting the varied abductions and retrievals of Helen and its relationship to the poetic tradition's treatment of the same theme, see Lilly B. Ghali-Kahil, *Les enlèvements et le retour d'Hélène, dans les textes et les documents figurés,* École Francaise D'Athènes, Travaux et Mémoires (Paris: E. de Boccard, 1955).

97. Semonides, 96,115, translation mine. For Greek text, commentary, and a complete translation, see Hugh Lloyd-Jones, *Female of the Species* (London: Duckworth, 1975).

98. Ibid., 1–2.

99. Ibid., 94–95.

100. Ibid., 96–100, 115–18, as above, translation mine.

101. See Herodotus, *The History* (Loeb), 1.105.

102. See Jeremiah 7:17; 44:18.

103. Aeschylus, *Eumenides* (Loeb), 1.

104. Farnell speaks of Demeter as "the brightest of all Gaia's emanations," and states that "her individuality was rooted in the primitive and less developed personality of Gaia" (*Cults of the Greek States,* 3:28; 3:30).

105. See Plato, *Menexenus* (Loeb), 238a.

106. *Homeric Hymns,* trans. Boer, p. 5.


## Chapter 4: The First Helen

1. Nikos Kazantzakis, *The Last Temptation of Christ,* translated by P. A. Bien (New York: Simon & Schuster, 1960), p. 457.

2. Elinor W. Gadon, *The Once and Future Goddess* (New York: Harper & Row, 1989), p. 3; see also Randall White, *Dark Caves, Bright Visions: Life in Ice Age Europe* (New York: American Museum of Natural History, 1986), p. 65.

3. The imprecise and uncertain scope of our understanding of human imaginative life may be put in a somewhat reassuring perspective by recalling that as recently as 1650, James Usher, the archbishop of Armagh, in what is now Northern Ireland, was confident in his calculations that creation occurred in the year 4004 B.C.E., calculations that John Lightfoot, Master of St. Catherine's College, University of Cambridge, made even more precise by adding the exact date and time of day: the twenty-third of October at 9:00 A.M. See Richard E. Leakey, "Prehistory," in *The Penguin Encyclopedia of Ancient Civilizations,* ed. Arthur Cotterell (London: Penguin, 1988), p. 9.

4. D. H. Trump, *The Prehistory of the Mediterranean* (New Haven: Yale University Press, 1980), p. 15.

5. Paleolithic dead were frequently buried in a contracted or fetal position, with the hands often folded across the chest. Their bones are found to be impregnated with red ochre, apparently symbolizing blood and the life-force; and they are accompanied by gifts. E. O. James suggests that the staining of skeletons with red ochreous powder, the color of blood, "the life-giving agent *par excellence* . . . was doubtless an attempt to make the deceased live again in his revivified body" (*Myth and Ritual in the Ancient Near East* [London: Thames & Hudson, 1958], p. 34). Usually these burials occurred close within the houses of the living, often beneath the family hearth. "That is to say," writes G. R. Levy, summing up the evidence, "the rich Paleolithic material of Europe and Asia combines to demonstrate a belief that the dead remained a part of the family or group, that they kept their association with the grave and its furniture, that their presence, if at all feared . . . was still more strongly desired, and sometimes at least retained by cult; that the attitude, in short, of the living towards the dead, bore less resemblance to the beliefs of recent primitives, than to those of the Neolithic and Bronze Age civilizations, which regarded the body and its tomb as a continuous link between the two phases of existence" (*The Gate of Horn* [London: Faber & Faber, 1948], p. 70).

6. Levy, *Gate of Horn*, p. 83.

7. Marija Gimbutas, *The Language of the Goddess* (New York: Harper & Row, 1989), p. xix.

8. "The earliest representations of the female divinity were vulvas as *pars pro toto*," writes Marija Gimbutas, "engraved on rocks during the Aurignacian period of some 30,000 years B.C.E. . . . The emphasis on vulvas in the figurine art of later epochs makes it clear that those of the Upper Paleolithic are not merely 'female signs' . . . but instead symbolize the vulva and womb of the Goddess" (*Language of the Goddess*, p. 99).

The later passage graves, including the *tholos* tombs of Mycenaean Greece, likely represented the vagina and uterus, the earth-womb from which the dead would be reborn. See M. Dames, *The Avebury Cycle* (London: Thames & Hudson, 1977), p. 30.

9. Eventually, these figurines provided the architectural pattern for recognizably anthropomorphic temples and tombs, most notably the temples of Malta. See E. O. James, *Prehistoric Religion* ( New York: Barnes & Noble, 1957), pp. 153 ff.; and Gimbutas, *Language of the Goddess*, pp. 153–54.

10. Marija Gimbutas's recent work *The Civilization of the Goddess*, cited above, offers the most thorough and insightful account to date of the virtual language of symbols encountered in the art of "Old Europe" (6500–3500 B.C.E.). Moreover, within this symbolic language, Gimbutas seems to have discerned an actual script, already in common use among all of the most advanced cultures of Old Europe some two thousand years prior to the appearance of writing in Sumer. Inasmuch as this Old European script is found exclusively on cult objects, Gimbutas suggests that it was a sacred script comprised of sacred hieroglyphs. Gimbutas has identi-

fied, within this script, roughly thirty core signs and over one hundred modified signs. Many of these signs are remarkably similar to those of the early Bronze Age scripts found, for example, on Crete and Cyprus. For a full discussion of this script, see Marija Gimbutas, "The Sacred Script," section 8 of *The Civilization of the Goddess* (New York: Harper Collins, 1991), pp. 308–21. Throughout this chapter I am particularly indebted to the work of Professor Gimbutas. See also Shan M. M. Winn, *Pre-writing in Southeastern Europe: The Sign System of the Vincâ Culture ca. 4000 B.C.* (Calgary: Western Publishers, 1981); and Harold Haarmann, "Writing from Old Europe," *Journal of Indo-European Studies* 17.3–4 (1989): 251–75.

11. With reference to the nudity of these female figurines of the Great Goddess, so closely identified with the Earth, it may be relevant to make note of a ritual practiced in India, even in modern times. It is said that when there is a drought women go out during the night into the parched fields and strip themselves naked. In twos, they yoke themselves to plows, as a third woman drives each "team," all the while crying out for relief to the Earth Mother. See William Crooke, *Religion and Folklore of Northern India* (Oxford: Oxford University Press, 1926), pp. 46–47.

12. Vincent Scully, *The Earth, the Temple, and the Gods* (New Haven: Yale University Press, 1962), p. 11.

13. In Paleolithic and Neolitihic art, black is the color of fertility and red the color of life. The significance of these colors is reversed in Indo-European art, wherein white and gold represent life, while black is the color of death.

14. This aspect of the Goddess as the "Terrible Mother" is later embodied and personified, for example, in the Egyptian underworld goddess Ammit, "the Eater of the Dead," imagined with the forequarters of a crocodile, the hindquarters of a hippopotamus, and the body of a lion or leopard. From her mouth come forth flames to consume the souls of the dead. On the day of judgment, when the heart of the deceased is placed in the balance with the feather of Maat, goddess of justice, Ammit waits, poised to seize and to swallow the too-heavy heart of anyone found unfit to live on in the land of the West, the kingdom of Osiris. See E. A. Wallis Budge, *The Gods of the Egyptians* (New York: Dover, 1969), 1:60, 218. Another, far more benevolent Egyptian "devouress" is the goddess Nut, the sky-goddess, sometimes envisioned as a celestial cow but most often taking human form, her naked body stretched out over the earth to form the vault of heaven. Her body is the wall between order and chaos, being and non-being. She is both the day and the night sky. At the end of each day, she swallows Ra and his entourage, circling the earth in his solar barque. All night, amidst the stars, they journey safely through her body and, at dawn, the "hour of labor," pass through her vagina into day, reborn (ibid., 2:100–112).

In the Sumerian underworld it is Erishkigal, dark—deadly sister and other self of Inanna, Queen of Heaven—to whom lost souls descend, passing through seven gates, which perhaps represent the seven planetary positions of Inanna/Ishtar

(Venus) on her descent and return. See Sylvia Brinton Perera, *Descent to the Goddess* (Toronto: Inner City, 1981), p. 61. In India, the "Terrible Mother" takes its most dreadful form in Kali, goddess of war and death, "dark, all-devouring time, the bone-wreathed Lady of the place of skulls," with whom Draupadi was eventually identified. See Heinrich Zimmer, "The Indian World Mother" in *The Mystic Vision*, Papers from the Eranos Yearbooks: 6, Bollingen Series 30 (Princeton: Princeton University Press, 1968), p. 81. Finally, in Greek myth, the gorgon Medusa is known as the mistress of the West gate, the mouth of death.

15. See W. K. C. Guthrie, *The Greeks and Their Gods* (London: Methuen, 1954), pp. 218.

16. Among the later incarnations of the crone are the Graiai—Fear, Dread, and Terror—who dwell in the west at the edge of the cosmic ocean, where day turns to night and life gives way to death. See Erich Neumann, *The Origins and History of Consciousness*, Bollingen Series 42 (Princeton: Princeton University Press, 1954), p. 214.

17. Gimbutas, *Language of the Goddess*, p. 321.

18. Ibid.

19. Gerda Lerner presents quite concisely the existing evidence for a prehistoric cult of the Great Goddess and discusses pointedly the methodologically precarious character of current reconstructions of that cult. "At best," she argues, "we can say that a profusion of female figurines with sexual features emphasizing maternity found in the Neolithic correspond to later mythological and literary material celebrating the power of female goddesses over fertility and fecundity" (*Creation of Patriarchy* [New York: Oxford University Press, 1986], p. 148; see pp. 146–49). On the question of reconstructing ancient religions from partial evidence and limited understanding, see also A. Leo Oppenheim, *Ancient Mesopotamia: Portrait of a Dead Civilization* (Chicago: University of Chicago Press, 1964), specifically his discussion entitled "Why a 'Mesopotamian Religion' Should not be Written," pp. 172–83.

20. Marija Gimbutas, "The Temples of Old Europe," *Archaeological Institute of America* 33 (1980): 46. The term "Old Europe" is used here and throughout our considerations to designate southeastern Europe, as far north as Czechoslovakia, southern Poland and the western Ukraine, during the Neolithic-Chalcolithic period, more specifically during the seventh, sixth, and fifth millennia. See Marija Gimbutas, *The Goddesses and Gods of Old Europe* (Berkeley: University of California Press, 1982), p. 17.

21. J. J. Bachofen, *Myth, Religion, and Mother Right*, Bollingen Series 84 (Princeton: Princeton University Press, 1973), p. 171. In fact, Bachofen adds: "and the higher woman's social position will be." On this point, however, there is nothing approaching consensus. If there exists any predictable correlation between the cult status of goddesses and the social status of women, it has yet to be demonstrated. For a careful, preliminary study of this question, see Peggy Sanday, "Female Status in the Public Domain," in Michelle Rosaldo and Louise Lam-

phere, eds., *Women, Culture, and Society* (Stanford: Stanford University Press, 1974), pp. 189–206.

22. Axel W. Persson, *The Religion of Greece in Prehistoric Times* (Berkeley: University of California Press, 1942), p. 1. Similarly, Alain Daniélou speaks of a single "great cultural movement extending from India to Portugal" in the sixth millennium B.C.E. (*Shiva and Dionysus,* translated by E. F. Hurry [London: East-West Publications, 1982], p. 32).

23. Ibid., pp. 32, 3, 163.

24. John Marshall, ed., *Mohenjo-Daro and the Indus Civilization: Being an official account of the Archaeological Excavations at Mohenjo-daro carried out by the Government of India between the years 1922 and 1927* (London: Arthur Probsthain, 1931), 1:76.

25. J. L. Myres, for example, suggests that the cult of the Mother Goddess traveled from Anatolia or Syria to Mesopotamia (*Cambridge Ancient History* [New York: Macmillan, 1924], 1:91). S. Langdon, on the other hand, argues for the reverse direction of influence, originating from Nippur, his candidate for the "pre-historic seat of the worship of the Earth Mother" (ibid., p. 444). Jacques Jean Marie de Morgan too would trace the diffusion of the cult westwards from Mesopotamia into Anatolia (*Prehistoric Man* [New York: Alfred A. Knopf, 1925], p. 250). Summing up this question in his own day, John Marshall says of the cult of the Great Goddess: "Wherever its cradle, it must have been spread over the Near and Middle East in the Neolithic, if not the Paleolithic age" (*Mohenjo-Daro and the Indus Civilization,* p. 50 n. 4). When due recognition is given, however, to the relevant archaeological discoveries from Old Europe, these earlier debates become largely moot.

26. Marshall, *Mohenjo-Daro and the Indus Civilization,* p. 51. "Nor can it be doubted," adds Ananda K. Coomaraswamy, "that a cult of the One Madonna existed already in the Paleolithic Age" (*The Ṛg Veda as land-náma-bók* [London: Luzak, 1935], p. 2 of Introduction).

27. See Martin P. Nilsson, *The Minoan-Mycenaean Religion and its Survival in Greek Religion* (Lund: Gleerup, 1950), pp. 392–96, for a thoughtful and provocative discussion of what he labels the "hypothesis of the Great Goddess."

28. On this question of monotheism confronting polytheism, see A. Leo Oppenheim, *Ancient Mesopotamia,* p. 182, where he proposes that "neither the number of deities worshipped nor the absence or presence of definite (and carefully worded) answers to the eternal and unanswerable questions of man separate decisively a polytheistic from a monotheistic religion. Rather, it seems to be the criterion of a plurality of intellectual and spiritual dimensions that sets off most of the polytheistic religions from the narrowness, the one-dimensional pressure of revealed religions."

29. See Nilsson, *Minoan-Mycenaean Religion,* p. 392; see also his *History of Greek Religion* (Oxford: Clarendon, 1925), p. 18. While this comment is made by Nilsson with specific reference to the question of Minoan monotheism, the arguments and

cautions that he sets forth would seem to have immediate relevance to the wider question of monotheism in the cult of the Great Goddess before and beyond Minoan Crete. Among the scholars whom Nilsson has in mind here are A. J. Evans, S. Marinatos, A. W. Persson, L. R. Farnell, and A. J. B. Wace, who stressed the unity of the Minoan Goddess amidst her many manifestations and cult names.

30. It is not surprising that the date of this discovery is difficult to determine. It is generally assumed that there was no understanding of the causal connection between sexual intercourse and human reproduction during the Upper Paleolithic period and quite possibly during the Neolithic period. The fact that in Paleolithic art the vulva is often associated with animal and plant life and that a phallus is sometimes depicted within the vulva suggests an appreciation of both intercourse and reproduction but not of the precise relationship between them. In this matter, metaphor alone is clearly insufficient.

31. Gimbutas, *Language of the Goddess,* p. 316.

32. Gimbutas, *Goddesses and Gods of Old Europe,* p. 9. Ithyphallic fertility daimones—likely the antecedents of later satyrs, sileni, and centaurs—are well known from Paleolithic and Neolithic art. Their function, suggests Gimbutas, "is to magically help the Earth Maiden rise from underground at spring, or to stimulate life powers in general, particularly the growth of plants" (*Language of the Goddess,* p. 178).

33. The unilateral starkness of this assertion pales, of course, before the counter-assertion of Paul: "For man did not come from woman; no, woman came from man" (1 Corinthians 11:8; *The Jerusalem Bible* [London: Darton, Longman & Todd, 1966]). Paul, unavoidably, concedes that men are born from women; but this fact is as irrelevant to his essential understanding of things as was the fact of intercourse to his stone-age counterparts.

34. After showing how the earth (*gē*) has proved that she is the mother of all humankind by bringing forth wheat and barley to nourish her children, Plato offers another proof that the earth is the true mother of all humankind: "it is not the earth who, in conceiving and in giving birth, imitates woman; rather, it is woman who imitates the earth" (*Menexenus* [Loeb], 238a, translation mine).

35. Budge, *Gods of the Egyptians,* 1:462.

36. See Alexander Marshack, *The Roots of Civilization: The Cognitive Beginnings of Man's First Art, Symbol, and Notation* (New York: McGraw-Hill, 1972), pp. 289–93. Gimbutas suggests that the divine bisexuality of the Neolithic Goddess "stresses her absolute power" (*Goddesses and Gods of Old Europe,* p. 196).

37. See H. Swiny and S. Swiny, "An Anthropomorphic Figurine from the Sotira Area," *Report of the Department of Antiquities Cyprus* (Nikosia: Department of Antiquities, 1983), p. 58.

38. See R. J. H. Jenkins in *Perachora* 1 (Oxford: Oxford University Press, 1940), no. 183, pp. 231–32; and P. J. Riis, "The Syrian Astarte Plaques and their Western Connections," *Berytus* 9 (1948–49), plate xix, 1.

39. "In Old Europe," writes Gimbutas, "the world of myth was not polarized into female and male as it was among the Indo-European and many other nomadic and pastoral peoples of the steppes. Both principles were manifest side by side. The male divinity in the shape of a young man or a male animal appears to affirm and strengthen the forces of the creative and active female. Neither is subordinate to the other; by complementing one another, their power is doubled" (*Goddesses and Gods of Old Europe*, p. 237).

40. The iconic divorce of male and female attributes, which can be traced to the sixth millennium, may provide some rough clue to the timing of this event in Old Europe. Regarding the introduction of the drama of hierogamy, Gimbutas suggests: "It seems unlikely to have been later than c. 6500 BC, when the 'phallic obsession' became manifest through representation of phallic stands, cups, and ithyphallic gods" (*Goddesses and Gods of Old Europe*, p. 230).

41. "With the establishment of husbandry and the domestication of flocks and herds, however," writes E. O. James, "the function of the male in the process of generation became more apparent and vital as the physiological facts concerning paternity were more clearly understood and recognized. Then the mother-goddess was assigned a male partner, either in the capacity of her son and lover, or of a brother and husband. Nevertheless, although he was the begetter of life he occupied a subordinate position to her, being in fact a secondary figure in the cultus" (*The Cult of the Mother-Goddess: An Archaeological and Documentary Study* [London: Thames & Hudson, 1959], p. 228). See also Elizabeth Fisher, *Woman's Creation: Sexual Evolution and the Shaping of Society* (Garden City, N.Y.: Doubleday, 1979), chapter 19.

42. In classical Athens, according to *The Athenian Constitution* (III.5), traditionally attributed to Aristotle, the sacred marriage between Queen Archon and Dionysos took place in the *Bucholion* or "cattle shed," the residence of King Archon of Athens. Fossilized in this custom and name is an image from a far earlier time. Indeed, thousands of years earlier throughout the Near East and in northwestern India, the ritual of the *hieros gamos* seems to have taken place, in a booth or hut, a *bucholion* of sorts. As a possible link between these times and between east and west, G. R. Levy points to the Greek legend of the Cretan Queen Pasiphae, who was enabled to mate with a sacred bull by means of a cow-effigy constructed by Daedalus, in which she was encased (*Gate of Horn*, p. 103; see also Jane Ellen Harrison, *Prolegomena to the Study of Greek Religion* [Princeton: Princeton University Press, 1991], pp. 534–37).

43. From the Paleolithic, the bison and, specifically, bison horns possessed a peculiar significance and power, which continued into the historic period, perhaps most notably in the omnipresent "horns of consecration" of Minoan Crete. Long before the bison or bull was understood as progenitor, however, it was seen as a prominent symbol and source of life energy. Indeed, the intimate connection, from earliest times, of the bull with the Great Goddess may be due to the remark-

able likeness of a woman's internal reproductive organs (possibly discovered as a result of the practice of excarnation) to the head and horns of a bull. See D. O. Cameron, *Symbols of Birth and of Death in the Neolithic Era* (London: Kenyon-Deane, 1981), pp. 4–5. The visual association of the bull's head with woman's uterus may account for myriad images in which new life—in the forms of flowing water, trees, butterflies, or bees—is seen to emerge from the bucranium or from between the abstracted horns of a bull. In this context, it is interesting to note that the only known word in ancient Greek for "butterfly"—often "born" from the skull or horns of a bull and perhaps taking stylized form in the *labrys* inserted into the Minoan horns of consecration—is *psychē*, "life-breath" or "soul." See Aristotle, *Historia Animalium* (Loeb), 551a; see also Jan Bremmer, *The Early Greek Concept of the Soul* (Princeton: Princeton University Press, 1983), p. 82.

Relevant to the emergence of bees and butterflies from bulls and to the association of these offspring with souls, we may note the following comments of Porphyry, *De ant. nym.*, 18: "The ancients gave the name of *Melissae* ('bees') to the priestesses of Demeter who were initiates of the chthonian goddess; the name *Melitodes* to Kore herself; the moon (Artemis) too, whose province it was to bring to the birth, they called Melissa, because the moon being a bull and its ascension the bull, bees are begotten of bulls. And souls that pass to the earth are bull-begotten." See Hilda M. Ransome, *The Sacred Bee in Ancient Times and Folklore* (New York & Boston: Houghton Mifflin, 1937), p. 107.

44. Hesiod, in the *Theogony* (477–84), acknowledges the birth of Zeus on Crete, where Gaia is said to have received him from his mother Rhea and to have hidden him away in a deep cave, safe from his father Kronos. Elsewhere, Zeus is said to have been born in a Cretan cave inhabited by bees and to have died and been buried in Crete, as well. The precise place of his burial was variously designated as Knossos, Mount Ida, and Mount Dikte. See Nilsson, *Minoan-Mycenaean Religion*, pp. 543, 553.

45. Universally, it seems, in the beginning and, in Minoan Crete, as late as the mid-second millennium, the Goddess is the dominant figure, and the god a quite lesser figure. The Goddess alone, the personification of everlasting life, is to be worshiped. "The young male god," write Persson, "embodies, not perpetual life, but transitory life—that which rises anew every spring, matures in the summer season, and withers away in the autumn" (*Religion of Greece in Prehistoric Times*, p. 122). Originally, it is the lesser god—a category including Zeus and Dionysos—not the Great Goddess who dies and is mourned, a pattern eventually broken and overturned by the removal of the gods from any contagion with death and their replacement by the dying *korē*, Persephone, the virgin daughter of Demeter.

46. The original throne of the Goddess seems to have been the very mountain of the Mountain Mother, the "lap" of the Mother of All. The Goddess herself is, then, "the throne" or "the seat," which is the meaning of the name *Isis*. All royal powers and prerogatives flow from her. See Erich Neumann, *The Great Mother: An Analysis of the Archetype*, Bollingen Series 47 (Princeton: Princeton University

Press, 1972), pp. 98–99. Thus, during the coronation ritual of ancient Egypt, the critical moment of royal accession occurs when the new king is enthroned and given his diadems and scepters. It is in this moment of "enthronement," when he is embraced by Isis, the deified throne, his very mother, that the king's supernatural powers pass to him. Later, when he dies, the dead king is said to go to heaven to sit on the "great throne which made the gods." See Henri Frankfort, *Kingship and the Gods* (Chicago: University of Chicago, 1978), pp. 43–44. Similarly, in Sumer, it is Inanna, Queen of Heaven and Earth, who invites her young consort Dumuzi to share her bed and her throne, both carved from the sacred *huluppu*-tree, once the house and body of the Goddess herself. See Diane Wolkstein and Samuel Noah Kramer, *Inanna: Queen of Heaven and Earth* (New York: Harper & Row, 1983), pp. 4–9, 42. Finally, in book 10 of the *Republic*, specifically in Plato's "Myth of Er," is a remarkable glimpse of the ancient Goddess as throne. After choosing their next lives—choices at once ratified and made irreversible by the Fates—the souls of the dead, Plato tells us, "without looking back passed under the throne of Necessity" (*Republic* [Loeb], X.620e–621a, translation mine), the goddess who turns in her lap the spindle which moves the sun and the stars and whose daughters weave the fabric of time, all of it, past, present, and future. The throne of the Goddess, through which souls pass on their way to birth and rebirth, is at the same time the gate of life, the gate of the universe, through which the sun is born with each new dawn. Caught in this one image is a timeless reflection of numberless prehistoric figures of the seated Goddess, some calmly enthroned, others braced to give birth.

47. The word *kóros* or *kouros* means both "lad" or "youth" and "sprout" or "shoot" (additionally, *kouroi* from *keirō*, "to cut" or "to clip," means "loppings" or "cuttings" pruned from a tree or plant), suggesting an originally vegetal conception of the Earth Mother's first male offspring, who like all young shoots would be cut back or would die as a matter of course in the winter's cold or the summer's heat, mourned by a Mother made barren until he is reborn from the same deep furrow or chasm in which he disappeared from life. A remarkable vestige of this primordial vegetal imagery may be found in the *Iliad*, wherein Thetis, the goddess-mother of Achilles, tells how "he shot up like a young branch, like a fine tree I reared him—the orchard's crowning glory" (Homer, *The Iliad*, translated by Robert Fagles [New York: Viking Penguin, 1990], 18.510–11 [437–38, Loeb]). Telemachos too, in the *Odyssey*, is likened to a young tree (14.175, Loeb). In fact, the goddess *Kourotrophos*, "Nurturer of Shoots," was reverenced as a distinct cult *persona* in Attica and elsewhere. See G. M. Quinn, "The Sacrificial Calendar of the Marathonian Tetrapolis" (dissertation, Harvard University Press, 1971), p. 153. Aphrodite's beloved Adonis, of course, seen in the microcosmic potted gardens left to perish prematurely in the sun—a Greek folk ritual with numerous counterparts throughout Europe and the Near East—is one more embodiment of the young *kouros*, beloved and mourned in his untimely death. Finally, in contrasting

the festival of Adonis with that of Demeter, John Winkler provides an interesting perspective on the appropriate subordination of the male in the celebration of life's mysteries. In the generation both of crops and of humans, writes Winkler, "Men's role . . . is to plow and to plant the seed. It is Mother Earth who does the eight months' labor, as it is human mothers who carry the long burden of human generation. . . . If any contrast is to be drawn between the respective roles of the sexes in cultivating these natural processes, men must be placed squarely on the side of Adonis, Aphrodite's eager but not long enduring lover. What the gardens with their quickly rising and quickly wilting sprouts symbolize is the marginal or subordinate role that men play in both agriculture (vis-à-vis the earth) and human generation (vis-à-vis wives and mothers)" (John J. Winkler, *The Constraints of Desire: The Anthropology of Sex and Gender in Ancient Greece* [New York Routledge, 1990], p. 205).

48. Marshall borrows this phrase from Monier Williams (see Sir Monier Monier-Williams, *Brahmanism and Hinduism* [New York: Macmillan, 1891], part 1, p. 180) to describe the underlying principle of Śaktism, an ancient form of worship that originated in India from the cult of the Mother Goddess and was closely connected with the cult of Śiva. So close is the resemblance between this cult and certain prehistoric cults in western Asia, that Marshall considers it likely to have existed among the Indus Valley people, despite the absence of any direct evidence to that effect among the finds at Mohenjo-daro or Harappa. In Śaktism, writes Marshall, "the goddess was transformed into a personification of female energy (*śaktī*) and, as the eternal productive principle (*prakriti*), united with the eternal male principle (*purusha*) and became the creator and Mother of the Universe . . . including the gods themselves" (Marshall, *Mohenjo-Daro and the Indus Civilization*, p. 57). This goddess, identified as the consort of Śiva, was herself "conceived as the creator of Śiva and superior to him . . . (and as) the supreme Goddess in the Śākta pantheon, reflecting in her own personality all female manifestations of the other divinities. Like Śiva himself she had a twofold nature. She was the power that creates and destroys; the womb from which all things proceed, to which all return; the mysterious force behind all appetites and passions. Like Śiva too, she was the archsorceress, giver of supernatural powers and magical faculties" (ibid).

Marshall is quite right, it would seem, in perceiving a number of parallels to Indian Saktism in certain pre-Aryan cults in the Near East, specifically the cults of Isis and Horus in Egypt, of Ashtaroth and Tammuz (Adonis) in Phoenicia, of Kybele and Attis in Asia Minor, and of Rhea and the young Zeus in Greece. "Everywhere," he writes, "she [the Great Mother Goddess] is unwed; but made the mother, first of her companion by immaculate conception, and then of the gods and all life by the embrace of her son" (*Mohenjo-Daro and the Indus Civilization*, p. 58). With reference to all of these cults, he points out: "Their central figure is a Mother or Nature Goddess, who out of her own being creates her partner God, just as the Indian Mother Goddess creates Śiva, and then in union with him becomes the mother of all things" (ibid.).

E. O. James accounts for these same parallels by arguing for an eastward diffusion of the western Asiatic cult of the Goddess and of her young male consort "from the Tigris to the Indus valley by way of the succession of tells along the foothills and valleys in western Iran, the Elburz, Makran and those of the uplands of Baluchistan to the plains of Sind and the Punjab" (*The Ancient Gods: The History and Diffusion of Religion in the Ancient Near East and the Eastern Mediterranean* [London: Weidenfeld & Nicolson, 1960], p. 296). Throughout this vast extension, notes James, "the female principle (*śakti*) in the form of the Earth-mother retained its earlier predominance" (ibid.) even after the Goddess began to lose her dominance and prestige elsewhere, owing to increasing emphasis on the male creative principle.

Finally, James concludes, as does Marshall, that the cult of Śiva and the Mother-goddess in later Hinduism is derived from the assumedly pre-Aryan Indus civilization, whose cradleland James tentatively locates "in the Iranian highlands where its founders shared a common origin with the Sumerians before they made their way into North-west India through Baluchistan" (*Myth and Ritual in the Ancient Near East,* p. 135).

49. Referring specifically to the Minoan-Mycenaean religion of Crete and of Mycenaean Greece, Persson claims: "Out of these two deities, the Great Goddess and the Boy God, there later developed a larger number of more or less distinct figures, which we meet in Greek religious myths. In my opinion, their multiple variety depends to a very considerable degree on the different invocatory names, the *epiklēseis,* of originally one and the same deity" (*Religion of Greece in Prehistoric Times,* p. 124).

50. All of these derivations are suggested by Persson, *Religion of Greece in Prehistoric Times,* pp. 125–36, with the exception of *Hera* as "the Lady," suggested by Nilsson, *Minoan-Mycenaean Religion,* pp. 395, 489 n. 9.

51. *Nysa,* a name given to several mountains sacred to Dionysos, is also, in the Homeric *Hymn to Demeter,* the designated location of the abduction of Demeter's beloved *korē,* who was picking hyacinths and narcissus "which Gaia, pleasing the All-Receiver, made blossom there, by the will of Zeus, for a girl with a flower's beauty" when "over the Nysian field the lord and All-receiver, the many-named son of Kronos, sprang upon her" (*The Homeric Hymns,* translated by Apostolos N. Athanassakis [Baltimore: Johns Hopkins University Press, 1976], 2.8–9 and 17–18, p. 2).

52. See Persson, *Religion of Greece in Prehistoric Times,* pp. 136–37.

53. For a critique of the view that Paleolithic and Neolithic figurines were pornographic objects representing prehistoric goddesses as sex symbols, see Marija Gimbutas, "Vulvas, Breasts, and Buttocks of the Goddess Creatress," in *Studies in Honor of Franklin D. Murphy* (Los Angeles: Institute of Archaeology, UCLA, 1981), pp. 15–42.

54. This ancient universal myth telling of the cosmic egg laid by a sacred waterbird finds wide iconic representation in numerous Minoan, Cycladic, and Hel-

ladic vases. This same cosmic egg, understood as the womb of the world, is often reflected in tombs, from the egg-shaped burial chambers of Hal Saflieni in Malta to the massive white egg-like dome of Newgrange in Ireland. See Gimbutas, *Language of the Goddess*, pp. 213–19. In Egypt, it was the Nile goose, worshiped as the "great chatterer," who laid the cosmic egg and thus created the world. See Hermann Kees, *Der Götterglaube im alten Aegypten*, Mitteilungen der Vorderasiatisch-Aegyptischen Gesellschaft 45 (Leipzig: J. C. Hinrichs, 1941), p. 309.

55. Nilsson discusses a variety of Cretan coins in which the youthful Zeus, the Minoan *megistos kouros*, appears in the branches of a tree, often together with a young woman who, on some coins, holds a scepter crowned by a bird. On other coins, the place of the young man is taken by an eagle. "A very remarkable type," writes Nilsson, "shows the eagle in the lap of the woman with outspread wings, a representation recalling that of the intercourse of Leda with the swan" (*Minoan-Mycenaean Religion*, pp. 550–51; see also A. B. Cook, *Zeus: A Study in Ancient Religion* [Cambridge: Cambridge University Press, 1914–1940], 1:528, figs. 391–400, particularly figs. 397, 398). These and other coins, concludes Nilsson, "show that there was in the district of Gortyn a belief that Zeus in the shape of a bird united himself with a tree goddess or nymph whose name is not given. But it may be remembered that some goddesses closely connected with the tree cult, e.g., Helen and Artemis, are of Minoan origin" (*Minoan-Mycenaean Religion*, p. 552). Finally, with reference to the appearances of Zeus as a swan at Sparta and at Argos, Nilsson adds: "I venture to guess that these myths, which appear in old Mycenaean centres, are remains of the Minoan belief that the gods appeared in the shape of birds" (ibid).

56. There is still another evident bond between these three, reflected in the explicit association of the Goddess, under her aspect as a bird, with the crafts of spinning and weaving, over which Athena later presides and which Helen plies so fatally in the *Iliad*. These crafts are, it will be remembered, Athena's personal gifts to Pandora, the negative image, as it were, of the Goddess.

57. Jack Lindsay, for one, finds iconic evidence of the conflation of their stories in the images engraved on a finely tooled cuirass uncovered at Olympia. Helen, standing between two pairs of men, her rescuers and her abductors, wears a robe bearing a meander pattern, a stylized version of the labyrinth. "So," concludes Lindsay, "Helen enclosed in a meander with Theseus holding her hand is close to Ariadne accompanying him through the maze, however different the situation is in other ways" (*Helen of Troy: Woman and Goddess* [Totowa, N.J.: Rowman & Littlefield, 1974], p. 278).

58. Wolkstein and Kramer, *Inanna*, pp. 4–5.

59. Ibid., p. 37, from "The Courtship of Inanna and Dumuzi."

60. See Budge, *The Gods of the Egyptians*, 2:106–7.

61. This tree, as legend has it, was eventually cut down and made into a column for the palace of the king of Byblos, who compassionately delivered it over to Isis when she begged for the body of Osiris contained within the column. This column may indeed be one source of the sacred *djed* column, said also to be the

spine of Osiris.

62. Whether the asherah represented, in Israelite religion, a distinct goddess, possibly worshiped as the consort of Yahweh, is a matter of considerable dispute. See Mark S. Smith, *The Early History of God: Yahweh and the Other Deities in Ancient Israel* (New York: Harper & Row, 1987), pp. 88–94, and his discussion of Yahweh and Asherah (pp. 80–114), on which I rely.

63. *ʿAbodah Zarah* 3:7; see H. Danby, *The Mishnah* (London: Oxford University Press, 1933), p. 441.

64. See O. Negbi, *Canaanite Gods in Metal: An Archaeological Study of Ancient Syro-Palestinian Figurines* (Tel Aviv: Tel Aviv University Institute for Archaeology, 1976), nos. 1661, 1664, 1680, 1685, 1688, 1692. Additionally, it may be relevant to mention in this context a seal, unique among the finds from Harappa, which depicts a naked female figure, upside down and legs spread apart, with a plant growing from her womb. See Marshall, *Mohenjo-Daro and the Indus Civilization,* p. 52.

65. Marshall, *Mohenjo-Daro and the Indus Civilization,* p. 63.

66. The Goddess, in the form of either a sacred tree or a pillar of life, is frequently flanked by heraldic animals. Goats were once common in this posture; but in the Bronze Age dogs became prominent in this context, only to be replaced in large part by lions. Thus the "lions gate," composed of a sacred pillar flanked by lions, was evidently a common feature of Mycenaean citadels. It is possible, of course, that the earlier association of the Goddess with dogs is reflected in Helen's identification with the dog in Homer, though the dog, by that time, had taken on a most dark and unsavory association with battlefield carnage.

67. Evans, Nilsson, Persson, and virtually everyone else recognize in the birds who frequent the shrines of the Goddess, perching in the sacred tree or surmounting the sacred column, the visitation of the Goddess herself. There is less than total agreement, however, regarding whether the vast majority of the birds depicted in Minoan art are to be hailed as doves, which would readily lend itself to a comparison of the Minoan Goddess with certain Oriental deities, most notably Aphrodite and Astarte. Evans and Persson represent the near consensus on the dovish character of the Minoan bird figures; but Nilsson has his doubts. See Nilsson, *Minoan-Mycenaean Religion,* pp. 336–38.

68. Nilsson, *Minoan-Mycenaean Religion,* p. 283. See also A. J. (Sir Arthur) Evans, *The Earlier Religion of Greece in the Light of Cretan Discoveries* (London: Macmillan, 1931), p. 13; he writes: "The sacred tree might itself be regarded as permanently fitted with divine life as manifested by its fruit and foliage." See also Evans's seminal work *The Mycenaean Tree and Pillar Cult and Its Mediterranean Relations* (London: Macmillan, 1901), *passim.*

69. Persson, *Religion of Greece in Prehistoric Times,* pp. 33, 123. See B. Schweitzer, review of "The Swedish Cyprus Expedition 2," *Gnomon* 9 (1937): 15; and L. Malten, "Motivgeschichtliche Untersuchen zur Sagenforschung," *Hermes* 4 (1939): 198.

70. See Plutarch, *Parallel Lives* (Loeb), "Theseus," 21. The eclipse of the Delian

cult of Ariadne by that of Aphrodite may be glimpsed in the story told by Plutarch regarding Theseus's dedication there of a statue of Aphrodite, a statue said to have been given to him by Ariadne. The dedication of this statue in the temple of Apollo and Theseus's subsequent introduction of the "Crane Dance" clearly describe the foundation of a cult, which is at the same time both old and new. The new cult, that of Aphrodite, may be seen to reflect the old cult of Ariadne, which it presumably now replaces.

71. See ibid., 20. There are, of course, many stories of Ariadne's death and many places where she is said to lie.

72. See A. W. Farnell, "Cretan Influence in Greek Religion," in *Essays in Aegean Archaeology Presented to Sir Arthur Evans* (Oxford: Oxford University Press, 1927), p. 18.

73. The tellurian stage was premarital and preagricultural, a time when open, unqualified hetaerism prevailed between the sexes and when swamp vegetation or wild plant life complemented the hunt. It was the stage of motherhood without marriage. Next, the lunar stage marked the beginning of settled agriculture, which provided the model for the transformation of culture. Thus the tilled field led to conjugal motherhood. This was the stage of matriarchal marriage. Finally, the solar or Uranian stage marked the emergence of cities and the liberation from nature through the assertion of will and of imagination over matter. This was, and is, the stage of conjugal fatherhood and of patriarchy. In the movement from one stage to another, Bachofen assigns a determinative role to violence; both the tellurian and the lunar stages were overthrown by force. More specifically, in the myth of the Amazons Bachofen finds a trace of the original uprising of women against the degradations of hetaerism, an uprising reflected in the legend of the Lemnian women. The eventual result, everywhere, was the full assertion and institutionalization of female power and privilege in matriarchy, which in turn, was overthrown by male violence and self-assertion. The legendary war against and defeat of the Amazons signaled the beginning of patriarchy, the work of many centuries of legislation, religion, poetry, and domestic practice. See Bachofen, *Myth, Religion, and Mother Right, passim.*

74. The earliest extant written record of mother-right comes from *The History* of Herodotus, wherein he comments on a curious custom of the Lycians, who Herodotus says came "in ancient times" from Crete. "Their customs are partly Cretan and partly Carian," he writes, "but they have one particular custom that they share with no people at all: they take their names from their mothers, not from their fathers. When one of them asks his neighbor who he is, the man will list his ancestry on his mother's side and call over his mother's mothers. And, indeed, if a woman of birth lives with a slave, her children are counted freeborn. But if a man that is a citizen, and even the first of them, has a foreign wife or concubine, the children are dishonored" (Herodotus, *The History,* translated by David Grene [Chicago: University of Chicago Press, 1987], 1.173, p. 112).

Clearly, what was once an all-but-universal custom in southeastern Europe,

Asia Minor, and the Near East—the focal area for *The History*—is already by the fifth century, for all Herodotus knows, a unique practice without precedent, even in Crete.

75. A few brief remarks here will suggest the scope and depth of these disputes. The Russian scholar N. S. Trubetskoy denied what is a baseline assumption of virtually every modern linguist, namely, the existence of a genetic or "family" relationship between the so-called Indo-European languages and thus the existence of an ancestral or proto-Indo-European language. More recently, Jean-Paul Demoule has raised the same doubts and adopted a position similar to Trubetzkoy's. For most scholars, however, the Indo-European question is focused in such challenges as reconstructing the *Ursprache* or source language of the original Indo-Europeans, the *Urvolk*; identifying the *Urheimat*, or original homeland, of those speaking the proto-Indo-European language; and, finally, tracing their migrations or invasions throughout Europe, the Near East, and India. On all of these and other relevant matters, there are vast differences of opinion, which have been carefully surveyed and assessed in a quite helpful recent study by J. P. Mallory, *In Search of the Indo-Europeans: Language, Archaeology and Myth* (London: Thames & Hudson, 1989). See N. S. Trubetzkoy, "Gedanken über das Indogermanenproblem," *Acta Linguistica* 1 (1939): 81–89; J.-P. Demoule, "Les Indo-européens ont-ils existé?" *L'histoire* 28 (1980): 109–20.

76. Colin Renfrew, *Archaeology and Language: The Puzzle of Indo-European Origins* (New York: Cambridge University Press, 1988), p. 285.

77. Inasmuch as patriarchy is most often understood as the all-but-unqualified domination of women by men, matriarchy is commonly understood as the reverse domination of men by women, which does not accurately describe what is known or surmised regarding the relationship between the sexes in Old Europe. Rather than use a single term such as "patriarchy" or "sexism," for instance, Gerda Lerner helpfully suggests and sorts out the respective connotations of a variety of terms, such as the "oppression of women," the "subordination of women," and the "deprivation of women" by men, a discussion equally useful when the sexes are reversed (*Creation of Patriarchy*, pp. 231–36). Riane Eisler, on the other hand, suggests a new term—*gylany,* derived from the Greek *gynē,* "woman," and *anēr,* "man"—"to describe the real alternative to a system based on the ranking of one half of humanity over the other," that is, an alternative to domination (*Chalice and the Blade* [New York: Harper & Row, 1987], p. 105). It is this term, *gylany,* that Gimbutas adopts to designate "a social order in which women as heads of clans or queen-priestesses played a special part." "Old Europe and Anatolia," she continues, "as well as Minoan Crete, were a gylany. A balanced, non-patriarchal and non-matriarchal social system is reflected by religion, mythologies, and folklore, by studies of the social structure of Old European and Minoan cultures, and is supported by the continuity of the elements of a matrilinear system in ancient Greece, Etruria, Rome, the Basque, and other coun-

tries of Europe" (*Language of the Goddess*, p. xx).

78. I have in mind here that account developed and documented over the past several decades in the published works of Marija Gimbutas, both because I find that body of work to present the single most coherent and compelling perspective yet offered and because her understanding of Old Europe and of "the coming of the Indo-Europeans" represents the currently most widely accepted understanding of these matters—the "vulgate" with a lower-case *v* as it were—found, for instance, in the *Encyclopaedia Britannica* and the *Grand Dictionnaire Encyclopédique Larousse*. Usage, however, does not determine truth; nor would I suggest that the views presented here stand for anything resembling a literal consensus among scholars of the subject.

79. Marija Gimbutas, *The Early Civilization of Europe*, Monograph for Indo-European Studies 131 (Los Angeles: University of California at Los Angeles, 1980), chap. 2, p. 32.

80. Ibid., chap. 2, p. 17.

81. Hesiod, *Works and Days* (Loeb), 116-20, translation mine. The Oxford edition questions the segments (comprising line 119) in brackets.

82. Ibid., 121.

83. See Marija Gimbutas, "The First Wave of Eurasian Steppe Pastoralists into Copper Age Europe," *Journal of Indo-European Studies* 5 (1977): 278–80. *Kurgan*, Russian for "barrow," points to a marked feature of these peoples: that they buried their warrior kings in shaft graves beneath barrows or mounds of earth. Their path across Europe can be traced by the locating and dating of these barrows, or kurgans.

84. As with every other element in this narrative, the number, timing, and names of the migrations of peoples which eventually formed the population of Greece are all matters for extensive and perhaps irresolvable discussion. We focus here on the Achaean and the Dorian inasmuch as it may be argued that they were centrally responsible for the rise and the fall, respectively, of the Mycenaean citadels, wherein the would-be "historical Helen" would have dwelt.

85. Gimbutas, "First Wave of Eurasian Steppe Pastoralists," p. 281.

86. Marija Gimbutas, "The Beginning of the Bronze Age in Europe and the Indo-Europeans: 3500–2500 BC," *Journal of Indo-European Studies* 1 (1973): 163–214.

87. See Gimbutas, "First Wave of Eurasian Steppe Pastoralists," p. 305.

88. Heraclitus, fr. 53; see René Girard, *Violence and the Sacred* (Baltimore: Johns Hopkins University Press, 1977), p. 144.

89. "A main theme," write Robert Graves and Raphael Patai, "of Greek myth is the gradual reduction of women from sacred beings to chattels" (*Hebrew Myths* [New York: Doubleday, 1964], p. 15). Samuel Noah Kramer makes a similar comment regarding early Mesopotamian myth, when he states that the goddesses "that held top rank in the Sumerian pantheon were gradually forced down the ladder by male theologians" and "their powers turned over to male deities" (*From*

*the Poetry of Sumer: Creation, Glorification, Adoration* [Berkeley: University of California Press, 1979], p. 27). "Similarly," write Graves and Patai, "Jehovah punishes Eve for causing the Fall of Man. Further to disguise Eve's original godhead—her title 'Mother of All Living' survives in Genesis—the mythographers represented her as formed from Adam's rib. . . . Still later mythographers insisted that she was formed from Adam's barbed tail" (*Hebrew Myths*, p. 15). Another telling example of the diminution and disempowering of the Goddess may be found in the fact that in Genesis it is Yahweh who "opens the womb" of, for example, Leah and Rachel (see Genesis 29:31 and 30:22–23). Formerly, it was the Goddess alone who opened women's wombs and brought forth new life. Commenting on this shift, Gerda Lerner writes: "Procreation, then, is clearly defined as emanating from God, who opens the wombs of women and blesses the seed of men . . . [which] acquires the power and the blessing of the procreativity which lodges in Yahweh" (*Creation of Patriarchy*, pp. 188–89). Thus, female sexuality is progressively severed from procreation; and the life-giving power is vested in the male, divine and human. Even Eve, "Mother of All Living," when she brings forth her firstborn, is made to say: "I have gained a male child with the help of the Lord" (Genesis 4:1; *Tanakh: The Holy Scriptures* [Philadelphia: Jewish Publication Society, 1988]).

## Chapter 5: The Truth of Helen

1. Hesiod, *Works and Days* (Oxford), 176–78, translation mine.

2. Dionysos, the god of theater, is not only the god of "revel" but also the god of "revelation." Nowhere is this made more clear than in Euripides' *Bakkhai*, a play manifestly about the theater and its god. Drama is not only the genre but also the subject matter of the *Bakkhai*, wherein Euripides may be seen to have offered in dramatic form his own poetics, a potent antidote to the *Poetics* of Aristotle, who was neither of the theater nor of the fifth century. I have argued elsewhere that in the *Bakkhai* the essence of all tragedy, as Euripides understood it, is distilled and disclosed. In a word, that essence is *vision*. See R. E. Meagher, "Revel and Revelation in the *Bakkhai*: Reflections on the Poetics of Euripides," *The Willamette Journal of the Liberal Arts* 5 (1990): 1–20. For a fuller discussion of vision and truth in classical Greek theater, and more specifically in the drama of Euripides, see R. E. Meagher, *Mortal Vision: The Wisdom of Euripides* (New York: St. Martin's, 1989), *passim*.

3. Both Plato's diagram of the divided line in book 6 of the *Republic* and his parable of the cave in book 7 present a layered world of many dimensions, arranged in ascending order, each the image of what lies above and beyond it. A similar scheme, I would suggest, is discernible in Greek epic and dramatic poetry, whose worlds are metaphysically and morally complex in ways more like than unlike Plato's. At the very least it is undeniable that the ancient Greek theater presents a world of images, wherein:

actors, masked and robed, become moving
    images of the otherwise unseen yet
    real figures of myth;
the now visible figures of myth become, in turn,
    images of the spectators themselves;
theatrical spectacle, in short, enacts myths
    transparent to what we call history.

If what is seen in the end is life as already lived and known by those who come
to the theater to see it, why such elaborate subterfuge? Why diffract what is essentially simple? What is there about the lives we live and the world we live in that a
direct gaze does not discover? Without pursuing here the full responses of Homer,
Euripides, or Plato to such questions—a project far beyond the reach of this discussion—a few suggestions are possible and pertinent. Poetry and philosophy, as the
ancients practiced them, are premised on the realization that imagination is
required to uncover reality precisely because reality is not straightforward or literal. Rather, it is devious and elusive and often unwelcome, requiring many different sorts of seeing: outward and inward, witting and unwitting, naïve, critical,
inventive, curious, and contemplative.

Thus Plato's Socrates, shortly before his death, describing in retrospect his own
spiritually arduous search for the ultimate cause (*aitia*) of all that comes and
ceases to be, told how "it occurred to me that I must guard against the same sort
of risk which people run when they watch and study an eclipse of the sun; they
really do sometimes injure their eyes, unless they study its reflection in water or
some other medium. I conceived of something like this happening to myself, and
I was afraid that by observing objects with my eyes and trying to comprehend
them with each of my other senses I might blind my soul altogether. So I decided
that I must have recourse to theories (*logous*) and use them in trying to discover
the truth about things" (Plato, *Phaedo*, translated by Hugh Tredennick, in *Plato:
The Collected Dialogues*, edited by Edith Hamilton and Huntington Cairns, Bollingen Series 71 [New York: Pantheon, 1963], 99d).

In addition to *logoi,* Plato's Socrates often had recourse to *mythoi,* stories that he
recommended might well be repeated over and over, like magic charms, in the
hope that their spell would grasp the soul when the simple truth would not. See
Plato, *Phaedo*, 114d.

In the wisdom traditions of the ancient world, moral and religious truths too,
like those of metaphysics, were often conveyed obliquely in stories or parables, in
which imagination and insight converge. Thus the prophet Nathan, wanting
David to see his own hideous crimes for what they were and knowing that David
could not or would not do so if confronted with them directly, told him a story on
the face of it far removed from David or from anything David had ever done.
David was, we are told, at once outraged by the comparatively minor misdeed of
the rich man in Nathan's story; and, as if the story were real, he said to Nathan:
"As the LORD lives, the man who did this deserves to die." Nathan's response was

simple: "That man is you." Nathan's story, once opaque and unthreatening, now became transparent to David's deeds, which David could no longer avoid seeing; and, at the sight of them, he said: "I stand guilty before the LORD" (2 Samuel 12:5; 12:7, 13; *Tanakh* [Philadelphia: Jewish Publication Society, 1988]). For an extended discussion of this parable, see W. M. W. Roth, "You Are The Man! Structural Interaction in 2 Samuel 10–12," *Semeia* 8 (1977): 1–13. Roth's discussion is particularly reliant on J. D. Crossan's account of the parable as a literary and theological genre in *The Dark Interval: Towards a Theology of Story* (Niles, Ill.: Argus, 1975).

4. The role of masks in ancient drama is often understated, as if their use might be explained in technical terms by the needs of classical actors, by convention always male and never more than three in number for any given production. Admittedly, masks made it possible for two or three men to play the many, diverse parts required by the repertoire of fifth-century tragedy; but this does not mean that the theatrical use of masks followed upon this happy coincidence. Beyond the demands of multiple impersonation, beyond any concerns of technique, masks are instruments of possession and empowerment. Their use in cultic dance and ritual drama is immeasurably older and wider in scope than their appearance in the theater of Dionysos. Masks clearly brought more than convenience and economy to Attic drama. Furthermore, it is important to note that the English word "mask" is itself misleading here; for whereas "mask" suggests concealment, its Greek counterpart, *prosōpon*, suggests disclosure. To "mask" any reality is, after all, to hide it, to allow it to escape notice, while a *prosōpon* is precisely that "look" or "countenance" that assures appearance and recognition. In the putting on of an ancient theatrical mask, one identity is surrendered to another; one presence makes another possible. The focus is relentlessly cast upon who or what becomes, in this process, present and visible, rather than upon who or what becomes, in the same instant, absent and lost to sight.

5. See T. Gaisford, *Etymologicum Magnum* (Oxford: Oxford University Press, 1848), pp. 51, 62. As Gaisford points out, *alēthes*, an adjectival form of *alētheia* meaning "something true" or "a truth," means literally "something that has not slipped into oblivion." Liddell-Scott translate this same word as "unconcealed."

6. Heraclitus, fr. 123, translation mine; see Hermann Diels and Walther Kranz, eds., *Die Fragmente der Vorsokratiker* (Berlin: Weidmann, 1956), p. 178. G. S. Kirk and J. E. Raven translate this fragment as "The Real constitution of things is accustomed to hide itself" (*The Presocratic Philosophers* [Cambridge: Cambridge University Press, 1957], p. 193, no. 211), while Martin Heidegger offers, as a starting point, "the essence of things likes to hide" (*Early Greek Thinking* [New York: Harper & Row, 1975], p. 113). Kant contributed relevant and historically crucial commentary on this matter when, in the preface to the second edition of his *Critique of Pure Reason,* he argued that the truths of nature are like secrets tightly grasped and not readily given up. Instead of expecting nature to reveal itself to random observation, he argued that nature must be sharply interrogated, forced to answer pointed questions. Reason, says Kant, "must approach nature in order

to be taught by it. It must not, however, do so in the character of a pupil who listens to everything that the teacher chooses to say, but of an appointed judge who compels the witnesses to answer questions which he has himself formulated" (*Critique of Pure Reason*, translated by Norman Kemp Smith [New York: St. Martin's, 1965], B xiii, p. 20).

One might well conclude from Heraclitus's aphorism and Kant's remarks that freely offered testimony is more suspect than testimony given under constraint or even torture. In fact, this was a working assumption in Athenian lawcourts with reference to slaves, whose testimony was legally admissible only if given under torture. That the citizens of Athens never chose to extend this practice more widely to include all witnesses may say more about their fear of torture than about their confidence in each other's veracity. Page du Bois, for one, has argued that the juridical use of torture to extract testimony reveals a great deal about the classical Greek understanding of truth (*Torture and Truth* [New York: Routledge, 1990], *passim*).

7. The antithesis between words or ideas, on the one hand, and actions or events, on the other, is also thematically central to Thucydides' account of the Peloponnesian War. While this antithesis occurs in many different formulations throughout Thucydides' history, Adam Parry found forty-two instances of the explicit use of *logos* and *ergon* to point to the disparity between what is thought or said and what is done or happens. In addition, Adam Milman Parry traced the appearance and development of this conceptual antithesis from Homer to Plato. It was, in his view, common to poets, philosophers, playwrights, and politicians. And, in his assessment: "There is reason to think that it was common coin in the Vth century. It is simple and ethical, placing value on *ergon* as unquestioned reality, and condemning *logos* as something purely delusive" (*Logos and Ergon in Thucydides* [Salem, N.H.: Ayer, 1988], p. 15 and *passim*). It would be a mistake, however, to understand *logoi* as "mere words," simplistically contrasted with "reality"; for words are themselves very real, powerful, and consequential, all of which was not lost on ancient minds, much less invented by modern ones. In his discussion of *logos* as one of the possible causes (*aitias*) of Helen's going off to Troy, Gorgias states: "The sovereign power of *logos* is great. Its 'body' is minute, even invisible; and yet it can do a god's deeds (*erga*)" (*Encomium of Helen*, edited by D. M. MacDowell [Bristol: Bristol Classical Press, 1982], 9, pp. 22, 24, translation mine). Paraphrasing Gorgias's discussion of *logos*, Parry claims: "Gorgias is saying, My style, my way of dividing the world into abstract concepts, is not mere words. It is in fact superior to what we call reality because it can *create* this reality" (Parry, "Thucydides' use of abstract language," *Yale French Studies* 45 [1970]: 18).

8. Euripides, fr. 2.439, translation mine; see August Nauck, ed., *Tragicorum Graecorum Fragmenta* (Hildesheim: G. Olms, 1964).

9. Euripides, *Iphigenia at Aulis* (Oxford), 333, translation mine.

10. Euripides, *Alkestis* (Oxford), 675, 695–96, translation mine.

11. Euripides, *Medea* (Oxford), 585, translation mine.

12. Euripides, *Hecuba* (Oxford), 187–88, translation mine.

13. Of the nineteen extant Euripidean dramas, fourteen have choruses composed of women, twelve are about women, and eight are named after specific women. Numbers aside, the focal presence and the resonant voices of women in Euripidean drama are all the more striking when set against the notorious words of Pericles to the women of Athens, reminding them that "the greatest glory of a woman is to be least talked about by men" (Thucydides, *The History of the Peloponnesian War*, translated by Rex Warner [New York: Viking Penguin, 1986], 2.46, p. 15). Indeed, it is usually assumed that, apart from funerals and certain specific festivals, Athenian women were expected to be neither seen nor heard outside of their homes. For an extended discussion of Euripides' treatment of women, see the section entitled "Women" in R. E. Meagher, *Mortal Vision: The Wisdom of Euripides*, pp. 115–42; also Philip Vellacott, *Ironic Drama: A Study of Euripides' Method and Meaning* (New York: Cambridge University Press, 1975), chapter 4, "Woman," pp. 82–126.

14. Euripides, *Iphigenia at Aulis* (Oxford), 1168–70, translation mine.

15. Euripides, *Hecuba* (Oxford), 442–43, translation mine.

16. Euripides, *Iphigenia in Tauris* (Oxford), 525, translation mine.

17. Euripides, *Hippolytos* (Oxford), 406–7, translation mine.

18. In that section of his history commonly referred to as "the Archaeology" (I.2–23), Thucydides states that the greatest war of the past was the Persian War, not the war against Troy, which was a relatively minor operation; and even the Persian War, he points out, was decided merely by two sea and two land battles. "As for this present war," concludes Thucydides, "even though people are apt to think that the war in which they are fighting is the greatest of all wars and, when it is over, to relapse again into their admiration of the past, nevertheless, if one looks at the facts themselves, one will see that this (the Peloponnesian War) was the greatest war of all. . . . Never before had so many cities been captured and then devastated . . . never had there been so many exiles; never such loss of life" (*History of the Peloponnesian War*, 21, p. 47; 23, p. 48).

Thucydides clearly believed that this war was *the* war, an upheaval so massive and deep that it divulged the very nature of war. Thus, in chronicling this event, Thucydides was convinced that he was writing not merely for his own generation but for all time. See W. Robert Connor's discussion of the Archaeology in *Thucydides* (Princeton: Princeton University Press, 1984), pp. 20–32.

19. The parallels between the Greek fifth century and our own twentieth century, and more specifically between the history of Athens and the history of the United States during those periods, are as evident as they are eerie. Rarely does one epoch so closely mirror another. Many scholars and statesmen have pointed this out, as did Secretary of State George Marshall, speaking at Princeton University on February 22, 1947. "I doubt seriously," he said, "whether a man can think with full wisdom and with deep convictions regarding certain of the basic international issues today who has not at least reviewed in his mind the period of the

Peloponnesian War and the Fall of Athens" (See W. Robert Connor, *Thucydides*, p. 3. Whether these words, or those of Thucydides, will speak with any point to the last decade of the twentieth century and to "the new world order," whatever it may prove to be, remains of course to be seen.)

20. Having scored a series of successes against the Syracusans and having nearly achieved total victory, the Athenian forces watched the tide of events turn decisively against them. Like their mother-city Athens, they were now besieged and left to fight for their lives. That fight was to take place, we know, in the great harbor of Syracuse. Facing his own desperate troops, Nicias, the Athenian commander, made explicit the stakes. They were about to fight not a battle but the war itself; for "if this action," said Nicias, "should end in anything else except victory for you, our enemies will at once sail against Athens, and those of us who are left at Athens will be incapable of resisting a combination of the forces they have against them there now and a new invasion force from here. So, while you will find yourselves at once at mercy of the Syracusans . . . your countrymen at home will be at the mercy of Spartans . . . therefore, the fate of both you and them rests upon this one battle" (Thucydides, *History of the Peloponnesian War*, 7.64, p. 519).

Later, after a disastrous naval defeat in the harbor, Nicias led those men still alive and able to walk into retreat. Victory was gone; survival was unlikely. Trying to keep his men from disarray and despair, Nicias reminded them: "if you escape the enemy now, you will all see again the homes for which you long, and the Athenians among you will build up again the great power of Athens, fallen though it is. It is men who make the city, and not walls or ships with no men inside them" (ibid., 7.78, p. 530).

In a similarly desperate moment, Themistocles had once urged that Athens should defend itself not from its walls but from its ships, clearly implying that "Athens" was a people, not a place. See Herodotus, *History* (Loeb), 7.143–44; 8.83. Indeed, the eventual decision to build both a navy and an empire may be traced in this movement of the Athenian imagination from walls to ships to men; for the Athenian empire was premised on the decision to become a sea power and to extend "Athens" to wherever its people would prevail.

In sum, what Thucydides makes clear is that the Sicilian campaign is a microcosm not only for the entire war but for the rise and fall of the Athenian empire as well.

21. The sketch of the Athenian "character" offered in the debate at Sparta in 432, prior to the declaration of war, would suggest that the Athenians were somehow following their own peculiar nature in pursuing the path of imperial self-aggrandizement. "Athenian daring" writes Thucydides, "will outrun its own resources . . . they [Athenians] are always abroad; for they think that the farther they go the more they will get. . . . If they aim at something and do not get it, they think that they have been deprived of what belonged to them already; whereas, if their enterprise is successful, they regard that success as nothing compared to what they will do next. . . . Of them alone it may be said that they possess a thing

almost as soon as they have begun to desire it. . . . And so they go on working away in hardship and danger all the days of their lives, seldom enjoying their possessions because they are always adding to them. Their view of a holiday is to do what needs doing; they prefer hardship and activity to peace and quiet. In a word, they are by nature incapable of either living a quiet life themselves or of allowing anyone else to do so" (*History of the Peloponnesian War*, 1.70, p. 76).

If, indeed, as Heraclitus states, a man's *ēthos* or "character" is his *daimōn* or "destiny" (fr. 119; see Diels and Kranz, eds., *Die Fragmente der Vorsokratiker*, p. 177; and Kirk and Raven, *Presocratic Philosophers*, p. 213, no. 250), an overweening power to which he succumbs as though it were dictating to him from beyond, then the same may be true, collectively, of cities. In this case, the tragic *mythos* or plot line of the empire was written in advance and delivered to the city, as a script might be handed to an actor, for its enactment. The very structure of Thucydides' history, however, wherein decisive actions (*erga*) are as a rule preceded by deliberative speeches (*logoi*), would seem to argue, on the contrary, that individuals and cities, up to a point, can and do confront and consider real alternatives. Eventually, however, the momentum of events may so constrict anyone's or any people's choices that they lose their initial freedom and find themselves riding out events over which they now have little or no control. M. Cogan suggests that it is the realization of this fact that may account for Thucydides' omission of any political speeches from his history once the debacle in Sicily is well under way and the exiled Alcibiades has sketched for the Spartans a plan for total victory. See Marc Cogan, *The Human Thing: The Speeches and Principles of Thucydides' History* (Chicago: University of Chicago Press, 1981), pp. 118, 165.

Thus Aristotle argues, in theory, that effective freedom can be lost through its exercise; for, as conduct shapes character, so character shapes conduct. The result is the knot of habit (*ēthos*), which, though tied freely, is no less binding for that fact. Both Pericles and Alcibiades, in practice, made very much the same point, when they argued on different occasions that Athens, though it had once been free to choose between leadership and tyranny, was no longer so. Having chosen tyranny, their choice became whether to continue to exercise it or to be destroyed by the forces they would release by loosening their grip. See Thucydides, *History of the Peloponnesian War*, 2.63, p. 161; 6.16, pp. 419–20; see also Aristotle, *Nicomachean Ethics*, II.i.

22. Pericles himself, in Thucydides account, uses all but the word "tyranny" to describe the Athenian empire, in that he admits that it was taken by force and must be held down by force. See Pericles' last recorded speech in Thucydides, *History of the Peloponnesian War*, 2.66, p. 161. Eventually, it seems, not only their enemies but the Athenians themselves accepted openly that their empire was a tyranny that would, if it could, extend itself over all of Greece. See, in particular, Thucydides' account of the debate at Camarina, ibid., 6.72-88, pp. 455–65.

Indeed, a central theme in Thucydides' history is the replacement of the Persian threat by the Athenian threat. The central irony here, of course, is that, whereas the Athenians endeavored to justify their empire on the grounds that they had defeated the Persians, Athens's critics and enemies endeavored to indict the empire on the grounds that it had simply substituted Athenian tyranny for Persian tyranny. This irony is nowhere more striking than in Thucydides' account of the final retreat of Nicias's forces in Sicily (see ibid., 6.72–87, pp. 525–37). Both sides—the Athenians and their enemies—evidently have an earlier moment in mind as the present tragedy unfolds. Both recall the second Persian invasion. The Athenian troops remember how their fathers quit the walls of Athens only to regroup and to meet the enemy at Salamis. A moment they hope to repeat. The Syracusans and Spartans, on the other hand, see in Nicias's troops an image of yesteryear's Persians permitted to flee for their lives after their defeat at Salamis. A moment they resolve not to see repeated.

23. Thucydides, *Peloponnesian War* (Loeb), 6.24.3, translation mine.

24. See Connor, *Thucydides*, p. 167.

25. Aeschylus, *Agamemnon* (Loeb), 341–42, translation mine. These words are echoed by those of Athena in the *Eumenides,* when she prays, as it were, to the Furies, the ancient goddesses, for her city: "Let our wars rage on abroad, with all their force, to satisfy our powerful lust for fame (*deinos eukleias erōs*)." See Aeschylus, *The Oresteia,* translated by Robert Fagles (New York: Viking, 1975), p. 282, lines 872–74.

26. Euripides, *Iphigenia at Aulis* (Oxford), 1264–65, translation mine. This use of *erōs* to describe the collective frenzy of an army on the brink of war reflects the very structure of the *Iphigenia at Aulis*. The entire play builds toward a preliminary sacrifice (*proteleia*) to which the girl Iphigenia will be central. Until quite late in the play, however, two very different ideas of that sacrifice survive intact. Klytemnestra, Iphigenia, and their attendants anticipate a sacrifice preliminary to the imminent marriage of Iphigenia and Achilles, while everyone else anticipates a sacrifice preliminary to the imminent war of Greeks and Trojans. The marriage is, we know from the start, a ruse, a grotesque charade, a vicious lie; but the war is real. Iphigenia and truth are its first victims.

The eve of a wedding, like the eve of a war, is fraught with a tension whose release will be accompanied by the spilling of first blood and by a piercing cry. The love-scream, the sacrificial *ololygē,* and the shouts of battle are expressive of a frenzy which the Greeks frequently saw as somehow one. Both war and marriage—the death-act and the love-act—were preceded by, and anticipated in, sacrifice. "Even marriage," writes Walter Burkert, "as initiation, is the product of sacrificial rites. The sacrificial meal that seals the new bond is permeated by rituals making the bride and the groom the butt of make-believe aggression. By hurling flowers and smashing pots, outsiders come to grips with the couple's new status. Above all the bride must suffer the male act. Defloration turns into sacrifice mainly because of the exclusively human phenomenon of shedding blood in the first intercourse" (*Homo Necans: The Anthropology of Ancient Greek Sacrificial Ritual and Myth* [Berkeley: University of California Press, 1983], p. 62). Burkert adds this chilling fact: "In Rome, for example, a spear was used to part the bride's hair, a spear that had dripped with blood and had killed men." See also M. P. Nilsson, "Wedding Rites in Ancient Greece," *Opuscula* 3 (1960): 243–50.

The consummate "male act" is, however, not making love but making war. This truth is, I believe, one that Euripides brings out of concealment in the *Iphigenia at Aulis*. This is the truth that remains hidden within a romantic lie until Klytemnestra discovers it and drags it into the open. The illusion and the reality, the lie and the truth—namely, the wedding and the war—at the center of this play correspond perfectly, after all, to distinct worlds: the women's world and the men's world, here the bridal party and the army camp. Klytemnestra—woman, wife, and mother—is sovereign over the one; Agamemnon—man, husband, and father—is sovereign over the other. The contrast drawn sharply between them is an essential one. "Motherhood," sings the Chorus, for all women, "is a strange, powerful thing (*deinon*), a great love-charm, giving this much in common to all women: there is nothing they will not do or endure for their children" (Euripides, *Iphigenia at Aulis* [Oxford], 917–18, translation mine). By contrast, for all his protestations to the contrary, Agamemnon indicates with his deeds, in concert with the chorus of men which he leads, that there is nothing men will not do *to* their children or make them endure. When all has been said and done, not *at* the altar but *on* it, Agamemnon rapes his own daughter, spoiling her life along with her virginity, in order to whet his army's appetite for battle and to rouse the winds of war. His idea of a wedding.

In sum, sacrifice, marriage, and war are not easily distinguished in the *Iphigenia at Aulis*. All three are violent, destructive acts, whose first and central victim is a woman. Even weddings, it seems, are not about love but about power and conquest.

For an extensive and excellent discussion of this play, see Helene P. Foley, *Ritual Irony: Poetry and Sacrifice in Euripides* (Ithaca: Cornell University Press, 1985), chapter 2, "The *Iphigenia in Aulis*," pp. 65–105.

In a wider discussion of "the spirit of strife" in which *Polemos* (war), *Eris*, and *Neikos* (feud) are said to represent "that same power of confrontation that Hesiod places at the origins of the world and Heraclitus celebrates as the father and king of the whole universe" (J-P. Vernant, *Myth and Society in Ancient Greece* [New York: Zone, 1980], p. 29). Vernant suggests further that "Ares and Aphrodite, *Polemos* and *Philia*, *Neikos* and *Harmonia*, *Eris* and *Erōs* also appear in the organization of the pantheon, in legends and in the theories of the philosophers, as pairs of powers that are opposed and yet closely linked, presiding over the complementary institutions that war and marriage represented so long as private revenge and the exchange of women took place within the same framework of interfamily relations" (ibid., pp. 30–31).

Although Vernant argues that the archaic complementarity between war and marriage disappears with the advent of the city-state, it is thematically evident, though transformed, in the *Iphigenia at Aulis,* as well as in other dramatic texts of the fifth century.

The homology of love and war underlying this entire discussion is as old as Greek poetry and, presumably, much older than. In Homer, for example, not only friends but enemies are treated as if they were lovers. Indeed, the intimacy of battle and the intimacy of the bed share, in part, a common language, both verbal and visual; for the ambiguity between "sex-play" and "war-play" is to be found in Greek art as well as in Greek poetry. See Emily Vermeule, *Aspects of Death in Early Greek Art and Poetry* (Berkeley: University of California Press, 1979), chapter 5: "On the Wings of the Morning: The Pornography of Death," particularly pp. 157–59.

27. See William Arrowsmith's discussion of this term and of the play as a whole in his introduction to his own translation of *The Birds* (Ann Arbor: University of Michigan Press, 1961), pp. 1–10, and in his essay entitled "Aristophanes' *Birds:* The Fantasy Politics of Eros," *Arion* 1 (1973–74): 119–67. In my treatment of this play, I am deeply indebted to both of these texts. See also, more specifically, Victor Ehrenberg, "Polypragmosyne: A Study in Greek Politics," *Journal of Hellenic Studies* 67 (1947): 46–67; and A. W. H. Adkins, "*Polupragmosune* and 'Minding One's Own Business': A Study in Greek Social and Political Values," *Classical Philology* 71 (1976): 301–27.

28. See Thucydides, *The Peloponnesian War* (Loeb), 6.18.4.

29. See ibid., 6.18.6.

30. Euelpides and Pisthetairos imagine themselves to be leaving Athens behind; but this is but one layer of the illusion in which they live. Athens, we recall, has long since construed itself not as a place but as a people with a certain character. Athenian to their core, Euelpides and Pisthetairos cannot but bring the idea or spirit of Athens with them. The fact that they have set out from Athens at their own private initiative, without official mandate, does not mean that they are not cleruchs or colonists, unwitting instruments of the Athenian *imperium.* They are, quite transparently, *agents provocateurs* of Athenian imperial theory and practice. Their alienation, so far from distancing them from Athens, bonds them to it; for alienation—from the past and from the timeless earth—resides at the core of fifth-century Athenian restlessness and ambition. Their nostalgia too, for a long-lost simplicity, likely has the same source: the deep cavity left by their essential uprootedness. They are by this time, in Thucydides' familiar words, constitutionally "incapable of either living a quiet life themselves or of allowing anyone else to do so."

31. The expansion of Athens's imperial design to include far-flung Sicily and the concomitant escalation in the war represented by Athens's Sicilian campaign are here raised, as it were, to the highest power. The truth revealed in this imaginative experiment is the *physis* or nature of imperial ambition, which as a rule likes to hide. The truth is that the desire for empire is infinite, though it mostly conceals itself within explicitly finite objectives, pursued one at a time, as if each one were final. Alcibiades, for whom Arrowsmith considers Pisthetairos a theatri-

cal stand-in, himself said as much in arguing for the Sicilian campaign. See Thucydides, *Peloponnesian War*, 6.18.

Plato, in the *Republic*, discloses the same truth, whose straw man in that text is the young sophist Thrasymachos. Plato, however, sees nothing essentially Athenian about the desire for absolute power or total tyranny. He finds it *in situ* not only in the Athenian character but in the human character, as well. The fact that fifth-century Athenians succumbed to this desire so fully means not that they possessed it but, rather, that it possessed them.

The *imperium* pursued by Athens and revealed in the *Birds* extended far beyond Sicily. Its theoretical scope, whatever its practical limits, was indeed cosmic. In the vision of what has been called the Athenian Enlightenment, man—not woman but man—was to be not only the measure of all things but their master, as well. Glimpses of this vision may be caught in every quarter of classical Greek philosophy, poetry, politics, and art. "For the first time," writes William Arrowsmith, "a city deliberately broke the bonds which bound it to the earth and the past and proclaimed its freedom of the wisdom and meaning accumulated through the millennial toil of the earth and the venerable patterns of culture and religion which grounded human life in the great cyclical life of nature" ("Aristophanes' *Birds:* The Fantasy Politics of Eros," p. 120).

What replaced the wisdom and meaning of the past was, in a word, *technē*, the unique fusion of will, imagination, and power that enables man to alter and to control his world in accord with his own freely conceived ideas. The promise and aim of *technē* are the dominion of mind and will over mere "material," which includes whatever or whoever is construed as such. Among the avatars or "heroes" of *technē* in Greek mythology and history are Prometheus, Oedipus, and Pericles, "the Olympian," all of whom, as paradigms, might well give one pause. Even the great hymn to *technē* and to "technological man," the second stasimon of Sophocles' *Antigone*, hesitates now and then. Amidst waves of enthusiasm, one feels the undertow. "Numberless wonders, terrible wonders walk the world," sing the Chorus of elders, "but none the match for man . . . man the skilled, man the brilliant!"

> He conquers all, taming with his techniques
> the prey that roams the cliffs and wild lairs . . .
>      Never without resources
> never an impasses as he marches on the future —
> only Death, from Death alone
>      he will find no rescue . . .
> Man the master, ingenious past all measure
> past all dreams, the skills within his grasp—
> he forges on, now to destruction
> now again to greatness.

(Sophocles, *Antigone*, 331–32, 347–50, 360–61, 365–67, in *Sophocles: The Three*

*Theban Plays,* translated by Robert Fagles [New York: Viking Penguin, 1982], 377–78, 389–92, 402–4, 406–9, pp. 76–77).

Death, which not even swift Achilles could outpace, is both the source of human longing and the reason for its futility. So long as death is loose and unchecked, man is always out of control, imaginatively winged and yet—given the gravity of his inescapable finitude—invariably too heavy to fly. "Bird-brained," as it were, nothing more. Indeed, in the confrontation between Pisthetairos and the Informer, it comes out that man's only wings are his *logoi,* his ideas and words. His only flights, therefore, are those of fancy, from which he is inevitably pulled down by the gravity of *erga,* deeds and events. The ageless, immortal Chorus of the Birds, led by the Nightingale, sings the laments, the truth, of wingless man:

> O suffering mankind,
> > lives of twilight,
> > > race feeble and fleeting,
> like the leaves scattered!
> > Pale generations,
> > > creatures of clay,
> the wingless, the fading!

(Aristophanes, *The Birds,* 685–87 trans. Arrowsmith, p. 50).

Pindar, no friend of tyranny or empire, addressing his magnificent eighth Pythian ode to *Hēsychia,* "kind goddess of tranquillity, daughter of Justice and lady of the greatness of cities" struck the same note, reminding anyone who would listen how fleeting is human splendor (*The Odes of Pindar,* translated by Richmond Lattimore [Chicago: University of Chicago Press, 1976], Pythia 8.1–2, p. 81). "In brief space mortals' delight is exalted," he sang, "and thus again it drops to the ground, shaken by a backward doom."

> We are things of a day. What are we?
> > What are we not? The dream of a shadow
> is man, no more.

(Ibid., Pythia 8.92–96).]

32. An intriguing dimension of the *Birds,* to which we can attend only briefly here, lies in the multiple, though masked, references in the *Birds* to the primordial reign of the Great Goddess, particularly the Minoan Goddess, whose most common zoomorphic association was with birds. Pisthetairos and his companion acknowledge, in a litany of praises, the temporal and metaphysical primacy of the birds. Their original and rightful sovereignty is beyond question. "Unhappy birds," laments Pisthetairos, "I grieve for you, you were once kings. . . . Kings of everything. Kings of Creation. My kings. This man's kings. Kings of King Zeus. More ancient than Kronos. Older than Titans. Older than Earth" (Aristophanes, *The Birds,* 466–69, trans. Arrowsmith, p. 38). "Think of it," warbles Pisthetairos:

the springtime of the world!
    The Age of the Birds!
Primal Lords of Creation! Absolute Masters of man!
But the gods are mere upstarts
    and usurpers of very recent date.
And proof abounds . . .
    Why even now memory of it remains. . . .
(Ibid., 481–82, 488, p. 39).

What Pisthetairos does not openly admit here is that the birds were images of female, not male, potency and prestige. All the same, the repeated insistence that once, in a time obviously remote and irrelevant, both heaven and earth were under the sway of birds, may contain an oblique yet considered acknowledgment of the Goddess and her regime. After all, it would hardly be uncharacteristic of Aristophanes to question the rule of men, divine or human, and to entertain a more elevated place for women in the city than that assigned to them by current custom.

Another trace of the primordial reign of the birds may be found in line 479, wherein Euelpides suggests that Zeus, unless he is forced, will never restore his scepter to the woodpeckers. A clue to why the god of thunder and lightning would owe his scepter to the woodpeckers may lie in the view that birds, even before they were portents, were themselves quite powerful. They were thought able to summon a storm, for instance, rather than merely serve as signs of its approach. The woodpecker, in this view, perhaps by sympathetic magic, was able to create thunder, thunder stolen eventually by Zeus. (See Jane Ellen Harrison, *Themis: A Study of the Social Origins of Greek Religion* [New York: Meridian, 1962], pp. 99–102. A further link between Zeus and the woodpecker lies in the word for woodpecker [*drykolaptē*] in the above text from the *Birds,* a word that literally means "oak-pecker," the oak [*drys*] being sacred to Zeus and, more widely, to other *personae* of the Indo-European sky-god. Furthermore, at Dodona, Zeus delivered his oracles from the sacred oaks, whose guardian was a bird, in this case a dove. At a similar oracle, however, at Tiora, the guardian-bird was a wood-pecker.)

33. Aristophanes, *The Birds,* 1759–62, trans. Arrowsmith, p. 107.

34. Arrowsmith, "Aristophanes' *Birds:* The Fantasy Politics of Eros," p. 130.

35. Although there is little doubt that in the *Birds* the primary sexual referent of "wings" is the phallus, there is a possible secondary referent to be considered. After all, birds, like gods and mortals—witness Prokne, Iris, and Basileia—come in female as well as male form. As either the subjects or, more often in Greek poetry, the objects of erotic desire, their participation in the frenzy of winged Eros would seem to require that they possess wings of a sort. Soranos of Ephesus, a physician famous during the reigns of Trajan and Hadrian, may provide more than one relevant clue: "The outer part of the female genital system which is visible has the name "wings" (*pteryges*), which are, so to speak, the lips of the womb.

They are thick and fleshy, stretching away on the lower side to either thigh, as it were parting from each other, and on the upper side terminating in what is called the *nymphē*. This is the starting point (*archē*) of the wings (labia), by nature a little fleshy thing and somewhat muscular" (Soranos, *Gynaecology,* 1.18, in John J. Winkler, *The Constraints of Desire: The Anthropology of Sex and Gender in Ancient Greece* [New York: Routledge, 1990], pp. 181–82. I am mostly guided by Winkler's commentary in the discussion that follows).

In most other contexts, the word *nymphē* means a young woman of bridal age—in ancient Greece a "teenager"—no longer quite a *parthenos,* or virgin, and not yet a *gynē,* or wife and mistress of a household. *Gynē* on occasion refers to a newly married woman, not yet a mother. From a fanciful male perspective, the *nymphē,* we might say, is woman at her sexual peak, like a rosebud opening for the first time, which happens to be another meaning of *nymphē.* Here, however, in the anatomical discussion of Soranos, as in other ancient sources, we learn that *nymphē* also refers to the clitoris. The labia, then, are not only the "wings" of a young woman in the perfect blushing moment of sexual awakening, but also the "wings" of the clitoris, thus creating a direct female analogue to the winged tumescent phallus identified with the youthful god Eros.

36. Arrowsmith, "Aristophanes' *Birds:* The Fantasy Politics of Eros," p. 136.

37. Aristophanes, *The Birds,* 693–99, trans. Arrowsmith, pp. 51–52.

38. Arrowsmith, "Aristophanes' *Birds:* The Fantasy Politics of Eros," p. 148.

39. Aristophanes, *The Birds,* 412–13, trans. Arrowsmith, p. 35.

40. The verb *chaskō* means "to yawn" or "to gape."

41. Thomas Hobbes, *Leviathan,* edited by C. B. MacPherson (Harmondsworth: Penguin, 1968), I.xi., pp. 160–61.

42. The fact that sexual power is so elusive of personal control may account for the hostility it arouses. Sexual desire happens whether we will it or not. It is an independent, invasive force, affecting not only the mind but the body, taking control, having its way with us. Thus Augustine, for one, found erotic desire so deeply disquieting and unacceptable, not because it was dirty but because it was domineering. It represented a rebellious affront to the human will. Like death, sex as we know it was seen as fundamentally unnatural, the unwanted legacy of original sin. Sex, like death, takes us, whether we are ready and willing or not, into chaotic powerlessness.

For man, it is mostly woman who embodies the alien, uncontrollable power of erotic desire. She provokes it and thus is identified with it. In the same moment, she becomes the object of both *erōs* and *eris,* the goal of all longing and the source of all frustration, the promise of bliss and the cause of chaos. She becomes the symbol of what must but cannot be tamed or overcome, an icon of the uncontrollable. Here, perhaps, we possess a possible clue to the meaning of misogyny and of the violence it breeds. In fact, the following testimony, given not many years ago by a law clerk in San Francisco, provides a confirming phenomenology of the relationship between *erōs* and *eris,* which I am here proposing for consideration.

"Let's say I see a woman and she looks really pretty, and really clean and sexy, and she's giving off very feminine vibes. I think 'Wow, I would love to make love to her,' but I know she's not really interested. It's a tease. A lot of times a woman knows that she's looking really good and she'll use that and flaunt it, and make me feel like she's laughing at me and I feel *degraded.* I also feel dehumanized, because when I'm being teased I just turn off. I cease to be human. Because if I go with my human emotions I'm going to want to put my arms around her and kiss her; so I just turn off my emotions. It's a feeling of humiliation, because the woman has forced me to turn off my feelings and react in a way that I really don't want to. If I were actually desperate enough to rape somebody, it would be from wanting the person, but also it would be a very spiteful thing, just being able to say, 'I have power over you and I can do anything I want with you'; because really I feel that *they* have power over *me* just by their presence. Just the fact that they can come up to me and just melt me and make me feel like a dummy makes me want revenge. They have power over me so I want power over them" (Tim Beneke, *Men on Rape* [New York: St. Martin's, 1982], pp. 43–44).

In a matter of moments, the discourse passes from *erōs* to *eris*, from desire to hate, from the experience of powerlessness to the instinct to control and to punish. Either, it would seem, there is little space between the two, or the leap from the one to the other is so familiar as to be easily, even inadvertently, made. Or both. One is left only to imagine the revenge evoked by Helen, Aphrodite incarnate, the queen of all beauty.

43. Euripides, *Helen,* translated by Robert Emmet Meagher (Amherst: University of Massachusetts Press, 1986), 1137–43 (Oxford), p. 78.

44. Arrowsmith, "Aristophanes' *Birds:* The Fantasy Politics of Eros," pp. 133, 134.

45. It is for this reason that, in discussing this tradition, I have frequently used the male pronoun or pronomial adjective when contemporary usage calls for a gender-neutral form.

46. Euripides, *Helen,* trans. Meagher, 16–23 (Oxford), pp. 3–4.

47. Ibid., 137–43, p. 14.

48. For example, Homer has Helen in Egypt, though *after* rather than *before* the war, while Herodotus is quite convinced that she never went to Troy in the first place, a view expressed much earlier by the sixth-century poet Stesichoros. Instead, Herodotus tells how Helen sojourned in Egypt for the duration of the war. See Homer, *Odyssey* (Loeb), 4.351–587; Stesichoros, "Palinode," *Lyra Graeca* (Loeb), 2.44; Herodotus, *History* (Loeb), 2.112–20.

49. From "Helen" in *George Seferis: Collected Poems, 1924–1955,* translated by Edmund Keeley and Philip Sherrard (Princeton: Princeton University Press, 1967), p. 353.

50. Euripides, *Helen,* trans. Meagher, 393–94 (Oxford), p. 26.

51. Ibid., 700–707 (Oxford), p. 51.

52. The same radical disparity between divine comedy and human tragedy is

revealed in the *Bakkhai* with a ferocity and clarity perhaps without dramatic equal. There, in the *agōn,* the contest, between Pentheus and Dionysos, the blaspheming king and the blasphemed god, the gulf separating humanity and divinity is revealed. In the next century, Aristotle will argue that there can be no *philia,* no true kinship or fellowship, between god and humankind. In the *Bakkhai* we see why. The reason is stamped into the dramatic masks of Pentheus and Dionysos, the one full of pain and the other smiling indifferently. From the outset, the masks of Pentheus and Dionysos reveal their respective characters; and "character," we know from Heraklitos, "is destiny." Greek masks do not lie. They tell the whole story of human tragedy and divine comedy and how the former provides the latter.

The delirium of Dionysos, as we know, comes with the drinking of the cup; and his cup brims over not only with wine but with blood and milk and honey and sap, with *hygra physis,* "fluid nature," all the flowing, flooding, gurgling forms taken by the fluid force of life. Truth, we might even say, is its final form. It is the last cup offered by the god, the ultimate decoction drawn from existence once it has been crushed beneath the god's feet.

53. Euripides, *Helen,* trans. Meagher, 78–79, 80–82 (Oxford), p. 7.

54. Ibid., 84 (Oxford), p. 7.

55. Ibid., 305 (Oxford), p. 21.

56. Plato, *Phaedrus* (Loeb), 243a-b, translation mine. See also *Republic* 586c.

57. See Hesiod, *Theogony,* 572.

58. See Hesiod, *Works and Days,* 63.

59. See Xenophanes, fr. 15, in Kirk and Raven, *The Presocratic Philosophers,* p. 169, no. 172.

60. Euripides, *Medea* (Oxford), 410–30, translation mine.

## Conclusion

1. Odysseus Elytis, *Maria Nephele, A Poem in Two Voices,* translated by Athan Anagnostopoulos (Boston: Houghton Mifflin, 1981), p. 25.

2. Albert Camus, *Notebooks: 1942–1951,* translated by Justin O'Brien (New York: Alfred A. Knopf, 1965), p. 141.

3. Euripides, *Trojan Women* (Oxford), 665–72, translation mine. Woman, in the Greek mythic imagination, was among those wild, liminal forces to be mastered and controlled by man. In the Sophoclean ode to *technē,* to which we will turn momentarily, one image of man's violent mastery over inhuman nature is his breaking of horses. This same image was applied to woman, who was often likened to the beast, the object of the hunt, and so required taming. Thus, in poetic diction, the word for "wife" is *damar,* "the tamed one," from the verb *damazō,* "to tame" or "to yoke." The sixth-century lyric poet, Anacreon of Teos, provides a rude introduction to this theme in the following poem to a virgin:

My Thracian foal, why do you glare with disdain
and then shun me absolutely as if I knew
       nothing of this art?
I tell you I could bridle you with tight straps,
seize the reins and gallop you around the posts
       of the pleasant course.
But you prefer to graze on the calm meadow,
or frisk and gambol gayly—having no manly
       rider to break you in.

(Anacreon, "On a Virgin," in *Greek Lyric Poetry,* translated by Willis Barnstone [New York: Schocken, 1972], no. 322, p. 123.)

4. See Saint Thomas Aquinas, *Summa Theologiae* (Madrid: La Editorial Catolica, 1955), II.i., Quaestio XXXVIII: "De remediis tristitiae seu doloris," Articuli 1–5, pp. 260–64. The remedies are as follows: the enjoyment of something delightful, a good cry, the compassion of friends, the contemplation of the truth, sleep, and a hot bath, all of which I recommend as fitting sequels to this volume.


## *Appendix: History and Imagination*


1. Thomas Hobbes, *Leviathan,* edited by C. B. MacPherson (Harmondsworth: Penguin, 1968), I.iv., pp. 100–110.

2. Ibid., p. 100.

3. Ibid., pp. 110–11.

4. George Steiner, *Real Presences* (Chicago: University of Chicago Press, 1989), p. 115.

5. Hobbes, *Leviathan,* p. 113.

6. Ibid., p. 114.

7. Aristotle, *Poetics* (Loeb), 1459a5–6, translation mine.

8. Ibid., 1459a6–7.

9. See ibid., 1459a7–8.

10. Hannah Arendt, *The Life of the Mind. Volume One: Thinking* (New York: Harcourt Brace Jovanovich, 1977), p. 33.

11. Ernest Fenollosa, "The Chinese Written Character as a Medium for Poetry," an essay edited by Ezra Pound, in *Instigations* (Freeport, N.Y., 1967). See Arendt, *Life of the Mind,* p. 241 n. 76.

12. Steiner, *Real Presences,* p. 89.

13. Ibid., p. 93, italics his.

14. Plato, *Republic* (Loeb), 607b, translation mine.

15. Ibid., 607a.

16. Homer, *Iliad* (Loeb), 23.384.

17. Ibid., 23.391–97.

18. See Cedric H. Whitman, *Homer and the Homeric Tradition* (New York: W. W.

Norton, 1965), chapter 10, "Fate, Time, and the Gods," wherein Whitman writes: "Every appearance of a god amid the deeds of a hero is an implied comparison, formalizing the event or character in the light of something other than and beyond itself. As possessors of pure being in various aspects, the gods in their presences lend to all humanity a fourth dimension, not of time, but of eternity, the essence of the heroic vision of glory and permanent value. The dimension added by an image may be of a different nature, but its function is essentially the same: to make an object or event more comprehensible through the simultaneous presentation of another object or event, somewhat after the manner of stereopticon vision" (p. 238).

19. *The Epic of Gilgamesh,* translated by Maureen Gallery Kovacs (Stanford: Stanford University Press, 1985), p. 18, line 129.

20. Ibid., p. 75, lines 2–4.

21. The question of influence here is very complex. Heracles, in that he spans the full range of bestial-human-divine, may be said to embody the characteristics of both Gilgamesh and Enkidu. The heroic-divine figure of the Master of the Animals is commonplace throughout the ancient Near East; and the *Epic of Gilgamesh* is, in the same period and place, the most widely disseminated text. More specifically, both are found among the Hittites, with whom the Mycenaean Greeks are known to have had contact. See Walter Burkert's summing-up of "The Oriental Influence," wherein he writes: "The gulf separating Early Bronze Age Sumeria from Archaic Greece is frightful; but there was a continuity of texts as of iconography, besides oral tradition which remains elusive" (*Structure and History in Greek Mythology and Ritual* [Berkeley: University of California Press, 1979], p. 80).

22. Euripides, *Alcestis* (Oxford), 780–84, 787, 799, translation mine.

23. There are exceptions to this oblivion. When gods and beasts associate with humans, particularly when gods mate with humans and produce mortal offspring, they can become vulnerable to grief. They reflect human emotions. Thus, Zeus feels death's sting when his son Sarpedon succumbs in battle; and Achilles' horses weep for fallen Patroclus, their beloved driver.

24. Possibly the editor of the late version of the *Epic of Gilgamesh.* His is the only name attached by tradition to any version of the poem, whose actual authorship is unknown. For a full discussion of the evolution of the epic, see Jeffrey H. Tigay, *The Evolution of the Gilgamesh Epic* (Philadelphia: University of Pennsylvania Press, 1982).

25. Steiner, *Real Presences,* p. 209.

26. *Natality,* as it is understood here, is a central concept for Hannah Arendt, who writes of it with characteristic insight and precision. See *The Human Condition* (Garden City, N.Y.: Doubleday Anchor, 1959), pp. 10–11, 157–58, 170, 221, 222.

27. Erich Fromm, *The Heart of Man: Its Genius for Good and Evil* (New York: Harper & Row, 1964), pp. 116–17.

# Other titles by Robert Emmet Meagher
*Published by Bolchazy-Carducci Publishers*

## *The Essential Euripides: Dancing in Dark Times*
Robert Emmet Meagher
### *Plays and Interpretation in One Affordable Volume*
In "Mortal Vision" Meagher endeavors to strike the core of what he takes to be
Euripides' abiding concerns: war, the plight of women, and the awful mystery
of the gods. The five plays selected for inclusion here embody those concerns as
fully and powerfully as any in the Euripidean repertoire. Finally, in "Revel and
Revelation," Meagher looks back at Euripides' consummate masterwork, the
*Bakkhai*, as a definitive response to the ancient quip that Athenian drama has little or nothing to do with Dionysos. Nothing could be further from the truth.
xii + 556 pp. (2001) Paperback, ISBN 0-86516-513-0

## *Euripides: Bakkhai*
Translated by **Robert Emmet Meagher**
Euripides' *Bakkhai* presents the inner conflict between the untamed, irrational
side of man represented by the god Dionysos and the rational side represented
by the god Apollo. Meagher offers a rich and revealing introduction to ancient
Greek tragedy—a remarkably appropriate alternative to Sophocles' *Oedipus the
King*.
vi + 97 pp. (1995) Paperback ISBN 0-86516-285-9

## *Euripides: Hekabe*
Translated by **Robert Emmet Meagher**
Euripides' *Hekabe* presents a spectacle of suffering, rage, and revenge that offers
compelling witness to the courage and solidarity of those who suffer the most
from violence. Meagher's brilliant translation is accessible yet does not diminish
the powerful impact of this extraordinary and timeless play.
vii + 55 pp. (1995) Paperback ISBN 0-86516-330-8

## *Euripides: Iphigenia at Aulis* and *Iphigenia in Tauris*
Translated by **Robert Emmet Meagher**
The story of Iphigenia's sacrifice and her legendary rescue is a story for our time
as much as any other. Meagher's insightful introduction and splendid translation illuminate this tale as never before, showing that the past is not past and
that the darkest and brightest truths never change.
176 pp. (1993) Hardbound ISBN 0-86516-266-2